SOCIAL ACTION AND HUMAN NATURE

Charles Taylor writes in his preface, 'This is a work in philosophical anthropology. That is, it explores issues of human nature. This is both terribly necessary, and also unbearably problematic. It is necessary, because all efforts to elaborate a science of human beings, in psychology, politics, sociology, anthropology (in the narrow sense), linguistics, etc., lean on certain assumptions about what human beings are like, which are often highly questionable. Certainly the big disputes about the methods and scope of science which rage in all these disciplines reach down into such deep underlying assumptions. And what affects these sciences doesn't matter only for the intellectual world in our day: their assumptions shape public policy and widely accepted images of human life, as we can see, for instance in the present vogue for computer-based models of the mind.'

Honneth and Joas begin with a critique of Marxian theory, which is especially sensitive to issues in the new social movements, ecological and feminist. They then discuss the work of writers such as Gehlen and Plessner, who are largely unknown in the English-speaking world but have written provocatively on exactly the issues now being debated in Britain and America. The authors conclude by examining the possibilities and risks of three types of historical anthropology through the work of Elias, Foucault and Habermas.

The book has been revised for its English edition and will be of interest to a wide range of students in philosophy, social theory and the social sciences generally.

SOCIAL ACTION
AND
HUMAN NATURE

AXEL HONNETH AND HANS JOAS

TRANSLATED BY RAYMOND MEYER

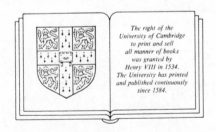

The right of the
University of Cambridge
to print and sell
all manner of books
was granted by
Henry VIII in 1534.
The University has printed
and published continuously
since 1584.

CAMBRIDGE UNIVERSITY PRESS
Cambridge
New York   New Rochelle   Melbourne   Sydney

Published by the Press Syndicate of the University of Cambridge
The Pitt Building, Trumpington Street, Cambridge CB2 1RP
32 East 57th Street, New York, NY 10022, USA
10 Stamford Road, Oakleigh, Melbourne 3166, Australia

Originally published in German as
Soziales Handeln und menschliche Natur
by Campus Verlag GmbH, Frankfurt-on-Main 1980
and © Campus Verlag GmbH, Frankfurt-on-Main 1980
First published in English by Cambridge University Press 1988 as
Social action and human nature

English translation © Cambridge University Press 1988

Printed in Great Britain by
Redwood Burn Limited, Trowbridge, Wiltshire

British Library cataloguing in publication data
Honneth, Axel
Social action and human nature.
1. Social anthropology
I. Title   II. Joas, Hans   III. Soziales
Handeln und menschliche Natur. *English*
306

Library of Congress cataloguing in publication data
Honneth, Axel, 1949–
[Soziales Handeln und menschliche Natur. English]
Social action and human nature/Axel Honneth and Hans Joas;
translated by Raymond Meyer.
p.   cm.
Translation of: Soziales Handeln und menschliche Natur.
Bibliography.
Includes index.
ISBN 0–521–32683–4.   ISBN 0–521–33935–9 (pbk)
1. Anthropology – Philosophy – History. 2. Anthropology –
Methodology – History. 3. Social history. 4. Social action.
I. Joas, Hans, 1948–. II. Title.
GN33.H6513   1988
306–dc 19   88–11913   CIP

ISBN 0 521 32683 4 hard covers
ISBN 0 521 33935 9 paperback

CONTENTS

v

FOREWORD by Charles Taylor

This is a work in philosophical anthropology. That is, it explores issues of human nature. This is both terribly necessary, and also unbearably problematic. It is necessary, because all efforts to elaborate a science of human beings, in psychology, politics, sociology, anthropology (in the narrow sense), linguistics, etc., lean on certain assumptions about what human beings are like, which are often highly questionable. Certainly the big disputes about the methods and scope of science which rage in all these disciplines reach down into such deep underlying assumptions. And what affects these sciences doesn't matter only for the intellectual world in our day: their assumptions shape public policy and widely accepted images of human life, as we can see, for instance in the present vogue for computer-based models of the mind.

But at the same time, we are very nervous and squeamish about 'human nature'. The very words ring alarm bells. We fear that we may be setting up some reified image, in face of the changing forms of human life in history, that we may be prisoners of some insidious ethnocentrism. The influence of Marxism, of Nietzsche, of anthropological theories, however opposed in other ways, converge on this warning. With the decline in influence of Marxism, the same distrust is being nourished by neo-Nietzschean theories like that of Foucault.

The authors of this book want to address this malaise. Philosophical anthropology starts from the belief that one can say something intelligible and important about 'the unchanging preconditions of human changeableness' (Introduction, p. 7). But these can't simply be read off human beings as they appear before us or are recorded in history. We can't get to any list of universal features by induction over human societies and cultures. Rather the attempt to define the unchanging preconditions proceeds by a critical examination of the body of scientific work which has already been accomplished. It digs into the unstated presuppositions of various theories and bodies of knowledge, points out their inconsistencies, narrowness, blindness to other assumptions which are also operative, and tries to develop out of all this a clearer conception of the human animal. The critical reflection here is what motivates the description 'philosophical'. In fact, this kind of study is a hybrid from a disciplinary point of view, irremediably athwart the boundary between philosophy and human science.

It is philosophical in another clear sense as well. Study in this domain is always not just arguing to certain substantive conclusions about what human beings are like, but also on a meta-level defending its right to state these conclusions. The cross pressures I described above, between the felt need to criticise the reigning assumptions of social science, and the doubts about what, if anything, can be put in their place, are continually felt throughout the whole process of reflection. They can never be definitively laid to rest and forgotten. This kind of critical, many-levelled argument is of the essence of philosophy.

This book, by Axel Honneth and Hans Joas, is a superb example of this kind of reflection, one which touches on the central issues of today. It comes out of a very rich tradition of philosophical anthropology largely in the German language, and picks it up at the moment when it is confronting a severe challenge to its whole way of thinking from contemporary French authors. It begins with a critique of the Marxian theory, one which is especially sensitive to the issues which have been put on the agenda by the new social movements, ecological and feminist. It then tries to explore how much the shortcomings that seem evident in Marxist theory can be made up by drawing on the work of other seminal thinkers. This second section of the book introduces very important writers who are almost entirely unknown in the English-speaking world, like Arnold Gehlen and Helmuth Plessner, but who have written provocatively and illuminatingly on exactly the issues which are now being debated in England and America. In their third part, the authors among other things confront the challenge to their enterprise in the work of Michel Foucault, and give an insightful account of the theory of Jürgen Habermas.

This penetrating and insightful book should knock down some barriers. It did so when it was originally published in German: barriers first between various theories on the German scene which are too often locked into ideological ghettos; and then between German and contemporary French thought, which have not really been confronted as they ought. These two authors, not only in this book but in their other work, have been seminal to this confrontation. Now I hope that the English translation will knock down other barriers, here those of unfamiliarity, which has kept many scholars and students in the English-speaking world from contact with a rich tradition of thought and argument, and with vital contemporary debates, which often bear most directly on the questions they are centrally concerned with.

PREFACE

This book has its origin in courses taught by the two authors in the late 1970s at the Free University of Berlin, and it gives sufficient indication of the background to their theoretical interests. The book is intended to give the English-speaking reader an introduction to the German tradition of philosophical anthropology and to a certain phase of neo-Marxist debate. Both authors have developed their ideas since the German publication of this book in 1980, and revision of this edition for the English publication incorporates some of this new thinking without fully integrating it.

The book is dedicated to our common friend Lothar Fichte. We are very grateful to Raymond Meyer, our translator, and to Linda Buechner for her patient and thorough work on the typescript.

AXEL HONNETH
HANS JOAS

TRANSLATOR'S COMMENTS

Since 'objective' carries too strongly the meaning 'expressing or dealing with facts or conditions as perceived without distortion by personal feelings, prejudices, or interpretations' (*Webster's Ninth New Collegiate Dictionary*), I have used 'objectual' to render into English the German adjective *gegenständlich*. 'Objectual' means 'having to do with, relating to an object or objects', as, for example, in the phrase 'objectual activity'; it can also mean 'relating to or being an object for a subject, for consciousness'.

As it was not always possible in translating this book to speak of human beings in the plural, I have, for the sake of stylistic simplicity, used the masculine pronoun to refer to the individual human being.

RAYMOND MEYER

INTRODUCTION

'Anthropology' does not have quite the same meaning in Germany as it has in English-speaking countries. As the word is used in the latter linguistic communities, it denotes a discipline that is chiefly concerned with the ethnological study of alien, usually 'primitive' cultures, while anthropology in the German sense is interested primarily in ascertaining the human being's fundamental biological nature through scientific investigation. Today, however, it is hardly necessary to give lengthy justifications for concerning oneself with anthropology in the German sense within the framework of the social and cultural sciences. The themes of various social movements lead all too clearly in this direction. The ecological, the counter-cultural and the women's movements – despite all the differences among the various shades in the variegated spectrum of these oppositional stirrings – have in common at least a concern with themes having to do with nature: with external nature and a humane relationship to it, as well as with the inner nature of the human being and its humane development. The prominence of these themes is due to a historical development in which the history of social movements is joined with a heightened awareness of the destruction of the environment and the exhaustion of the supplies of raw materials in a complex manner that is difficult to disentangle. In this development, crucial parts of the conception of progress guiding liberals and leftists were shaken to their very foundations. The development of the productive forces, advancement in the technological mastery over nature, had appeared, for long periods of time, to be a reliable guarantee for the further development and expansion of human freedom; even when the social content of a technological formation was criticised, there was nevertheless a trust in the gradual expansion of human freedom in the process of the perfecting of the technological domination of nature. However, the destruction of the environment, which menaces the very conditions of human beings' physical existence, and which is capable of destroying their material living conditions in the foreseeable future, has led to a flood of doubts not just about the emancipatory progress arising from unbridled exploitation of nature, but also about the progress supposedly implicit in all the radical socio-cultural changes that have accompanied this technological development during the last three or four hundred years. The life-threatening consequences of uncontrolled technological development have called into question many of the steps in social and psychical development that are the foundation of the development of industrial society. The growing emotional distance and alienation of societies from immediate contact with nature, the replacement of personal and direct power relations by internalised, psychical mechanisms of control, hence phenomena that could be regarded as the self-evident preconditions of an expansion of human freedom, are today increasingly looked upon as indications of a process of destruction of possibilities for the realisation of the full humanity of human beings, a process that began with the start of the modern era. For that reason, the ecologically grounded doubt about the emancipatory potential of industrial growth has called forth doubts about what Marx called the 'civilising effect of capitalism'. The history of industrial society, and not only of its capitalist form, is now interpreted primarily by means of the categories of a refinement of relations of mental and emotional coercion, of the dissolution of personal and direct social relations, and of the destruction of vital experience of nature.

The concerns of the women's movement could be easily integrated with this shift of attitude and of assessment, especially when this movement was directing its attention and efforts no longer, or no longer solely, to achieving the political, legal, social and economic equality of women, but to elaborating the critique of a male and patriarchal rationality. When this was the case, a specifically feminine relationship to one's own body, to partners in social relations, and to the world in general, could serve as a yardstick with which the deformations not only of the male sex role, but also of the dominant model of civilisation in its entirety could be revealed. Is the possibility of an 'historical compromise' beginning to emerge here, one that cuts across all the old political camps and is occasioned by the undeferable problem of safeguarding the survival of the human race? Is the apolitical myth of a complete decentralisation, or a rightist or a leftist variant of asceticism and of the state as the agency and guarantor of an equitable distribution of goods, or the notion of democratic planning of society, accompanied by the breaking of the power of the dominant economic interests, gaining general acceptance as the guiding idea of the ecologically inspired resolve to achieve political change?

This book gives no answers to these questions. They are mentioned not to prepare the way for prognoses about the political future of our society, but merely to indicate the authors' motives and the historical setting of the problems treated in the present work. The legitimacy of the question of the relationship of the human being to nature and of nature in the human being is today beyond all doubt. This was not always the case. At the acme of the renaissance of Marxism and of Marxist approaches in the social and cultural sciences at the beginning of the seventies, those who argued for the necessity of studying anthropology were unfailingly met with doubts and objections that joined together to make an adamantine wall of refusal. Epistemologial criticisms of the alleged objectivism of anthropological assertions and social–scientific arguments against the claim of universal validity for them made it difficult, especially in the theoretical discussion revolving around Marxism, to deal directly with anthropology. This field of investigation in its entirety was suspected of fostering ahistorical thinking, of being irredeemably entrapped in ethnocentric perspectives, and of serving as an ideal means of conservative argumentation against progressive commitment to effect social change. For long periods of time, these objections confined the discussion of anthropology to merely epistemological disputes about anthropology's claim to be a science and permitted hardly any examination of factual anthropological statements oriented to their substantive content. At the same time, those who were not ready to accept the existing form of Marxism as the full realisation of its inherent potential saw grounds enough for believing that an anthropological approach might be necessary for elaborating an interpretation of Marxism that was adequate to the present historical period.

The form assumed by Marxist theory in the representative interpretations of it sufficed to demonstrate this necessity. That theory's categories had been integrated to such an extent into the system of predications of a global philosophical science that it was difficult to perceive the historically practical reference of those categories or their connection with historically practical action. It was therefore necessary to begin the reconstruction of Marxist theory at such a deep level that its politically practical dimension was again accorded its theoretical rights in the theory's fundamental premises. This undertaking amounted to rooting the categories of Marxism in a theoretical model of human praxis in such a way that the independence of social conditions was neither denied nor reified, but could be recognised rather as the product of social action. This task was carried out chiefly by means of interpretative study and analysis of so-called Western Marxism, by means of the reconstruction of a 'philosophy of praxis', and less through the independent attempt scientifically to determine the anthropological characterisation of human action in contrast to animal behaviour.

However, such a step became unavoidable when to the awareness that present-day Marxism was not founded in the category of praxis there was added the insight that Marxism had not yet developed a set of conceptual instruments for identifying and describing, in a consistent manner, communication processes and interactional relationships. These insights guided the various attempts to supplement historical materialism with the dimension of individual psychical processes and specifically human action by means of psychoanalytic approaches or of certain theories of action. In his critique of political economy, Marx, for the purpose of that critique, reduced the nexus of social action to a great extent to instrumental action or to instrumentalised social relations. He did so in order to be able to depict the process of capital accumulation as a process that represses human possibilities for free, self-determined action. As a result, however, for long periods of time the Marxist tradition sought to force its investigations into this narrow conceptual framework. In this way, the conscious abstraction of Marx's analysis of capital from the plexuses of interaction that shape personality became the model and thus the fetter of historical–materialistic research, even though a politically efficacious analysis of processes of social change in particular requires an internally nuanced concept of communication.

Ignorance of the methodologically conscious reductionism of Marx's analysis of capital is also an important cause of the third shortcoming of historical materialism that can direct attention to the necessity of an anthropology: the lack of a concept of human needs with a substantive content. In this regard, too, the abstraction of the critique of political economy from qualitative needs unchannelled by capitalism could legitimate the general neglect of the category of need in historical materialism. This deficiency was magnified, certainly, both by the general lack of methodological clarity about just how specifically human needs were to be scientifically ascertained, and by incertitude about whether and how the assertions of biological theories regarding human beings were to be taken into account in historical materialism. In the Marxist tradition, the question of what latitude the human being's organic endowment allows to the cultural and historical shaping of human needs has to a large degree remained unanswered. In the analyses of historical materialism, neither the natural basis nor the substantial impact of human needs has been clearly in evidence.

When the hegemony of Marxism was broken, in the intellectual Left of many European countries the hegemony of scientific and systematic theoretical effort in general was also shattered. Within a short span of time, the gates were opened for all variants of long-forgotten theories of cultural decay, which reappeared clad in fashionable new clothes, for the most part of French design. Consequently, in both phases of recent intellectual history, anthropology comported itself in an anti-fashionable manner. Whereas it first had to defend the legitimacy of anthropological concerns in an atmosphere of unquestionable benevolence towards science, today, despite the acceptance of its concerns, anthropology must deal with a scepticism about, and a hostility to, science that do not emanate only from a dullwitted conservatism, but are even emerging in the heart of the remnants of the progressive movements and in the midst of the new social movements.

It is no longer 'bourgeois' science – whatever that might be – but science as such that is being called into question in various ways. There are, first of all, carefully calculated attempts to efface the boundary separating theoretical argumentation from aesthetic experience, to abolish the distinction between science and literature. These efforts see in science a system of propositions that is unable to allow room either for expressive–emotional, or for moral experiences and sentiments. The subjectivity lying beyond the reach of scientific concepts is supposed to find a much more suitable form of expression in literature, to which, accordingly, an authentically cognitive function is attributed. This elimination of distinctions appears in a variety of forms, ranging from the opening up of scientific accounts in relation to literary sources or moderated forms of communicative social research – that is, forms in which the goal of scientific cognition is retained – to attempts to construct a poetological cognition that seek to overthrow the primacy of abstractly conceptual cognition by means of aesthetic modes of expression, and thus ascribe to literarily presented feelings and expressions the status of arguments that are capable of pronouncing the truth.

Another variant of this profound critique of science can be found in the efforts that have been made to interknit with each other modern and pre-modern forms of consciousness. The cognitive claims of a science confined to the empirically perceptible world are thereby relativistically called into question, inasmuch as the character of pre-modern modes of experience is played off against them: what we impute to our psyches is assigned in pre-modern experience to the reality about us. The range of this critique of science extends from the reports of Carlos Castañeda to Paul Feyerabend's 'anarchistic' theory of science. Its fundamental criticism results from the ethnological recognition of the manner in which the conception of reality developed in the modern period of European history has arrogantly destroyed the experiential horizon of archaic societies, within which nature was regarded as a living partner in interaction and dialogue, and which today appears fantastical. However, this position utilises the aforesaid recognition more for the sceptical relativisation of its adherents' own culture than for improving understanding of the oppressed cultures.

Lastly, a third variant consists in the attempts to efface the distinction between conscious experience and unconscious emotional feelings. These attempts call into question science as a system of propositions that are instrumentally subordinated to a cognitive goal, but that have isolated themselves from the ingress into our speech of meanings from our unconscious. With the aid of literary protocols of experience that is open to sexual, traumatic and indeed even demented feelings, the system of a linguistic order that defines the meaning of the words we use is to be made problematical. These attempts arose and were carried out subsequent to a discussion that made evident the social character of our notions of normality; they criticise as a fiction the subject that disposes over itself, that is self-determining.

Thus, in opposition to the objectivity that theory is obligated to preserve by methodological rules and prescriptions of neutrality, in order to be intersubjectively verifiable, all these attempts adduce the particularity and uniqueness of subjectivity, the claim of non-European experience to provide valid knowledge, and the primordial character of emotional feelings that cannot be consciously monitored. In the end, all these attempts no longer subject to criticism the relations of domination implicit in our social conditions, but instead conceive scientific theories in detachment from their content as part and essential component of these relations of domination on the basis of those theories' systematic exclusions. On this view, science leaves unaffected the goal of a utopian and radical revolution of these relations of domination. The objectivating form of scientific theories is considered as much to be an instrument of administrative and technical disposition over human beings. Consequently, impulses arising out of individual needs are not translated into effort to achieve theoretical understanding of them, or at least not into a striving to achieve communicatively validated generalisation with regard to them; rather, these impulses are demarcated from, and set over against, unchanged science.

Now, what is the appropriate status of anthropological reflection in the field of problems and discussion that has been sketched out? It is certain that an anthropology confined within the boundaries of a special branch of science has no future. Neither can a subdiscipline of biology serve to establish what enters into the central categories of the social and cultural sciences as the fundamental characters of the human being; nor can philosophy immediately grasp cognitively the 'essence' of the human being by means of abstract definitions. This is not a new insight, and the intent to overcome the disciplinary boundaries is constitutive for most anthropological theories. However, the grandly conceived 'New Anthropology' of Hans-Georg Gadamer and Paul Vogler (1972–4) has made emphatically clear that this surmounting of disciplinary boundaries cannot be accomplished by means of an unstructured collocation of what the various individual sciences have to contribute. The theme of the unitary theory that must enter into dialogue with natural–scientific knowledge, but cannot be derived from that knowledge, must have its origin in the problems of the social sciences. Nor is an advance to be gained in this regard from any attempt to escape from this task in an historicist way, that is, by pointing to the historical mutability of all human circumstances. Such a position might seem plausible in view of the great diversity of cultures and societies from the standpoints of history and ethnology, but it is untenable in the face of biology and even of the concrete comparison of animals and the human being. However, anthropology must not be understood as the theory of constants of human cultures persisting through history, or of an inalienable substance of human nature, but rather as an enquiry into the unchanging preconditions of human changeableness (Kofler, 1967, p. 28).

These unchanging preconditions of human changeableness cannot, though, simply be factually ascertained; they are not evident in nature. They present themselves only in the form of reconstructed inceptive conditions of the species' history and of the individuals' development. In our opinion, anthropology should be understood neither as the basis of the social and cultural sciences, which has a priori precedence over them, nor as a synthesis of the knowledge of the particular sciences or as a mere hodgepodge of their bodies of knowledge. Rather, anthropology is a reflective step in the scrutiny of the suitableness of social–scientific theoretical frameworks that has become autonomous. This radical self-examination requires the identification and the making explicit of the natural bases and the normative implications that are always assumed in the substantive work of the social sciences, in face of the findings of biology, palaeontology, and other natural sciences. Thus this process of self-reflection draws its questions from the problems of the social and cultural sciences and returns to them with its theories clarified and internally differentiated by anthropology.

This conception of anthropology differs not only from the claims of a *fundamentalistic* anthropology, but also from the 'negative' anthropology of Ulrich Sonnemann and Dietmar Kamper and from the 'experimental anthropology' of Wolf Lepenies and Helmut Nolte. In his definition of anthropology, Kamper starts from the assumption that it is a self-reflection and a striving to achieve clarity about its own premises and principles. He does not seek to replace false anthropologies with a correct one; rather he considers the enterprise 'anthropology' as such to be misguided so long as the recognition of the changeableness of the human being and of his capability to attain self-understanding have not been made a part of the very heart of anthropology. That does not mean for him – as it does for us – regarding self-reflexivity, on the one hand, as an essential component of anthropology's field of investigation, and on the other hand as a determination of the relationship between anthropology and the other sciences. Instead, Kamper wants to conceive a concept of the human being 'that permits the conceptual demonstration of the impossibility of a concept of the human being' (Kamper, 1973, p. 26). In a banal interpretation, this formulation reveals of course the essential logical impossibility of Kamper's approach. His argument, however, is not all that banal, even though the poverty of substantive content in his studies certainly is one of the consequences of this theoretical self-frustration. For he draws near to the above-mentioned radical questioning of the validity and limits of science. According to Kamper, the theories of the human sciences should 'cling to the character they have as only partial explanations and no longer exercise an effect on praxis in the manner of a total theory, but rather by delimiting themselves, practically setting free human intellectual and cultural many-sidedness, and postulating the reflexivity of every single concrete individual' (*ibid.*, p. 237). With his reference to praxis, however, Kamper shows the problem of his approach, which makes possible only the destruction of concepts and counsels abandonment of clear and established determinations. If the anthropological finding is correct that self-reflection is functionally correlated with action, then it is not just self-reflexivity that is a critically important part of anthropology's object of investigation, but in particular the relationship between action and reflection. On the level of the definition of the status of anthropology, though, that means that this theory, like all others, is dependent on the clear and settled formulation of propositions, owing to the pressure of time and the pressure to decide produced by the will to act. These propositions can be as revisable and falsifiable as may be – without them everything remains obscure. Kamper's position is very strongly influenced by Heidegger's critique of the efforts to elaborate a philosophical anthropology having a reference to science (*ibid.*, p. 22 and pp. 139ff.); he does not, however, see that Heidegger leaves science no substantive function whatsoever.

The position of Wolf Lepenies and Helmut Nolte, taken by them in their publications at the beginning of the seventies, appears to be more convincing. The theoretical framework of their experimental anthropology sets anthropology in relationship with the problem of practical reflective self-examination. Lepenies and Nolte reject the limitation of social changes on the basis of the limits of human nature, just as they reject immediate, over-optimistic grounding of programmes for social change in human needs: being experimental, anthropology can tell from the results of attempts to achieve social progress whether or not the bounds of human nature have been overstepped. This anthropology takes into account not only praxis-related reflection, but even the historical context. On closer examination, though, the proposed solution proves to be a merely verbal one: for neither can politics assume the task of experimentally testing-out anthropological hypotheses (indeed, society and history in general are to a high degree not amenable to experimentation in the sense of being observably repeatable); nor can anthropology postpone the clarification of its hypotheses until the occurrence of great social revolutions. Science requires its own pragmatics, even though the fact that it is an integral part of the historical processes and social movements is of fundamental importance.

Our approach to anthropology regards it as self-reflection of the social and cultural sciences on their biological foundations and on the normative content of their bodies of knowledge, considered in relation to determinate historical and political problems, and its viewpoint is that of a humanisation of nature. This is to be understood in three ways. First, the human being humanises nature; that is, he transforms it into what is life-serving for himself and thereby creates, in an interknitting of the transformation of nature and the development of the human personality which requires more exact clarification, the cultural shapings of his nature. Second, the human being humanises nature within himself in the course of the long civilising process that has been engaged in by the human species. Lastly, the human being himself is a humanisation of nature, being an upstart out of the animal kingdom; in the human being, nature becomes humane. What might sound here, in anticipatory summary, like an abstract definition or unctuous pathos over humanity, is developed in detailed argumentation in the three parts of this book.

In the first part, we ascertain, through examination of discussions of Feuerbach and Marx, just what is the exact meaning of Marx's 'transcending' of Feuerbach, and pose the question of the extent to which productive moments of Feuerbach's thought were lost in Marx's 'surpassing' of it.

The second part is devoted to elaborating the human being's capability for social action, in contrast to animal forms of behaviour. Following an introductory account of the German tradition of anthropology, attention is focused first on Arnold Gehlen's anthropology, for it is conceived as a theory of action. His understanding of the specifically human endowments and capabilities is derived from the structure of human action; he does not, however, detach his concept of action consequently enough from the solipsistic framework of his philosophical presuppositions. Thus, our next step is to set forth George Herbert Mead's theory of intersubjectivity, with the aid of which the theory of action can be transformed into an anthropology of intersubjective action, of practical intersubjectivity. Upon this foundation are then treated the three domains in which the human capacity for action differs in its presuppositions from animal behaviour. These domains are: motility, motivation and perception. First, through examination of the anthropology of Helmuth Plessner, human motility is presented and discussed, in particular as it manifests itself in communicative expressivity. Then, guided by the critical and constructive studies of Agnes Heller, we deal with the human being's structure of needs. Finally, the distinguishing characteristics of human perception are set forth, with reference especially to Klaus Holzkamp's writings, on the one hand, and to the phenomenology of Maurice Merleau-Ponty on the other. In all three cases, though, the theoretical framework underlying the discussion requires both critique and emendation of the approaches taken by the aforenamed authors.

The third part considers the necessity and the dangers of an historicisation of anthropology through examination of three major theories of history. Norbert Elias's theory of the civilising process, which links the development of affective self-control with the centralisation and monopolisation of power in the modern state, is historically and psychologically relativised. Next, Michel Foucault's studies on the development of the exclusions effected by our Western rationality, with their wealth of historical material, are closely scrutinised as they are exemplified in his analysis of power, in order to uncover their implications for the theory of history. Lastly, we consider critically Jürgen Habermas's grandly conceived attempt, which draws upon a plethora of philosophical and social–scientific, Marxist and non-Marxist approaches, to reconstruct historical materialism in the form of a theory of social evolution that is inspired by the theory of communication.

This book is a contribution to the discussion of anthropology that has a systematic intent. It does not itself offer an anthropology. The substantive content presented in it is gained through examination of theories, a fact that might make it easier for the reader to orient himself. However, in comparison with the procedures of the great anthropologists, which are, certainly, theoretically mediated, but which make their arguments chiefly in direct reference to the phenomena themselves, the substantive content of this book can only be regarded as epigonous. For a complete overview of the subject, important fields of investigation are lacking, the discussion of which would require in each instance a separate volume. These are: ethology, sociobiology and psychoanalysis. Nevertheless, we hope that with this work we have not only provided a critical introduction to anthropological theories, but have also made a contribution to the grounding of the social–scientific and philosophical debates about the centrally important notions of action and praxis. These concepts might yield arguments in defence of a meaningful notion of historical progress within the framework of well-founded argumentation against fashionable scepticism about civilisation as well as against technocratic confidence in civilisation.

1

ANTHROPOLOGY AND HISTORICAL MATERIALISM

Ludwig Feuerbach's anthropological materialism

The philosophy of Ludwig Feuerbach is of central importance for the relationship between anthropology and historical materialism. It was from their intense study, appropriation and criticism of this philosophy that Marx and Engels went on to evolve the basic premises of historical materialism; and it is therefore no accident that present-day discussions of the legitimacy of anthropology in relation to historical materialism continuously refer to this threshold in the history of ideas. Only too often, though, Feuerbach's contribution is considered merely in its function as precursor of historical materialism, and not with regard to the specific problem it addresses, and to how it poses that problem; only as the point from which Marx's thought 'pushed off', and not as the point at which, and with which, that thought began. In order to avoid this mistake here, Feuerbach's anthropological materialism will first be presented in its fundamentals and in its own right. Proceeding in this way will make it possible to grasp historical materialism's transformation of Feuerbach's materialism, including the possible unsuitableness of that transformation. The crucially important basis of the following reflections consists in Feuerbach's writings from the beginning of the 1840s, in particular his *Principles of the Philosophy of the Future*, which appeared in 1843.

These writings were composed at a high point of the development of Feuerbach's thought and of his public influence. In many stages of thoroughgoing self-criticism carried out in the course of, and founded upon, studies in the history of philosophy and especially a critique of religion, Feuerbach had advanced from being a follower of Hegel to a point where neither German idealism nor the materialism of the eighteenth century any longer appeared sufficient to him. From criticism of religion he arrived at a radical questioning of the validity, tasks and nature of philosophy, as well as at political conclusions that found great interest in the period preceding the 1848 Revolution among the democratic intellectuals who were then becoming politically radical. Feuerbach himself, however, remained at some distance from the political struggles of the day and continued his work in the areas of investigation in which his earlier intellectual development had taken place. The strongest theme of the evolution of his thought is the effort to free philosophy from the false opposition between rationality and emotionality through his concept of the human being, and from the false opposition between conceptual thought and intense sensuousness through his conceiving of the philosophy of the future as an anthropology.

From the standpoint of the history of philosophy, Feuerbach's decisive step in effecting this liberation was his critique – the first ever – of transcendental philosophy. As Feuerbach understood this philosophy, it had arisen out of the supplanting of the naive realism of pre-critical consciousness, and had profoundly shaken the simple conviction regarding the independent existence of the world that appears to us. However, at the end of the comprehensive, methodologically unconditioned doubt, the self-certainty of the thinking subject was all that remained to this self-grounding of philosophy which originated with the rise of the bourgeoisie and the development of self-aware subjectivity and individual autonomy. Consequently, accounting for the givenness and determination of the external world by means of the cognitive achievements of the subject now became a philosophically crucial problem, although an absurd one for 'common sense'.

Feuerbach's critique does not offer one of the innumerable proposals for solving this complex of problems that were presented until into the twentieth century; his aim, rather, is to go completely beyond the transcendental enquiry as such. In pursuing this goal, he does not retreat to rehabilitation of naive realism, but subjects the steps of transcendental philosophy's reasoning to a new scrutiny. He uncovers the two implicit presuppositions that any question posed by transcendental philosophy always contains. Feuerbach's procedure does not consist in assuming the ego as a first principle, in order then to enquire about the possibility of a cognition of the external world, but instead asks: 'How are we able to suppose the existence of an ego that thus enquires and can thus enquire?' (from 'On "the beginning of philosophy"', in *The Fiery Brook: Selected Writings of Ludwig Feuerbach*, translated and with an introduction by Zawar Hanfi, New York, 1972,

p. 140). The thinking ego that presupposes itself forgets that it is not just a thinking being, that indeed it could not even exist as such, if it were not first of all a *corporeal ego endowed with needs*. Further, it forgets that it becomes *an ego only by means of its relation to others*, that the very talk of an 'I' is meaningless if it is not accompanied by the thought of a 'you'. Hence, empirical, corporeal communities are prerequisite for all cognition.

In this manner, Feuerbach avoids the cul-de-sac of an ultimate grounding of philosophy without surrendering the insight into the constitutive accomplishments of cognising subjects that had been gained by idealism. To be sure, these cognitive achievements are no longer sought in solitary thinking as such, but accounted for as arising out of intersubjective praxis that is guided by needs. For him, epistemology no longer consists in establishing what the a priori preconditions of thought are, but is rather the self-reflection of contentual thought. In this way, the two presuppositions tacitly posited by transcendental philosophy, the human being's sensuousness and his innate impulse towards union with others, become the guiding threads of Feuerbach's philosophy. It joins together a theoretical consideration of man's organic structure of needs and perception with the presupposition of a specifically human form of communication and interaction. The former can be followed in Feuerbach's thought in his notion of 'sensualism'; the second of Feuerbach's central ideas, in his notion of 'altruism'.

Feuerbach himself had begun by assuming that sensuousness was a deficient mode of cognition in comparison with thinking, in order to defend the universality of thought against the claims of the particularity of the individual, sensing human being. His critical study of religion, which takes the sensuousness and particularity of the individual into consideration more strongly than does philosophy, along with the paradigm of sexual love that played an important role in all his thought, led him to reformulate the problem he was investigating: he primarily conceives of the relation of subject to object not as one effected through thought, but as one founded on and determined by need (*Philosophy of the Future* § 33; in *The Fiery Brook*). Love and need become the proof for the existence and structuredness of the external world, which cannot be obtained in a purely intellectual fashion. Natural objects possess their own proper structures, which become experienceable as the resistance of objects in relation to the subject's neediness; Feuerbach thus contradicts the Kantian notion of a chaotic external world, which becomes categorised only through the cognitive achievement of the transcendental subject. He rehabilitates sensuous pre-philosophical experience of the world not only as the foundation, but also as the medium and end of thought. Thus, even before the advent of the Darwinian paradigm – the organism that secures its survival in its environment, which was to become crucially important for *Lebensphilosophie*, pragmatism and philosophical anthropology – Feuerbach supersedes concretely the aporiae of transcendental philosophy. By following this path, however, he is not led to an epistemological relativism, as were many of the aforementioned intellectual schools. For Feuerbach does not treat the specifically human mode of perception and capacity for action, which have been modified in comparison to those of animals, as a special faculty; instead, he situates them in the total organic structure of the human being. He can therefore understand human sensuousness as being, by its essential nature, 'open to the world' (*Philosophy of the Future*, § 53)[1] and see in it the foundation for the human being's potential universality.

Feuerbach complements the idea of a sensuousness rooted in the human organism with the notion of an a priori intersubjectivity of the human being. He was the first to take into consideration both epistemologically and substantially the significance of the specifically human structure of intersubjectivity. German idealism had, it is true, produced important contributions to an intersubjectivistic theoretical conception of the human being. Fichte, in his *Science of Rights (Grundlage des Naturrechts nach den Prinzipien der Wissenschaftslehre*, 1796), had understood that the conditions for the ego's experience of itself as a free being lie in its intersubjective recognition by another subject. Only when an ego is, so to speak, 'summoned' by another ego to put its freedom into action, can it catch sight of, and thereby become conscious of, its own freedom; hence, intersubjective recognition constitutes the condition of the possibility of practical self-consciousness (Siep, 1979, pp. 26ff.). It was from this postulate of intersubjective recognition, which Fichte had developed for the purpose of a deduction of the concept of right, that the theoretical impulses emanated which led Hegel to elaborate a theory of mutual recognition in his Jena writings. In them, Fichte's leading idea is joined with elements of Hölderlin's philosophy of unification (Henrich, 1971, pp. 9–40) and developed further into the fundamental principle of a practical philosophy. Hegel understands the processes of the unification and separation of subjects as a movement brought about by the struggle for recognition, a movement by means of which forms, first, of

---

[1] The notion of 'sensualism' is the central theme of Alfred Schmidt's interpretative study of Feuerbach's philosophy (Schmidt, 1973).

individual, then of collective identity are developed in stages. Thus personalities and moral conditions of life only evolve at all in performances of action that have the intersubjective structure of recognition given between human beings (see, in its entirety, Siep, 1979). Certainly, Hegel soon forced this theory of recognition, which still entered into the dialectic of master and slave in his *Phenomenology of Mind*, back into the mentalistic framework of his systematic philosophy and thereby deprived it of the explosive power it has from the viewpoint of the theory of intersubjectivity (Habermas, 1968, pp. 9–47). The principle according to which philosophy was to be grounded had not changed. In contrast, Feuerbach takes as the starting point of his reflections the sensibly given 'you'. Like empiricism, he also begins his epistemological investigations with sensuous experience; however, he criticises the monological character of empiricism, which forgets

> that the most essential sensuous object for man is *man himself*; that only in man's glimpse of man does the spark of consciousness and intellect spring. And this goes to show that idealism is right in so far as it sees the origin of ideas *in* man; but it is wrong in so far as it derives these ideas from man understood as an isolated being, as mere soul existing for himself; in one word, it is wrong when it derives the ideas from an ego that is not given in the context of its togetherness with a perceptibly given You. Ideas spring only from conversation and communication. Not alone but only within a dual relationship does one have concepts and reason in general. It takes two human beings to give birth to a man, to physical as well as spiritual man; the togetherness of man with man is the first principle and the criterion of truth and universality. Even the certitude of those things that exist outside me is given to me through the certitude of the existence of other men besides myself. That which is seen by me alone is open to question, but that which is seen also by another person is certain. (*Philosophy of the Future*, § 41, pp. 231–2)

The cognising subject is to be conceived only as a community of subjects, because becoming a subject is possible solely by means of processes of interactive communication; intersubjectivity is thus not just the precondition for sensuous certainty about the existence of objects, but is also the criterion for the validity of all cognitive judgments whatsoever (*ibid.*, § 41). Feuerbach develops in many respects this theoretical insight into the nature and function of intersubjectivity. He sketches a consensus theory of truth based not on the fact of assent, but on agreement reached through reasoned argument. He derives the ontogenetic constitution of things from the schema of the action that occurs in interaction:

An object, i.e., a real object, is given to me only if a being is given to me in a way that it affects me, only if my own activity – when I proceed from the standpoint of thought – experiences the activity of another being as a *limit* or boundary to itself. The concept of the object is originally nothing else but the concept of another *I* – everything appears to man in childhood as a freely and arbitrarily acting being – which means that in principle the concept of the *object* is mediated through the concept of You, the *objective²* ego. To use the language of Fichte, an object or an alter ego is given not to the ego, but to the non-ego in me; for only where I am transformed from an ego into a You – that is, where I am passive – does the idea of an activity *existing outside myself*, the idea of objectivity, really originate. But it is only through the senses that the ego is also non-ego. (*Philosophy of the Future*, § 32, p. 224)

With such formulations, Feuerbach gropes his way forward as far even as the achievements of interactionist social psychology. He evolves a concept of dialogue, understands reflection as dialogue that has been transposed into the interior of the human being, elaborates the dialectic of the formation of the self in communities, sketches a model of role-taking, and even uses the expression 'role':

How do matters stand, then, when I as a particular individual have intercourse with others and in an appropriate manner exchange remarks and responses with them, stand outside myself, and in the case of a dispute, in which the one party is the opponent of the other, the two parties assume different roles, so to speak, that is to say, when I am thinking, am concentrated in myself, am absorbed by myself as it were. (*Dissertation*, pp. 312f. Bolin/Jodl edition)

Anticipating the theses of psychoanalysis and interaction theory, he interprets conscience as an internalised attachment figure.

These insights into the nature and function of interaction, together with his fundamental sensualist premises, make it possible for Feuerbach to elaborate an anthropologically grounded materialism. Feuerbach is not a materialist at the price of a reduction of all that is specifically human to the structure of moving bodies; he does not fall into the mechanistic materialism of the eighteenth century, which decomposes the world into physical objects; nor is his materialism like the dialectical materialism of Soviet Marxism, which ontologises the world into matter that moves itself. Feuerbach, it is true, places nature at the centre of his philosophical theory, but the nature in question is precisely none other than *human* nature in its interactively oriented and sensuously open capability for action. In *The Essence of Christianity*, he wrote:

---

² I.e., 'objectual'; see 'Translator's comments'.

The obtuse Materialist says: 'Man is distinguished from the brute *only* by consciousness – he is an animal with consciousness superadded'; not reflecting, that in a being which awakes to consciousness, there takes place a qualitative change, a differentiation of the entire nature. (p. 3, note 1)

The cognitive intent of this materialism is defetishisation: the attempt to explain all pseudo-nature, all forms of action and consciousness that have slipped away from human control and become autonomous, by tracing them back to need-guided structures of action. Religious conceptions of the world and of life become the object on which Feuerbach's critique of ideology focuses. He not only unmasks them as cognitive errors, but also grasps and demonstrates their great emotional and communicative importance (cf., e.g., Löwith, 1984, esp. part 1, chapters 2 and 3); thus he criticises religion less as a false or deficient form of human cognition, than as an illusory form of the satisfaction of human needs.

Having concluded our brief presentation of Feuerbach's theory, we come to the question of the degree to which the critique of Feuerbach's philosophy in *The German Ideology* may lay out in appropriate fashion the guidelines of an historically grounded materialism as distinct from Feuerbach's anthropological materialism, but under-appreciates the significance of Feuerbach's fundamental interactionist and sensualist convictions.

Marx's critique of Feuerbach

In his surmounting of Hegelianism through a critique of religion, Feuerbach was a model for Marx. However, while Feuerbach made that project into his life's work, Marx was interested chiefly in the results of that critique that were pertinent to the theory of society. He enquires into the consequences for Hegel's philosophy of the state and of right that ensue from Feuerbach's attack on the very foundation of Hegel's systematic philosophy of identity; he asks about the structure of a society that makes religious interpretations of the world necessary. This interest, it is true, led Marx not just to apply Feuerbach's philosophy, but also to go beyond it.

Marx transforms the critique of transcendental philosophy into *a philosophy of praxis*, and anthropological materialism into *historical materialism*. The road Marx followed did not lead to a dialectical materialism that at the outset forces an arbitrary choice between the two equally speculative philosophical positions of idealism and materialism, abandons constitutive subjectivity through acceptance of the copy theory of perception, and lapses back into pre-critical metaphysics in a dialectics of nature. Rather, Marx surpasses Feuerbach's critique of transcendental philosophy by employing, in a manner specifically his own, the category of praxis, which is present in germ in that critique, as the central category of his reflections in the areas of epistemology, anthropology and politics.

The *Theses on Feuerbach* find fault with Feuerbach for conceiving and defining praxis 'only in its dirty-Jewish form of appearance', that is, as purposively rational, calculating 'commercial activity' (Marx and Engels, *Collected Works*, vol. 5, p. 3). Now, this mode of action is, according to Feuerbach, wrong in relation to nature, and thus unworthy of human beings; consequently, he is ultimately compelled normatively to prefer a merely contemplative form of life: 'Hence he does not grasp the significance of "revolutionary", of "practical–critical", activity' (*ibid.*, p. 3), that is, of a politically oriented action that transforms social institutions. From this fact Marx draws the epistemological conclusion that the notion of 'constitutive subjectivity' remains limited in two respects in Feuerbach's thought. On the one hand, Feuerbach does not see that all objects are practically constituted prior to their cognition. Marx expressed this criticism as follows: Feuerbach

> does not see that the sensuous world around him is not a thing given direct from all eternity, remaining ever the same, but the product of industry and of the state of society; and, indeed, [a product] in the sense that it is an historical product, the result of the activity of a whole succession of generations, each standing on the shoulders of the preceding one, developing its industry and its intercourse, and modifying its social system according to the changed needs. (from *The German Ideology*; Marx and Engels, *Collected Works*, vol. 3, p. 39)

Feuerbach does not take into consideration the fact that the things which the human being sensuously encounters, while indeed natural, are objects that have nevertheless always been 'fashioned' in some way and to some extent by human activity. On the other hand, the preconditions of cognition that are specifically human are developed by Feuerbach not out of the human being's capacity for action, but solely out of the receptive, i.e., 'contemplative', sensuousness of the human organism. This idea is expressed in the fifth thesis on Feuerbach: 'Feuerbach, not satisfied with *abstract thinking*, wants [*sensuous*], *contemplation*; but he does not conceive sensuousness as *practical*, human-sensuous activity' (Marx and Engels, *Collected Works*, vol. 5, p. 4; as edited by Engels). In contrast, Marx understands the human being's sensuous–cognitive capabilities as achievements that are integral to the process of the very activity which transforms nature. The human species, therefore, gains access to nature for itself only through praxis, by means of which it also emancipates itself from the dominion of nature, in socially organised work.

In this manner, Marx develops in his early writings a concept of praxis which is a criticism both of Feuerbach's philosophy and of German idealism. In opposition to Feuerbach's notion of man's purely passive sensuousness, he argues for and demonstrates that activity is a character of human subjectivity, which character the idealism of Kant and Hegel had made into the basis of an epistemology; on the other hand, to that epistemology's notion of an incorporeal, world-making subjectivity, the 'ego', Marx opposes sensuousness as a character of human subjectivity that Feuerbach had, for his part, made into the foundation of an anthropological philosophy. The two components of this double critique – corporeal receptivity and creative activity – are combined by Marx in the concept of 'objectual activity'; this notion thus becomes the key category of his theory. Marx establishes all further determinations of this concept within the framework of the modern concept of labour. In his own understanding of 'objectual activity', he implicitly brings together the various elements of meaning with the help of which modern social–philosophical theories have attained to an understanding of the process of historical transformation that has gradually brought about awareness of socially organised production as the practical foundation of all social development (cf., e.g., Conze, 1972, pp. 134ff.).

With this intent, Marx begins by taking over, albeit critically, the definition of the concept of labour through which classical political economy explained the epoch-making expansion and acceleration of economic growth as arising from labour as a factor of production. Considered from the perspective of economics, then, 'labour' is the performance of action, by means of the social organisation of which plexuses of social relations attend to the material conditions of their own reproduction. Marx, however, understood human labour not just as a value-creating form of activity, but also as a means of education; to the economic significance of the concept of labour, he always joined an emancipatory aspect of its significance. In doing so, he was allowing himself to be guided, via Hegel, by the central themes of the anthropology of expressiveness that can be regarded as one of the most important achievements of the romantic wing of the German Enlightenment that originated with Herder. In this tradition, as Charles Taylor, following Isaiah Berlin, has shown (Taylor, 1975, esp. pp. 27ff.), all effectuations of action by the human being are interpreted as the means of expressing an essential nature that is different from one individual to the next; on this view, then, human action is a process of active realisation of a self, a process of self-realisation. Hegel had taken over into his own thought this theme of expressiveness and interpreted work as a process of externalising human capabilities (see Riedel, 1973; Löwith, 1984, pp. 286ff.). In his turn, Marx was able to build on that position by conferring on the economically defined activity of labour the additional dimension of human self-realisation. This enables him to regard that instrumental form of activity which he, with the political economists, considers to be the decisive factor of production, also as a unique vehicle of expression. The romantic undertone that characterises long stretches of Marx's early writings is nourished by the synthesis which British political economy and the German anthropology of expressiveness have entered into in his concept of labour (cf. the exemplary study by Berki, 1979). Human labour is understood to be just as much a process of productive expenditure of the human being, as a process of the manifestation of the forces of his essential being: labour is simultaneously a factor of both production and expression.

Both semantic components of the modern concept of labour merge so thoroughly in Marx's concept of 'objectual activity' that it permits, with no difficulty, a historicisation of Feuerbach's anthropological materialism. Because Marx interprets the mode of activity through which human beings are distinguished as a species both as nature-transforming production and as an educational process that shapes subjectivity, he is able to interpret the historical development of human life-relations as a process in which the social reshaping of external nature and the social elaboration of inner nature reciprocally advance one another to ever higher levels. In the very same labour process in which it increases its knowledge of, and control over, its natural environment, the human species also expands its needs and its capabilities. From this perspective, therefore, history is – according to Marx –

the succession of the separate generations, each of which uses the materials, the capital funds, the productive forces handed down to it by all preceding generations, and thus, on the one hand, continues the traditional activity in completely changed circumstances and, on the other, modifies the old circumstances with a completely changed activity. (*The German Ideology*, *Collected Works*, vol. 5, p. 50)

Within the framework of this conception of history, anthropological theory clearly assumes the function of providing the conception's material grounding. Marx allows historical materialism to remain dependent on a reflection upon itself in which are established the natural, organic conditions that are fundamental to the social integration of human beings:

> The first premise of all human history is, of course, the existence of living human individuals. Thus the first fact to be established is the physical organisation of these individuals and their consequent relation to the rest of nature . . . All historical writing must set out from these natural bases and their modification in the course of history through the action of men. (*ibid.*, p. 31)

The points of reference of this anthropological reflection performed by historical materialism are provided by the fundamental Feuerbachian themes of 'sensualism' and 'altruism'. The concept of 'sensuousness', freed from Feuerbach's contemplative restrictions upon it, enters into Marx's concept of labour; while Feuerbach's ascription to human beings of an inborn propensity to enter into community with one another, liberated from its confinement to love and friendship, is taken over into Marx's concept of the form of intercourse, and later into the concept of relations of production. In this manner, Feuerbach's anthropology accompanies Marx along his intellectual itinerary as a system of thought giving impulses to the various stages of the elaboration of the latter's own theory. In the *Economic and Philosophical Manuscripts*, Marx acknowledges Feuerbach as the founder of 'true materialism and of real science', inasmuch as he made 'the social relationship of "man to man" the basic principle of the theory' (*Collected Works*, vol. 3, p. 328). In a letter approximately contemporaneous with the aforementioned work, Marx states that Feuerbach has similarities with the 'culturally revolutionary' French communists, and accords to *The Philosophy of the Future* pride of place among the works that had contributed to the philosophical foundation of communism:

> The unity of man with man, which is founded upon the real difference among human beings, the concept of the human species pulled down from the heaven of abstraction upon the actual earth, what is it but the concept of history. (Quoted from Schuffenhauer, 1972, pp. 202f.)

Admittedly, Marx makes both of Feuerbach's central ideas into fundamental premises of his social theory only at the price of neutralising that which is truly critical about them. Marx, together with Engels, passes beyond Feuerbach's conception of a contemplative anthropology that is limited to interhuman relations, for the benefit of a theory of society that is systematically grounded in the co-operative reshaping of nature; in this radicalisation of Feuerbachian philosophy for the purposes of a theory of society, however, Marx robs it of part of its emancipatory power. Thus the question can be asked regarding Marx's transformation of Feuerbach's notion of sensuousness into a concept of sensuous, objectual activity, whether in this transformation the aesthetic and contemplative dignity of 'emancipatory sensuousness' is preserved, and the human being's powerful inner, drive-fraught nature, which is not fully determined by social history, is sufficiently taken into consideration. This is the theme of Alfred Schmidt's book on Feuerbach (1973). In Marx's transformation of the Feuerbachian idea of 'altruism' into the notion of human relations of co-operation, a remnant of interactionism is, to be sure, preserved, as witness the famous passage about Peter and Paul, in which it is asserted that Peter becomes Peter only through Paul (*Capital*, p. 144, note 19). However, not only does Marx make these remarks as it were in passing; he also does not draw from his observations the epistemological and social–psychological conclusions which Feuerbach had already formulated with great clarity. For Marx was so little aware of the categorial limits of his concept of labour that he was unable seriously to investigate a domain of social interaction. In consequence, in Marx's works the anthropological analysis of the labour process is not matched by a comparable account of interhuman relations (*Capital*, pp. 283ff.; see also Habermas, 1971a, chapter 1); at the point where the 'reshaping of men by men', i.e., socialisation, was to be treated, the manuscript of *The German Ideology* breaks off (*Collected Works*, vol. 5, p. 50; see the editors' note). Early in his study of Feuerbach's philosophy, Engels had disparaged his dialogics as trite and commonplace (*MEW*, vol. 3, pp. 541–3; the passage referred to here occurs on p. 542); he did not see that this criticism also held good for all assertions made in *The German Ideology* which were meant to be self-evidently valid, and which for that very reason preclude all speculation.

However, the anthropological frame of reference that Marx had gained from his critical study of Feuerbach's thought, and in which, in the early stage of the development of his ideas, his construction of a theory of society is explicitly embedded, retreats more and more into the background as Marx's work on his critique of capitalism progresses. To the extent that Marx tailors his theory of society to the mode of production of capitalist societies, the anthropological moment of historical materialism, which Marx after all regards as its basis, becomes effaced. In the early phase of its development, Marx directly gives to his theory of capitalism the form of a theory of labour that is alienated from itself; this theory criticises capitalism as a mode of production grounded in private property in the means of production that makes it impossible for the labouring subjects, the workers, to recognise themselves in the products they themselves have made (see Reichelt, 1970, chapter 1). But the Marx of *Capital* employs an entirely different approach to the critique of capitalism (see Reichelt, 1970; Theunissen, 1975; Bubner, 1973, pp. 44ff.; Krahl, 1971, pp. 31ff.). He no longer describes the capitalist social relation directly from the perspective of subjectivity-forming labour as a social relation of alienation; rather, he traces out, implicitly, the process of capitalist repression of human subjectivity. Marx makes the historical fact that the capitalist process of valorisation has become independent the starting point of his analysis of capital by making value that effects its own growth in quantity the subject of his theory. Because he assumes the 'structural identity', to borrow Reichelt's expression, of capital with Hegel's 'spirit' or 'mind', Marx can also systematically make use of the structure of argumentation of Hegel's *Logic*: capital's becoming autonomous can be presented in the same terms used to describe the process of the spirit's coming to know itself. Thus, in the systematic works of his late period, Marx, like Hegel, abstracts from all human subjectivity in order to be able to employ for the analysis of capital Hegel's logic as a methodological model suited to the abstraction that is really effectuated by capitalism. However, the relationship between the anthropological moment of his thought and his critical theory of society is thereby shifted. Certainly, the critique of political economy, too, remains embedded, in the final analysis, in the anthropologically grounded theory of Marx's early writings, because only thus can the subject capital be recognised as a pseudo-subject that is in fact founded in human labour (see Reichelt, 1970, pp. 150–62; Theunissen, 1975, pp. 328f.; Bubner, 1973, pp. 58f.); the early anthropological reflections, however, seem to lose all importance for the steps of argumentation in which the analysis of capital is carried out.

In this manner, the anthropological foundation of historical materialism retreats completely into the background in the late stage of the development of Marx's theory. To be sure, Marx continued to follow with great interest the ethnological and anthropological literature of his time; his careful study of both contemporary ethnology and Darwin's theory of biological evolution has been well documented and investigated (cf. Krader, 1973; Lucas, 1964a, 1964b). On the basis of this knowledge, Marx was able to expand the explanatory horizon of historical materialism to encompass also humanity's early history. This research, however, enters only very indirectly into the systematic construction of his critique of political economy. As a result, the relation between anthropology and historical materialism has remained a matter of controversy up to the present day.

Positions in the Marxist discussion of anthropology

Up to the Second World War, the significance of anthropological theories for historical materialism was not really discussed, even though they played a not unimportant role in Marxist attempts to elaborate theories. The social-democratic movement tried anthropologically to ground historical materialism in universal history, but did so from a perspective that was almost completely evolutionary (Weiss, 1965). Hegelian Marxism, on the other hand, was concerned with defending Marxism's historicity by criticising all anthropology (see Cerutti, 1970). Between these two interpretations of historical materialism, though, the theoretical importance of anthropology within the framework of Marxism, as well as its substantive content, remained as such unexamined. Only after the war was the discussion begun by the position, unequivocal at least in its intent, taken by a Western Marxism that had become critical of Stalinism. In this position, important parts of the analysis and argument of Marxist theory are joined together to make a positive theory of human possibilities of self-realisation in such a way that the processes of alienation visible in Western capitalism, and also those of bureaucratised socialism, become equally criticisable against the normative background of a conception of the human being obtained by the methods and theoretical tools of anthropology. However, in its efforts to achieve clarity about its philosophical premises, post-war Western Marxism did not succeed in making anthropology's fundamental determinations more than tenuous guiding notions and so extending them into the establishing of the natural preconditions of social history through biological investigation. Nor did it succeed in making clear, even in its theoretical approach, how anthropological, normative lines of argument might be combined with Marxism's construction of history, grounded in political economy. Since then, the significance of anthropology for historical materialism has been vigorously discussed in Western Marxism. In contrast, in Eastern Europe, that is, in the sphere of influence of Marxism–Leninism, anthropological questions have served as the starting point for a critique of Stalinism and of bureaucratic domination that has often been timid and has usually remained philosophical (cf. Schaff, 1970).

Many interpretations in Western Europe of the significance of Marx's early writings within the framework of his *oeuvre* simultaneously made the attempt to answer the question of anthropology's theoretical relevance to Marxism. Althusser, with his structural Marxism, was the first to try to achieve clarity regarding the level at which anthropology and the argumentation of the Marxist critique of society are situated. In his interpretative reconstruction of Marxist theory, he distinguished so rigorously between the scientific structure of the grounding of Marx's analysis of capitalism and the anthropological construction of theory in the early writings that all attempts to ground historical materialism anthropologically come under the suspicion of being ideological (a). In the French discussion of Marxism, however, the personality theory of Lucien Sève turned the anthropological themes of Marxist theory against the structuralist critique of anthropology. According to Sève, these themes give even to the construction of the Marxist critique of political economy its specific emancipatory orientation. But in making his interpretation of Marxism, Sève neglects the theoretical goal of an anthropological grounding of historical materialism, namely the normatively oriented determination of the natural basis of specifically human sociality (b). This theoretical scope of the anthropology of Marx's early writings can be grasped with the aid of György Márkus's study *Marxism and 'Anthropology': The Concept of Human Essence in the Philosophy of Marx*. This study will therefore be presented last (c). In this manner, the fundamental theoretical framework will be established within which historical materialism can be grounded in the anthropological reconstruction of the specifically human capacities for action.

(a) Althusser's structuralist critique of anthropology

Althusser's interpretation of Marx's thought and writings is shaped by the crucially important experience of Stalinism. From its very beginning, it was intended to be a critique of the Marxist tradition that would explain both how Stalinism was theoretically possible, and why the

Marxist critique of Stalinism was so ineffectual.[3] Althusser's structuralist version of Marxism therefore concentrated all its scientific energy on seeking the answer to the question of what errors in interpretation caused Marxist theory to become perverted either into Stalinist economism or into the humanism of Western Marxism. In his 'symptomatic reading' of Marx's works, Althusser sought to answer this question in ever new attempts to interpret those works. He conceives of the development of Marxist theory not in the chronological sequence of the phases of a theoretical conception that unfolds itself in successive stages, but rather from the standpoint of centrally important problematics that structure the thematic horizons of the individual writings (Althusser, 1969). This problem-oriented reading is aimed at demonstrating the existence of an epistemological rupture in Marx's development of his theory. The anthropological grounding of the theory presented in the early writings, of which both Stalinism and the Marxist critique of Stalinism are, so Althusser maintains, imitative in their explanation of the historical process by a centre of a system or of action that constitutes history, is replaced in Marx's economic writings by a scientific, structural grounding of theory. According to Althusser's line of argument, at the present time a Marxism that is applicable to the social conditions of Western Europe can be legitimately elaborated only by using such a grounding of theory. Althusser's interpretation of the 'scientific' phase of Marx's theoretical development is guided by the model provided by the latter's analysis of capital which Althusser takes as his standard (Althusser and Balibar, 1970). In contrast, he attempts to account for the early anthropological stage of Marx's theory by the paradigmatic importance for Marx of Feuerbach's critique of Hegel. Althusser's image of Feuerbach is thus of paramount importance for the global critique of anthropology that guides his interpretation of historical materialism.

At bottom, Althusser's line of argument is aimed at demonstrating that Feuerbach's anthropologically grounded critique of Hegel's idealism adopts the structure of the latter's philosophical argumentation (Althusser, 1969, pp. 41ff.). Althusser establishes Feuerbach's philosophical humanism by examining Feuerbach's critique of religion.

---

[3] An article by Althusser that is paradigmatic in this regard is 'Something new', in Althusser, 1976, pp. 208ff.; Valentino Gerratana has given a critique of Althusser's critique of Stalinism in his article, 'Sur les difficultés de l'analyse du stalinisme', in *dialectiques* 15/16 (Paris, 1976), pp. 43–53.

Feuerbach recognises the ideological systems of interpretation proper to the history of religion as projections of a species that is unconscious of its constitution of the objects of its religious beliefs. He generalises the original motive of his investigations, namely the critique of religion, into the thesis that all socio-cultural phenomena can be shown, through their deciphering, to be projective self-realisations of the human species-nature. Even Althusser acknowledges the revolutionary anti-feudalism of this anthropological materialism:

> It must not be forgotten that this discourse, of which I can only sketch the premises here, had a certain grandeur, since it called for the inversion produced by religion or political alienation to be itself inverted; in other words, it called for the inversion of the imaginary domination of the attributes of the human subject. (Althusser, 1976, pp. 197–8)

Nonetheless, Althusser undertakes to establish within the structure of Feuerbachian materialism's philosophical grounding the theoretical problematic which, despite its critique of idealism, that materialism shares with the Hegelian system. For the purpose of philosophically maintaining reasonableness in opposition to an unreasonable reality, Feuerbach, like Hegel, takes recourse to a subject standing behind the historical process which is in itself reasonable and is constitutive of history. However, while Hegel demonstrates the reasonableness of spirit which objectifies itself, and thereby alienates itself from itself in history, in contrast to the bad facticity of history, Feuerbach establishes in his study of social and cultural objectivations the natural wealth of the human being's species-capabilities. The thought of the young Marx, as well as of the Young Hegelians, was guided by the problematic of this philosophy of reason, the Feuerbachian version of which only replicated Hegel's idealism, in a mirror image, so to speak, in its theoretical humanism. This position enables Althusser to place various of Marx's early writings within the whole problematic of humanism. Thus the early writings of Marx are humanistic in the procedure of their philosophical grounding because they, following Feuerbach's anthropological materialism, seek to understand unreasonable reality as the masked objectification of the essential forces of human beings, in order thereby, and by that means alone, to break the spell of alienation binding the contemporary present. Marx's humanism, asserts Althusser, shares with bourgeois philosophy in general the latter's premises regarding the philosophy of history, inasmuch as his humanism, both in its arguments and in its political positions, postulates a naturally given substrate from the standpoint of which history can be construed as the 'Entäußerung', the externalisation and estrangement of human beings' essential powers. In his attack on the theoretical humanism of Marxism, then, Althusser intends to strike a blow against the entirety of an anthropological grounding of historical materialism that considers the natural preconditions of human sociality to be the developmental framework of the historical process (Althusser, 1969, pp. 219ff.).

In the course of his own attempts to interpret Marx's works, Althusser has over and over again assigned a new date to the epistemological rupture that is suppposed to separate the humanism of Marx's early writings from the scientific theory of history to be found in the mature writings. At first, the fundamental criticism that he makes of Marxism's anthropological method of grounding itself is directed only against the early writings which are informed by Feuerbachian themes, especially *The Economic and Philosophical Manuscripts*. Later, however, in the form of a systematic critique of Hegelianism, he tracks down the humanistic Marx even into single steps of the argumentation presented in the later writings.[4] But Althusser is chiefly interested in those passages of Marx's *oeuvre* which reveal, in the manner in which the assertions are grounded, the fundamentals of a post-humanist problematic. This problematic, Althusser claims, forms the integrative framework of the whole of the scientific theory used for the analysis of capital. This problematic enables one to discern the structure of argumentation that is proper to structural Marxism: a centre of history that has been tacitly imputed to historical materialism is replaced by the structure of a mode of production, within which the relatively autonomous societal subsystems enter into regulated relations with one another by means of the economic subsystem which is, in the last instance, determinative; and instead of a temporal continuum of history, there are discrete temporalities which are independent of one another, and each of which is defined by the particular mode of functioning of the societal subsystem that is its basis. Thus Althusser attempts to show that Marx's later writings on economics should be understood as interpretative indications of a scientific type of critique which replaces anthropological materialism's 'centralistic' mode of argumentation with the structuralist mode of argument employed by a theory of history that has been purged of philosophical presuppositions. In his essay 'The concept of critique and

---

[4] On the re-dating of the epistemological rupture in Marx's thought, see for example Louis Althusser, 'Preface to *Capital* volume one (*March* 1969)', in Althusser, 1971, pp. 71ff.

the critique of political economy', which forms a part of the original version of the collectively written work *Reading Capital*, Jacques Rancière contrasts these two modes of argumentation, presenting them as ideal types. He understands *The Economic and Philosophical Manuscripts* paradigmatically as an anthropological theory which explains in a critical manner the economic phenomena of social production by their secret centre, the species-life of human beings. In contrast, in *Contribution to the Critique of Political Economy*, Marx is supposed to have purified the economic concepts he uses of all anthropological resonances and associations so radically that he can depict the process of capitalist accumulation as a structural process devoid of all intentionality, and that regulates itself through its contradictions. Thus, in this scientific model of critique, the critique of capitalism obtains its standard from the structural self-contradictoriness of the investigated social formation alone, a standard that demonstrates in a normatively neutral fashion, as it were, the necessity of overcoming and going beyond capitalism. In this way, Marxism seems able to renounce and to do without any reflection in which specifically human possibilities of development are theoretically recognised, without therefore having also to abandon its claim to being critical.

However, this structuralist purification of Marxist theory results in a critique of society that is completely ineffectual. In his critique of political economy, Marx abstracts with conscious method from all possibilities inherent in human nature for humanising the world because he wants to present and examine only the domains of reality that have already been made subject to the capitalist process of accumulation, in order, by so doing, indirectly to give evidence of the degree to which capital has become independent of human direction. Althusser and his followers, in contrast, take this procedure used by Marx for the analysis of capitalism as the gospel truth of a Marxism that has been made scientific. It is only the tacit transformation of the restricted view of reality employed in Marx's critique of political economy into the whole truth of a Marxist theory of society that allows the Althusser school to reconstruct historical materialism upon the foundation of structuralist theory. Solely the assumption that the social reality theoretically admitted by Marx's *Capital* is co-extensive with the human sociality that can be at all scientifically studied makes it possible to detach the object of investigation so rigorously from the plexus of social action that ultimately it can be comprehended, in structuralist fashion, in a theory of the subjectless rules of systems. Even in his analysis of capitalism, Marx must ultimately find the grounding of the critique of capitalist society in an anthropological reflection that remains conscious of the possibilities inherent in human sociality for realising humanity, in contrast to the process whereby capital becomes independent which he presents and analyses. Althusser, however, excises this critical moment from Marxism. His interpretation of Marxism thus leads to a theory that can understand social interrelations only as subjectless functional units, and that is completely incapable of taking into consideration the social praxis in which even a society that is alienated from the goals and needs of the socially integrated subjects is grounded (see Honneth, 1977; Rovatti, 1977). Now, how is a theory of society supposed to be able to understand in any way and to any degree the social learning processes in which it, as an interpretation of the given situation, could acquire political power, if it previously believed that it had to leave out of consideration all historical nexuses of action? The structuralist interpretation of Marxism has purged its fundamental concepts so radically of all anthropological determinations of social action that it can no longer perceive historical processes as inherent in the contemporary social struggles and collective processes of reaching agreement.

In the French discussion of Marxism, Lucien Sève has posed questions aimed at this de-anthropologising of historical materialism which are clearly unavoidable. For how should it be possible to advance as grounded a Marxist perspective that points beyond capitalism, if Marxism forgoes a reconstruction of the human potentialities that are repressed under capitalism, and if the mere presentation of the structural contradictions of capitalism is not accompanied by consideration of the possibilities for praxis? By raising this question Sève has surely put his finger on the weak points of structural Marxism, without, however, succeeding in drawing all the conclusions implicit in his line of critical reasoning.

(b) Lucien Sève's theory of personality

Lucien Sève's *Man in Marxist Theory and the Psychology of Personality* was published in France in 1968. This work is a systematic attempt to formulate the approach required for solving the fundamental problems posed by a scientific study of the individual personality within the horizon of a politico-economic theory of society based on the works of Marx. Sève begins his books by distinguishing categorically his own methods and investigations from the physiological reductionism of a tradition in Soviet psychology that has its origins with Pavlov. He does so, however, without taking notice of the immanent transcending of the tradition in the 'cultural–historical school' of Vygotsky and Leontiev.[5] This fact alone shows that he does not hope to find the solution he is seeking in a more exact determination of the human being's peculiarities as a natural being, but by means of philosophical clarifications. His choice of the second path compels him to make an extensive and detailed critique of two prominent interpretations of Marxism that are battling with one another. In opposition to a Marxist humanism oriented exclusively to the theory of alienation presented in Marx's early writings, Sève asserts the importance of historical materialism's true grounding in history and economy. He refuses to purchase the salvaging and valorisation of Marxism's anthropological moments at the price of making Marxism ahistorical and excluding the economy from its analyses and theory. On the other hand, Sève counterposes to the structuralist de-subjectification of historical materialism the continuity in Marx's works of questions relating to anthropology and the theory of personality: the paradigmatic importance for Marxism of the analysis of capital must not be paid for with the renunciation of all theory of subjectivity. What is novel and fruitful about the approach worked out by Sève, who was later regarded as one of the most important theoreticians of the 'Euro-Communist' shift of the French Communists, is the fact that he undertakes to extract Marx's anthropology from the latter's mature works. He thereby joins in the revival of the claim that Marx's critique of political economy is scientific, a movement for which Althusser's writings were the clearest sign. Despite Sève's concurrence with Althusser in this general claim, he disagrees with the details of the latter's interpretations of Marx's writings.

At the heart of Sève's line of argument is Marx's sixth thesis on Feuerbach. There Marx asserts that:

> Feuerbach resolves the religious essence into the human essence. But the human essence is no abstraction inherent in each single individual. In its reality it is the ensemble of the social relations. (Marx and Engels, *Collected Works*, vol. 5, p. 4)

Sève interprets these statements to mean

> that men's being, their historically concrete 'humanity', in no wise has its seat

[5] For an overview of Vygotsky's work, see James V. Wertsch, *Vygotsky and the Social Formation of Mind* (Cambridge, Mass., 1985).

or its origin directly in human individuality considered in general but rather
. . . above all . . . in the economic development of society. The *6th Thesis*
therefore establishes a fundamental distinction between the objective human
essence and the form of individuality, and asserts the basically subordinate
character of individuality with regard to the objective social basis. (Sève,
1978, p. 159)

Refusing all speculation about the essence of 'the' human being, Sève
maintains that the theory of personality must take this distinction into
account in its entirety and from the very beginning. However, he also
recognises that the sixth thesis by no means rejects the concept of
human essence itself. In the later part of the thesis, Marx criticises
Feuerbach because the latter's non-social formulation of the concept of
human essence forces him '(1) to abstract from the historical process'
and in so doing 'to presuppose an abstract – *isolated* – human individual',
wherefore (2) the human essence can 'be comprehended only as a
"genus",[6] an internal, dumb generality which merely *naturally* unites the
many individuals' (Marx and Engels, *Collected Works*, vol. 5, p. 4).
According to Sève, Marx, in making these assertions, is not at all
rejecting the concept of human essence per se, 'but *abstract understanding* of this concept, replaced at the same time by *further*, historical,
scientific, concrete *understanding* of the *human essence*: the ensemble of
social relations' (Sève, 1978, p. 166). Sève attempts to bring the early
Marx's concept of 'human essence' within the framework of the critique
of political economy. By refusing to understand human essence as an
abstract quality inherent in each individual human being, while at the
same time adhering to a concept of human essence that is referred to the
social relations, Marx opens two paths of reflection for a Marxist theory
of subjectivity. First, his position conceives of the human individual as a
socially integrated subject, with the result that, second, attention is
directed to the question of the material processes of social integration in
which individuals collectively reproduce themselves by means of the
appropriation of natural resources in determinate, historically concrete
relations of production. It is the achievement of Sève's interpretation,
and his superiority over a representative of 'speculative humanism' like
Adam Schaff, that he does not stop at the definition of the human being
as a social being which is capable of objectifying actions, but goes on to
seek the adequate concept of society based upon this definition. Sève

---

[6] Here 'genus' is the translation of 'Gattung', which is rendered into English as 'species'
by Martin Milligan in his translation of *The Economic and Philosophical Manuscripts of
1844*, used as the source of the English translations of terms taken from that work.

rejects a psychologising concept of society that does not permit the conceiving of the autonomy of the objectifications, of the stabilised nexuses of action and expectational patterns, of the institutions and traditions. The position of that which is individual, then, is to be determined on the basis of an adequate concept of society. In this regard, though, Sève's proposals become unsatisfactory. Since he clings to a relatively crude schematisation of society into 'base' and 'super-structure', he must attempt to assign to the individual a place within this framework. Since it is obviously nonsensical to ascribe the individual either to the base or to the superstructure of society, and since Sève is incapable of dissolving these rigid concepts by means of a logically consequent conception of the social plexus founded upon the category of praxis, he hits upon the notion of 'juxtastructure':

> Thus although [individuals] are functionally determined by the social base (and its superstructures) *quite as much* as the superstructures themselves, individuals do not arise *on* this base with superstructural characteristics but are as it were *laterally meshed in* with it and become wholly subordinated to it – although it is not their *actual source*. (Sève, 1978, p. 144)

On the basis of this fundamental notion, Sève then seeks to elaborate the determinations of forms of subjectivity that are typical of capitalism, in terminological parallel to Marx's analysis of capital. Even on this level, his theoretical programme reveals a reductionism that pervades all stages of his personality theory. For his attempt to take the early Marx's notion of human essence out of the abstract framework of a pre-sociological anthropology and to integrate it into the scientific frame-work of a politico-economic theory of society leaves out of consideration two central dimensions of the anthropology that is present in germ in Marx's early writings: neither the normativity of Marx's concept of human essence, nor his attempt to formulate a determination of human essence that also takes man's natural being into account are in any way taken over into Sève's investigation.

As far as normativity is concerned, Marx's critique of Feuerbach goes far beyond the conception of anthropology that is a component of Sève's personality theory. Marx criticises Feuerbach for establishing the es-sence of human beings solely in light of their actually observable being, rather than conceiving of the human being, in contradistinction to the given social reality, as something that has first to be realised (see Marx and Engels, *Collected Works*, vol. 5, p. 58). To an anthropology that restricts itself to the subjectivity given in a particular historical period,

Marx counterposes the human being's broad possibilities of development. Marx's definition of human essence as the 'ensemble of social relations' can thus no longer be interpreted merely as an, as it were, materialist rooting of the concept of human essence in the 'objective social base' of the given economic social formation. The human essence is, certainly, 'in its reality' not an 'abstraction inherent in each single individual', but instead is theoretically accessible only in its social integration, which is effected by means of socialisation processes. However, the human being's subjective, specifically human possibilities of action are not exhausted by the form they have under capitalist social integration. In Marx's writings, both the concept of human essence and the concept of praxis or society have a normative moment that goes beyond the conditions obtaining under capitalism, and that Sève does not grasp.

It is not just the normative dimension of the anthropological concept of human essence, which is to be found also in the concept of personality, that is lost in Sève's interpretation of Marx's works. He also does not take into account the fact that Marx's critique of Feuerbach, despite its line of argument aimed primarily at the scientific apprehension of social relations, does not by any means deny the importance of the naturalness of human beings, thus of the natural foundation of human subjectivity which Feuerbach emphasised. Marx's objection in the sixth thesis that, within the framework of Feuerbach's thought, the essence of the human being 'can . . . be comprehended only as "genus", as an internal, dumb generality which merely *naturally* unites the many individuals' (Marx and Engels, *Collected Works*, vol. 5, p. 4) does not preclude the possibility that it is both meaningful and necessary to enquire about the natural preconditions underlying human activities and forms of praxis, even though the latter are, certainly, not co-extensive with the former. To that extent, the question of the natural basis of specifically human sociality remains centrally important for the grounding of a Marxist theory of personality. In any case, the way the theses on Feuerbach are worded does not permit the playing off against each other of the two sides of the twofold determination of the human being developed in the young Marx's anthropology, namely of the human being as a natural being endowed with consciousness and, on the other hand, as a social being.

Because he neglects the natural fundamental features of specifically human sociality, Sève is uncritical with regard to the domain that he calls 'neurophysiopsychology' – the neologism with which he designates this domain is sufficient to signal his deep disinterest in this domain's objects of enquiry. Because he neglects the normative moments of human sociality, Sève is not only no longer able to ground the necessity of human beings' emancipation, but he also attenuates the meaning and the substance of that emancipation. His ideal of full personal development is the attainment of polytechnical skills and knowledge, but not in addition political socialisation for the purpose of self-determined action in democratic decision-making processes. His concept of the forms of individuality remains vulgarly functionalistic, insofar as that concept contains only the determination of individuals by social requirements, but not the individual's self-definition and practical contributions. In his concept of 'biography', there is lacking self-determination with respect to one's own future life, as well as the dimension of a unity in meaning of the life-course effected by synthesising achievements of the ego. On the most diverse levels of his formation of concepts, Sève reproduces the opposition between individual and society, which he had set out to overcome. Thus his reconstruction of Marx's anthropology remains half-hearted in every respect, and in its substantive proposals does not even rise to the level of its interpretation of Marx's writings. It is true that he rightly incorporates the concept of species from the early writings into his construction of a Marxist theory of personality, in opposition to Althusser's structuralism; but he leaves out of consideration the organic conditions of human sociality and its possibilities of historical development.

György Márkus undertakes to investigate these two topics in his study *Marxism and 'Anthropology': The Concept of Human Essence in the Philosophy of Marx* (1978). His philosophically oriented efforts are aimed at formulating a concept of human essence that is open to history, and that would lie between the abstract alternatives of an ahistorical anthropology establishing the human being's species-specific endowments and a subjectless structuralist conception of history. Márkus's study has the form of a detailed interpretation of the anthropology present in germ in Marx's early writings, and the influence of which is to be found even in the structure of argumentation of the later writings on economics.

(c) György Márkus's interpretation of Marx

Márkus begins his study with the immanent reference which Marx's economic theory of capitalism makes to the fundamental anthropological premises of the early writings. With his concept of 'communism',

Marx claims not only to characterise from the standpoint of politics and economics the social formation that follows of economic necessity upon capitalism, but also to describe, from the moral and practical standpoint, the developmental stage of the history of the human species that is normatively superior to capitalism, in that it admits of greater latitude for freedom. The critique of political economy immanently points to a process of progress in the history of the human species that brings to realisation the possibilities of freedom naturally present in germinal form in human beings. These anthropologically rooted possibilities of the species' development are the object of Márkus's interest. He starts with the special position occupied by the human species in virtue of the fact that, although it is the biological result of natural evolutionary processes, it steps outside the limits of this natural evolution with its socio-cultural form of living. To use Marx's words, the human being is both a sensuous natural being and a specifically human species being (Márkus, 1978, pp. 4ff.). The human being distinguishes himself from all subhuman life forms through the kind of activity called work; on the basis of this difference between the structure of animal behaviour and the human capability for action, Márkus seeks to determine the species-specific developmental possibilities of the human being:

> Work constitutes the real, historical relation of man to nature and at the same time it determines the fundamental relations between man and man and so it forms the basis of whole [sic] human life. (*ibid.*, p. 5)

The animal is limited by its life activity, which is guided by a deep-seated system of instincts comprehending both perception and voluntary movement. In contrast, with work there appears a form of action by the human species that interposes itself with an intermediating function between the needful subject and the satisfaction of the subject's needs. Through the gradual dismantling of instinct-guided behaviour, the human species frees itself from the limits of nature. Now the human being can relate himself to nature in work without immediate pressure from need. In the tool he gives an objective form to this mode of activity that distinguishes him from the animal. The traces of the human being's shaping persist to an increasing degree in the object of work, in the natural objects, until the human being's original 'natural environment' has been transformed into his 'cultural environment'. In the reverse manner, it is with his historically advancing fashioning of nature that the human being appropriates his organically possible capacities for action. In work, he can, to an ever increasing extent, make the regularities of nature into the guiding principle of his own activity. At the same time, as the possibilities of satisfying his needs increase through his action upon nature, the pretensions of the human being's needs also become greater; the appropriation of nature follows a spiral consisting of the satisfaction of needs made possible through particular labour processes and of the expansion of needs produced by the satisfaction of needs. Using a pair of concepts borrowed from Marx, Márkus calls the totality of this interrelation and interplay of the human appropriation of nature and the unfolding of human subjectivity the 'naturalisation of man' and the 'humanisation of nature' (*ibid.*, p. 14).

Marx assumes that in work, the form of activity specific to the species, the human being relates himself consciously and socially to the nature environing himself. On the basis of this structure of human action, therefore, Márkus can identify and describe two further peculiarities of the human being which establish the conditions in which the species' developmental history begins. First, their collective working upon nature causes the subjects of this activity to relate themselves of necessity to the operations of their particular partners in this activity. The intersubjective construction of societies grows out of the co-operative relations found in the original division of labour. Furthermore, in the labour processes the technical knowledge of a given generation must be passed on to the following one; in such socialisation processes, the human species gives permanence to its chances for survival. Second, these labour processes are also the, as it were, organically rooted precondition for the self-awareness that is proper to the human being. Since, in contrast to the instinctually guided behaviour of animals, the activity of the human being that is directed to natural objects is not immediately fused with the satisfaction of needs, he is able to become conscious of the intentions of his own actions in relation to nature, which no longer makes *direct* appeals to his instincts and has become objective for him. In work the human being experiences himself as an agent, a subject of action, who has stepped outside of nature and who follows his own need-dispositions. With this psychical distancing of himself from nature and from his own activities, he develops the capability to hold his natural environment away from himself, so to speak, in such a way that he can consciously influence it.

Intersubjectivity and consciousness are thus species characters which are, in Marx's anthropology, embedded in the structure of work, and for which the human being has acquired the capability only in the process of natural evolution. Together with work, they constitute the three specifically human particularities to which the development possibilities of the human species are tied. Following Marx, Márkus defines the process of social emancipation as the process of the universalisation of these capabilities which are essential to human life. This understanding of social emancipation makes the history of the human species appear also as a process of progress, in which the scope for the realisation of human possibilities for action also increases as the extent of the economic appropriation of nature grows (*ibid.*, p. 62). In this manner, Márkus can carry out the critique of political economy as a critique of the capitalist social formation using not only the criterion of economic rationality, but also the criterion of practical and moral rationality. The universalisation of the species-specific capability for work can be presented using a pair of axes to demonstrate that with the cultivation of nature, the human being's cognitive capabilities are further developed. The universalisation of the intersubjectivity that is structurally embedded in labour processes can be projected on to a single axis, along which the initially merely assumed unity of the human species ultimately becomes a 'world-historical, empirically universal fact' with the advance of the economically necessitated, gradual interlocking of all separate production communities. Lastly, the universalisation of the human faculty of consciousness can be displayed conjecturally along an axis, on which forms of the appropriation of reality that have become increasingly freed from the demands of survival become prevalent, as the gradual detachment of productive thinking from the societal labour process advances.

Thus, in his interpretation of the anthropological bases of Marx's theory, Márkus succeeds in effecting a mediation of anthropology and historical materialism that is able to bring the theoretical recognition of the organic conditions in which human sociality has its beginning into harmony with the construction of an open historical process using political and economic categories. In the anthropological reconstruction of the possibilities of action specific to the human species, historical materialism holds fast to the social dimensions in which human subjectivity, in a process whose success is always uncertain, learns to unfold, to realise itself, as the human shaping of nature becomes more extensive in the course of history. In this manner, Marx historicised the concept of 'human essence' without divesting it of its biological points of reference:

> Marx meant, it seems, by 'human essence' primarily those characteristics of the real historical existence of mankind *which make it possible to comprehend history as a continuous and unified process that has a developmental tendency*. The *universality* of man . . . mark[s] the general direction of the historical progress of humanity, while the characterisation of man as a *conscious social* being engaged in material *productive self-activity* refers to those necessary traits,

those dimensions of this total developmental process on the basis of which the above historical tendency unfolds and in the spheres of which it becomes manifest. (Márkus, 1978, pp. 39ff.)

2

ANTHROPOLOGICAL FOUNDATIONS OF SOCIAL ACTION

Preliminary remarks on the German tradition of 'philosophical anthropology'

In the form anthropology has generally taken in Germany – and the present work stands undeniably in this tradition – it has its origin in one of the philosophical and scientific currents that were characteristic of the Weimar Republic. The name given to this current of thought, 'philosophical anthropology', is in fact very misleading, for merely philosophical definitions were precisely what it did not aim at. Rather, this intellectual current undertook, in a non-speculative manner, to grasp the 'fundamental structures of humanity' through comparison of man and animal, and through critical examination and appropriation of as many findings of the natural and cultural sciences as possible. This anthropology developed in the context of more general tendencies to turn philosophy away from its concentration on mere epistemology, and to help it regain substantiality of its object, as well as to find a way out of traditional impasses. Thus, this movement called for the clarification of the relationship between the natural and the socio-cultural sciences, not by means of definitional demarcations, as had been done previously, but through investigation of the subject matter of mediating scientific domains, such as biology. Philosophical anthropology met with great public interest and assumed an almost fashionable character, which was to be surpassed only by existential philosophy. The following thumbnail characterisation of the principal motives, controversies and authors of this intellectual current that arose out of the ferment of the twenties has the immediate purpose of situating at the outset the anthropologies of Arnold Gehlen and Helmuth Plessner, which have great importance for our development of a theoretical framework, in an historical context, in order thereby to show that the relationship between factual assertions and political volition is not at all as simple and straightforward as many of Gehlen's critics suppose.

However, the antecedents of philosophical anthropology extend of course much farther back in history. To give an account of them would be almost tantamount to portraying the entire, specifically German history of idealist and post-idealist philosophy.[1] Kant's anthropology was still a traditional attempt to combine and unify diverse knowledge about human beings. The sources of this knowledge were to be found in the description of nature and in life-experiences, not in metaphysical speculation or in physical analysis. The true starting point of the German anthropological tradition, however, is the Romantic reaction to the ethics and philosophy of history of the Enlightenment, as represented by Kant. Herder is to be numbered among the precursors of anthropology insofar as his work was a precursor of this Romantic critique. In Romanticism, the philosophy of history yielded primacy to the philosophy of nature. It was not, though, a matter of a philosophy of nature per se, but of an attempt to understand the human being by means of the philosophy of nature. This effort made the confused anthropological theories of the German Romanticism the common point of origin for two traditions of anthropological thought and research. On the one hand, Feuerbach can be understood as a defender of the aforementioned themes against Hegel's attempt to re-integrate the Romantic critique into a philosophy of history. Thus Feuerbach's writings and the message of his anthropology, which has remained vital and pervasive in Marxism, originate in the same impulse as do, on the other hand, Schelling's late philosophy and the radical new approach of Schopenhauer. However, Schopenhauer, in particular, and his admirer Nietzsche are the thinkers whom German 'philosophical anthropology' invokes again and again. In comparison, Herder and especially Feuerbach are scarcely mentioned. Schopenhauer's philosophy represents what is surely the most radical break with the Western metaphysics of reason. Certainly, this metaphysics too had always been aware of a tension between the human being's rational nature and his corporeal nature. But there had been no doubt that reason had a powerfulness properly its own, and that a greater value had to be accorded to it. In Schopenhauer's thinking, these unquestioned assumptions were rendered ineffectual. He conceives of a human will that is animal-like in nature, and that is primary and independent of the human being's

[1] A useful discussion of this history can be found in Herbert Schnädelbach, *German Philosophy 1831–1933* (Cambridge, 1983).

inherent reason. Schopenhauer sees happiness in salvation from the will. Nietzsche turns Schopenhauer's metaphysics of the will around and replaces the longing for salvation from the will with the affirmation of an unbridled will to live, to intensify life, a will to power. Regardless of the differences in the way these two thinkers assign value, their radical refusals to ascribe central importance to reason share the problematic question of whether they constitute a surmounting of the Cartesian dualisms, or whether they are merely an inverted Cartesianism (Schulz, n.d., p. 401), that is, a simple reversal of the relationship between the body and reason. The tension among the various forms of solution to this problem, between the abandonment of the metaphysics of reason on the one hand and on the other the preservation of the distinguishing features of the human being established by that metaphysics, character-ises the field in which the empirical attempts to elaborate an anthropo-logical theory have taken place.

The first motive of philosophical anthropology (cf. Seifert, 1934–5; Haering, 1929–30) was to overcome the disciplinary boundaries within the organisation and conducting of scientific investigations, and to bring together not only philosophy and the sciences, but also the various sciences among themselves in their assertions about man. Knowledge that was divided into special sciences was, it appeared, by and large useless if these sciences could not be joined together in a synthesis. Behind the desire for such a synthesis, however, stood not an abstract yearning for universal knowledge, but rather – and herein lies philo-sophical anthropology's second principal motive – the urgently felt need for practical understanding, for the 'strength to direct and shape one's own life', according to Seifert, a 'need for a world view', in Haering's words. Science was regarded as an enterprise that gave a sense to life only when it was related back to the problems of a cultural crisis that was understood as epoch-making. Of course, it remained an entirely open question, what world view would emerge from this synthesis, and whether this *Weltanschauung* was to have the effect of binding individ-uals together socially, or was supposed to enable the individual to find a meaning in his life. In any case, though, these possibilities sufficed to burden the debates about anthropology with serious questions that were central to the period.

The lines of thought tending towards anthropology shared the in-tention of going beyond a rationalist and individualist limitation of the notion of the human being. Now, it is unclear, in the case of such an intent, whether the critique of rationalism is to be understood as the search for a higher rationality or as a retreat into irrationality, whether the critique of the individualism of bourgeois society is to be understood as a higher form of the embedding of the individual in a solidary society or as a repressive subordination of the individual to a collectivity. In any case, a conception of the 'whole person' was another of philosophical anthropology's major themes. Finally, mention should be made of the intent to place the human being, considered as a part of the world, not alongside the other parts, but at their centre. At this point, the relationship between anthropology and ontology necessarily became controversial.

It is only too clear how strongly all of these concerns were linked to the attempts of intellectuals to achieve clarity about the premises and principles of their thought, to gain a firm standpoint in the midst of the crisis-shaken Weimar Republic. Nevertheless, it seems inappropriate to measure the different attempts by a single yardstick from the critique of ideology. The most important expressions of the first stage of the anthropology discussion came from Max Scheler and Martin Heidegger. In his early preliminary study, published in 1914, Scheler already attempted an exact determination of the human specifica, and then continued this undertaking at greater length at the beginning of the twenties. Since death interrupted his reflections, Scheler's most important statement is to be found in his work *Man's Place in Nature*.

There he developed an hierarchical schema which was intended to contain the essential structures of the processing of the environment, extending from the plant to the human being. For Scheler, the development within this schema culminates in the spirit, which is conceived of as possible, independent of man, in the framework of a highly speculative, religious interpretation of history as God in the process of becoming. This succinct statement of Scheler's position is at the same time an indication of his limits. In spite of his affinity with science, he considers it incapable of the requisite synthesis; for this synthesis, philosophy and its ability to grasp essences are needed. Entirely parallel to his deprecation of civilisation and high estimation of culture, and to his restriction of the extent of science's capability, Scheler draws a boundary between man's 'practical intelligence' and that which is truly spiritual in the human being. This position is the basis of this philosopher's creative originality in anthropology, for it safeguards him against attempting to find the differentia of the human being in a merely gradual increase of practical intelligence or of brain size. To such attempts he opposes a radical discontinuity, which he founds on the human being's personhood. What the phenomenological procedure accomplishes in philosophy becomes for Scheler the guiding thread for anthropological insights. The phenomenological reduction is for him the model example of the human being's capability for distancing himself from the data of his environment and from his own drives and affects. This distance makes possible objectivity, adequation of perception to its objects, the human being's becoming conscious of himself, and his openness to the world. Scheler derives the development of the human being from the nature of a defective life form that is badly integrated into its environment, and that must compensate for its natural deficiencies through its cultural achievements.

Martin Heidegger sets out upon his philosophical quest in a quite different manner, and does not by any means regard himself as a philosophical anthropologist. Nonetheless, he belongs to this discussion, inasmuch as his thought unquestionably shares some features with Scheler's shift of perspective. Heidegger does not undertake to ground the differentia of the human being by scientific means; rather, he presupposes it. As Plessner once inimitably expressed the matter, Heidegger's philosophy takes no more notice of the human being's nature than it needs for dying (Plessner, 1974, p. 24). In lengthy sections of *Being and Time*, Heidegger analyses the structure of *Dasein*, of human existence, not with the intention of thereby elaborating a scientific theory, but in order to elucidate the nature of existential problems, which are always individual. The framework of these analyses is given by his intent to develop an ontology and to answer the 'question of the meaning of Being', inasmuch as he takes recourse to the life form that alone is capable of both an understanding of Being and an understanding of itself. Heidegger thereby places himself in a peculiar intermediary position between anthropology and transcendental philosophy. He too makes the anthropological turn of transcendental philosophy, up to a certain point, but refuses to decompose philosophy into anthropology. His 'analysis of *Dasein*' does not seek to fulfil the task of anthropology, although it undeniably has anthropological implications that were, moreover, developed in its reception. While *Being and Time* still admits the task of an anthropology (Heidegger, 1962, p. 71), this is no longer true of Heidegger's later thought. Thus, although in many respects, especially in virtue of his deprecation of science as merely derivative and secondary knowledge, Heidegger cannot be accounted a philosophical anthropologist, and although his philosophy both aims further and remains narrower in scope than philosophical anthropology, the question can nonetheless be asked: what does Heidegger's thought yield that is useful specifically for anthropology? This contribution consists chiefly in the fact that Heidegger resolutely calls attention to the structure of the human being's self-reflectivity and thereby – as did Scheler with the concept of person – throws into relief a fundamental character of the human being that cannot be decomposed in the manner of faculty psychology. He conceives this self-reflectivity in its temporal structure, hence not merely as a backward-looking coming-to-terms with the past and freeing oneself from it, but as necessarily referred to practical projects extending into the future. However, as far as the intermediary position between anthropology and transcendental philosophy is concerned, which position is of paramount importance for the principal themes of his thought, Plessner has persuasively criticised it with arguments that are reminiscent of Feuerbach's critique of Hegel, even in their tone:

> Only he can exist who lives, regardless of the level on which he lives. To close oneself off to [life in its wholeness, Trans.], and to found living upon just one of the human being's possibilities, namely existing, means to let the pursuit of the human being's enquiry about himself for the sake of this relatedness to himself count as the sole legitimate directive for an anthropology carried out with practical intent . . . What conditions must be fulfilled so that the dimension of existence is founded upon that of living? (Plessner, 1976, pp. 188ff.)

Serious criticism of the whole enterprise of philosophical anthropology was voiced even as it was being launched. In his demarcation of his position from anthropology, Husserl (1941) was much more radical than his student Heidegger and even accused him of anthropologism, inasmuch as the latter made use of the finite consciousness of the existing individual instead of the transcendental dimension of consciousness, and no longer denied to all scientific and pre-philosophical cognition participation in providing the foundation for philosophy. With his unconditional defence of his transcendental approach, Husserl sought to ward off the irrationalist dangers that were undoubtedly appearing as a result of the work of Heidegger and some proponents of philosophical anthropology. Joachim Ritter's important, carefully pondered assessment of philosophical anthropology was also dictated by his scepticism about the possibility of safeguarding the sciences against being overcome by needs for a consistent world view. Only his position had the weakness that, while formulating a refusal of these needs, it was not able to propose a more rational form for them (Ritter, 1974, pp. 36–61). Unlike Dilthey, who had still believed in the possibility of world views as enlightened forms of practical reason, Ritter could only advise stoical endurance of the compartmentalisation of scientific knowledge. In his writings, one can find neither an alternative synthesis nor ideas for reorganising the scientific enterprise in order to increase its capability for synthesis.

Here only a few of the multitude can be named who thought and wrote within the framework of philosophical anthropology. Erich Rothacker's original contribution consisted chiefly in his counterposing to the notion of the human being's openness to the world his embeddedness – necessitated by action – in particular, culturally and linguistically mediated environments, and in thereby linking philosophical anthropology and cultural anthropology in a fashion that resolved the tension between action and an 'idea of the world'. Ernst Cassirer's anthropology, published in English during its author's exile from Germany, drew strongly on the findings of empirical research and led Cassirer to understand the human being no longer as an *animal rationale* but as an *animal symbolicum*, that is, to regard the capacity for creating and using symbols as the decisive differentia of the human being. The anthropology of Werner Sombart is lacking in any fruitful insights and is of interest only as evidence of the extent to which Sombart adapted himself to Fascist ideology. Paul Ludwig Landsberg also made the turn to existential anthropology, but his work remains purely intraphilosophical. The writings of Viktor von Weizsäcker do not go from philosophy to biology, but rather from medicine and biology to philosophy, and are full of stimulating ideas and insights; however, their substantive content can also be found to a large degree in the principal systematic theories of philosophical anthropology.

Without doubt, the oeuvres of Arnold Gehlen and Helmuth Plessner must be considered as presenting the two major theories of philosophical anthropology. In many respects converging, while in many other respects radically different, they are the first focus of the following discussion. However, between them there stands a body of work and thought that originates within a completely different horizon, and that solves problems which remain unsolved in the theories of Gehlen and Plessner: George Herbert Mead's anthropologically grounded theory of practical intersubjectivity.

Philosophical anthropology as a theory of action. Arnold Gehlen's attempt to construct a systematic anthropology

Arnold Gehlen combined central concerns of philosophical anthropology with the findings of biological and ethnological research to make a systematic anthropology. In it, the special position of the human being is not accounted for with the classical philosophical dualisms of body–soul and body–mind, which were still accepted by Scheler, for example, but is explained, rather, by the structure of human action. In his system, Gehlen accounts for the human being's specific capabilities by arguing that they have their origin in compensation for the organic deficiency that is peculiar to the human being, a compensation which is successful only in action. So unequivocally does the concept of action become the centre of this anthropological theory that even an historical materialism derived from the Marxist notion of praxis could allow itself, in the first steps of its development, to be guided to a great extent by Gehlen's anthropology.

Arnold Gehlen was led to his discovery of the anthropological significance of human action along the path of an ambivalent critique of traditional epistemology.[2] In his early philosophical writings, the epistemological presupposition of an order-creating ego was the point of departure for his reflections; the self-certainty of the solipsistic subject led Gehlen to the questions of the possibility of certainty about the reality of the external world, of a continuity of intersubjective relations, and of an identity of perception in the multiplicity of sense impressions. These questions, which have compelling force in the tradition of Descartes's rationalism, were answered by Gehlen with a line of argument that sees through the philosophical apriorism of an order-creating subject, without, however, overcoming the solipsism of this basic model. To the rationalism of an epistemology focused on the reflexive ego, Gehlen opposes the dimension of irrational *Erlebnis*, deeply subjective mental–emotional experience, which comprehends consciousness; in this turning towards *Lebensphilosophie*, though, he does not fundamentally free his thinking from the solipsistic presupposition of a solitary subject. With the concept of *Erlebnis*, Gehlen does indeed break

---

[2] This thesis was presented and defended by Dietrich Böhler in his excellent interpretation of Gehlen's early writings. See Böhler, 1973. Böhler's interpretation is chiefly of Gehlen's *Habilitation* dissertation, *Wirklicher und unwirklicher Geist: Eine philosophische Untersuchung in der Methode absoluter Phänomenologie* (Leipzig, 1931), and the articles published in his *Theorie der Willensfreiheit und andere frühe Schriften* (Neuwied and Berlin, 1965).

through rationalism's restriction to the philosophy of consciousness, for the sphere of consciousness is now 'embedded in a more comprehensive sphere, which often can be surmised only from within the sphere of consciousness, and which announces itself in antinomies and paradoxes' (Gehlen, 1927, p. 31); but the act of *Erlebnis* is itself rooted just as much in the isolated subject as was previously the activity of consciousness recognised by rationalist epistemology. This critique of epistemological solipsism, which itself remains solipsistic, marks the beginning of a decisionistic fundamental theme of Gehlen's theory that was in agreement with the pre-fascist conservative cultural critique. Contrasted with a reflexivity that did not issue in action, the decision to engage in an action oriented to irrational certitudes assumed an almost philosophico-political dignity; because the irrational act of *Erlebnis* can be referred back solely to the solitary subject, the action ensuing from it cannot enter into an intersubjective process of deliberation. In his interpretation of Gehlen's early works, Dietrich Böhler put a political construction on this theme:

> The 'inability to act' of the university-educated 'declining bourgeoisie' that has been laid bare here in the sense of the 'bourgeois self-hatred' (Habermas) typical of the twenties, or of 'anti-bourgeois bourgeoisness' (von Krockow), is interpreted by Gehlen as a sign of a decaying senescent culture, incapable of commitment and lacking fighting spirit, as mediocre as it was indecisive. Indeed, like his elder contemporaries before him, like Ernst Jünger, Carl Schmitt and Martin Heidegger, who had grown up in the putrid atmosphere of bourgeois security and enervated prosperity of the years prior to 1914, while he had experienced only their cultural offshoots in the Weimar Period, Gehlen sees in the ineffectuality of 'mere knowledge' and in historical relativism the roots of the amorality and the inability to act of the age, of the final epoch of the bourgeoisie in its decline. In contrast, Gehlen, in adopting a decisionistic stance much closer to existential philosophy than he would have us believe, and differing from that philosophy solely in the authoritarian role it assigns to community, calls upon his audience to make the decision to take upon themselves the risk of active life, and that means to subject themselves to any system of action whatsoever. (Böhler, 1973, pp. 238ff.; see also Lepenies, 1967, pp. 41ff.)

His going beyond epistemological idealism by means of *Lebensphilosophie* led Gehlen into a political decisionism that, with the abrupt transformation of an empty aesthetic subjectivism into a heroism of action modelled on the valour of the battlefield, became a central motif of pre-fascist thought (cf. Hillach, 1978). However, Gehlen's critique of

idealism does not exhaust itself in this political theme of an ultracon-
servative critique of culture. For the same philosophical reflection also
opens to him the possibility of radicalising the concept of *Erlebnis* that
had been opposed to the apriorism of the philosophy of consciousness,
to make of it an understanding of the practical significance of cognition
for action. The original category of 'irrational mental–emotional experience' that constituted the consciousness-encompassing point of reference of the early critique of rationalism could then be developed further
into a category of action that makes it possible to conceive of consciousness as a phase in the execution of an action, in the manner of pragmatism. This train of thought forms the foundation of Gehlen's
anthropology. He would reject, though, any suggestion that his work
contains echoes of Feuerbachian themes; historical ancestors whom he
would recognise are, rather, Schopenhauer and Nietzsche.

In his principal anthropological work *Der Mensch* (Man) (Gehlen,
1971), Gehlen takes up again the critique of idealism begun in his early
writings on epistemology, giving it the form of a rigorous obligation on
the part of theory that is concerned philosophically with 'man' to be
based on and guided by empirical data. He studies and assimilates the
findings of biological and ethnological research for the purpose of
elaborating an *empirical philosophy*, and thus energetically preserves
philosophy's claim to scientificity. In his thought, however, this concept
of scientificity has deserted the banner of the Enlightenment and gone
over to the side of a programmatically elitist counter-Enlightenment:

> Every science consists in the formulation of hypotheses, the conformity of
> which with the facts is to be proven, and every science must draw its concepts
> from the facts, and not arrange the latter in accordance with already estab-
> lished concepts. If this science is philosophical, then that means, as I have
> said, not 'metaphysical' but, if you will, 'overarching' . . . thus a philosophical
> science of the human being includes the attempt to make assertions about the
> human being as a totality, using the material of these special sciences and
> going beyond their boundaries, and to make assertions that are themselves
> empirico-scientific: it is precisely in this [the nature of a philosophical
> science of man, Trans.] that the presupposition consists that it is possible to
> make such assertions, and it is of course in this [the nature of a philosophical
> science of man, Trans.] that the difficulties consist. (Gehlen, 1971, p. 16)

Anthropology lays claim to a theoretical status unique to itself between the special scientific disciplines and a purely metaphysical philosophy. It is therefore opposed to all attempts to ground the human
being's peculiarity by means of particular biological features (such as the

impoverishment of instincts), or philosophical attributes (such as mind or will), or by combining both these lines of argument in a vulgarly materialistic fashion to advance the thesis that the human being's brain is his specialised organ. Rather, Gehlen wants to make the structure of his anthropology dependent, both categorically and methodologically, on an integral life principle characteristic of the human being in his physical endowment as well as in his psychical capacities; he conceives of the human being's organic peculiarities as the presuppositions for, and his cultural achievements as the results of, the 'capacity for action' as the unitary structural law of human life. In this way, the concept of 'human action', obtained from the early concept of *Erlebnis* under the theoretical influence of American pragmatism, becomes the categorial basis of philosophical anthropology:

> Certainly, however, we can and shall demonstrate how the human being's determination for action is the pervasive structural law of all human functions and achievements, and that this determination results unequivocally from the human being's physical organisation: a life form that is physically so constituted is viable only as an acting life form; and the structural law of all human effectuations, from the somatic to the mental, is thereby given. (Gehlen, 1971, p. 23)

Gehlen finds the explanation of the specifically human capacity for action in the biological thesis that the human being is a *defective life form*. From the physiological standpoint, man is to a great extent unspecialised, hence organically adapted to specific environments only to a small degree. In evolutionary theory, organic non-specialisation is regarded as the general prerequisite for higher development, as specialisations that have already been attained evolutionarily are irreversible; in the case of the human being, though, decisive organic specialisations do not occur even after the species has arisen, hence not in the course of the species' history, inasmuch as the socio-cultural mechanism of environmental adaptation encompasses the continuous alteration of the natural environment and the cultural self-shaping of the social world. The organic, life-threatening defects of the human being thus become opportunities for the occurrence of a self-directed process of development. For the human being's natural

> non-specialisation means the lack of an environment that is naturally adapted to him, with which he lives in biological equilibrium, and, second, it means the necessity of making the whole exposed, organically helpless and

unprotected life system capable of prevailing by means of its own spontaneous activity, hence the necessity of first rendering at all possible the
human being's physical survival by means of consciously experienced and
monitored actions. (*ibid.*, p. 131)

The human being would then be able to free himself from his organic
deficiencies only in spontaneous actions that have been uncoupled from
instinct-like mechanisms. Scientific evidence for the thesis that the
human being is a defective life form, which thus sees the structural
peculiarity of the human being in action, is found by Gehlen in some
physiological characters of the species: the human being is distinguished (a) by numerous instances of organic primitivism (cranial
curvature, a poorly developed lower jaw, orthodontia; the only exception, i.e., organic advantage, is the development of a freely movable and
opposable thumb); (b) by the lack of a pelt that would protect him against
the elements, a low degree of natural keenness of his senses, no con-
genital organs of attack; and (c) by the extreme helplessness of the
human offspring, its lengthy childhood, and its extremely late sexual
maturity (*ibid.*, pp. 86ff.).

From the standpoint of evolutionary theory, Gehlen accounts for the
organic non-specialisation of the human being with the thesis that man
is born prematurely. According to this thesis, the human being's primitive organs and other species-specific deficiencies are fetal conditions
that have become permanent. The helplessness of human progeny and
the general retardation in its development reinforce the impression that
man is a prematurely born embryo. The conditions of the human being's
socialisation result in essence from his premature birth: critically important stages of the human being's process of organic maturation take
place outside the womb, hence under worse natural conditions but with
the opportunity for the human being's cultural moulding. These reflections have their origin with the Swiss zoologist Adolf Portmann. The
evolutionary causes of this 'normalised premature birth' are a matter of
dispute. Gehlen himself names the probably most plausible thesis,
according to which a change of position of the female's pelvis caused by
the human being's upright posture – which in turn was made necessary
by climatic changes in some regions, presumably in the veldts of East
Africa (cf. Richard Ardrey) – and a consequent change in the conditions
for carrying a child to term in pregnancy were decisive (*ibid.*, pp.
123ff.). This thesis of man as a defective life form is, of course, a philosophical exaggeration; however, its empirical content cannot be

disposed of with the simple objection that an absolutely defective life form would not have the opportunity to invent compensatory artifacts with which to supply its deficiencies. Even in ontogenesis, especially, however, in phylogenesis, there is ascertainable a complex relationship between the loss of restrictive determinations and the origination of learning possibilities, a fact which gives to the aforementioned thesis a dynamic form, and which can show the structure of the phylogenetic production of higher ontogenetic modifiability (on this point, see Holzkamp-Osterkamp, 1975, vol. 1, pp. 135ff.).

These altered organic preconditions of ontogenesis lead to *a rupturing of all three sides of the triangle consisting of impulsional system, perception of triggering stimuli and motory reactions, which is characteristic of instinct-governed life forms.* Gehlen enquires into the structure of human impulses, perception and voluntary movement in order to demonstrate human action's function of compensating for the human being's organic deficiencies:

(a) The human being has only remnants of instincts – in the case of the infant, sucking and grasping reflexes; later care-taking behaviour in response to the infant-schema; and rudiments of form and colour perception. In the great majority of domains, however, there result from these and other instinctual residues no fixed behavioural patterns, but only dispositions that might express themselves in certain, only very generally determined readinesses for action and in states of excitation. Often, though, such dispositions are completely lacking. Of decisive importance for Gehlen is the fact that the principal impulses become autonomous. Sexuality, for example, is 'chronic' in the human being, thus not operative only during periodic mating seasons; moreover, human sexuality is capable of entering into all the human being's motivations. Gehlen summarises all of the foregoing in the notion of the plasticity of human impulses. He writes:

> The plasticity of human impulses is a biological necessity that corresponds to the retrogressive metamorphosis of human organs, or, better, to the human being's lack of organs, to the human being's non-specialisation and capacity for action. The term 'plasticity' is very polysemic and has several facets. It means, first, the absence of originality determined, individual instincts, and thus the impulses' capability to develop, i.e., their ability to enter into or to terminate combinations with one another, to find new orientations, to arise out of actions, to distribute themselves over similar objects or objects that belong together in some way, and even to originate newly: even in the later course of a human being's life there arise new and original needs and wants.

Third, the expression means the 'openness to the world' of the impulses; fourth, their susceptibility to influence from an individual human being's attitude in a particular regard and their capacity for being inhibited, guided, or being made superordinate or subordinate. Fifth, it means the fact that all impulses are capable of undergoing higher development and sublimation, so that, given certain inhibitions, conditioned and selectively 'bred' needs and wants make their appearance. And lastly, plasticity also means the impulses' vulnerability, their readiness to degenerate, their ability to 'luxuriate': when the human being's structure of behaviour is perturbed and the tasks of the impulses disappear or merely change very significantly and too rapidly for the impulses to keep pace with them, then a human existence is possible that is 'disengaged' or 'alienated', when human beings' impulses no longer find any points of attachment in the objective circumstances. (Gehlen, 1971, p. 351)

A further important law of the impulses, according to Gehlen, is presented in the thesis that the human being has a constitutional surplus of impulses resulting from the chronic character of his needs and wants and from the prolonged inhibition of voluntary motion during his physical and mental development. Gehlen found the germs of this idea in Alfred Seidel's *Bewußtsein als Verhängnis* (Consciousness as Fate, 1927). From this surplus of impulses Gehlen infers the importance of the fantasy as the unconstrained processing of needs and wants not exhausted in action. As the capacity for placing himself in situations other than the one an individual human is actually in, and in courses of movement other than the one he is in fact executing, the fantasy is for Gehlen the root of many accomplishments specific to man (on the whole complex, see H. Ottmann, 1981). In play, in art, and, as we shall see, in speech, a capability for experimentation with alternative actions that goes beyond the particular situation is operative. Later, in his theory of institutions, Gehlen again took into account this special importance of the fantasy for human beings by attributing the formation of institutions to a collective ability creatively to place oneself in an imaginary world.

In comparison with the theories of drives or instincts, a concept of human needs and wants defined in the above-described way yields a more complex relationship between needs and wants and the lack thereof, on the one hand, and between needs and wants and action taken to satisfy them, on the other. Needs and wants do not simply subsume objects or other subjects under themselves, but rather alter themselves in the latter and due to the effects of their commerce with the latter, developing themselves so that they are able to take into consideration the qualities proper to the objects and the other subject's own rights.

Needs and wants are, furthermore, 'postponable'; they can accept detours in the actions taken to satisfy them. Finally, actions are not merely executed for the purpose of satisfying needs and wants, but can themselves become sources of pleasure for the actor; thus they can themselves become needs and wants. These new needs and wants arise out of the actions and attach to them. Gehlen summarises as follows:

> We can therefore distinguish the following important characteristics in all higher-level attitudes and enduring interests.
>
> (a) They are conditioned by impediments; the reduction of mere coping with the circumstances and problems of the present moment is presupposed by them. And this mere coping is unsatisfying; that is, the strong organic need of the impulses to be given a higher degree of form becomes palpable.
>
> (b) They are enduring interests; i.e., they are directed into the future, have the stability of habit, and are invariant relative to changes of situation, hence are first meaningful for an acting and foresightful being in this form.
>
> (c) They have an intimate relationship with their objects. Capable of qualitative development to the highest degree precisely because of their exclusivity, they become accustomed to their respective objects and acquire a highly refined sensitivity.
>
> (d) They become 'secondarily drive-like'. All attitudes and orientations of activity that are characterised by their content become habitual, and the human being experiences in them an ultimately immediate satisfaction.
>
> (e) They finally become combinable and 'shiftable' to an especially great extent. They are amalgamated with sensations, skill in action, and experiential knowledge to such a high degree that they conform both to the requirements of the pertinent material and of the action, and to the acts of thinking and mental presentation, and under the influence of both these requirements and these acts they, so to speak, shift their position; however, they are thereby also able to establish interrelations among themselves and to develop further. (Gehlen, 1971, pp. 352f.)

(b) Human perception, which is to a great extent liberated from permanent ties to objects that are useful or harmful specifically to the human species, carries with itself the danger of the unprocessable abundance of sense impressions, but for that very reason also the opportunity for the development of a flexible perception, one that has 'an intimate relationship with its objects'. In the grasping play of early infancy and in the discovery of his own body, the human being begins to construct for himself a visual field that is structured with meanings, hence that is relieved of the burden of the immediate plethora of stimuli; in the knowledge he acquires from his everyday commerce with things, the human being saturates this perceptual space with modes of symbolic signification to such a degree that he finally also perceives a reality which has been thoroughly worked upon and fashioned by cognition. When we perceive things, we perceive more than would 'in fact' be possible: for example, their hardness or wetness, their front and back sides:

> Thus we orient ourselves in the sensory world according to certain optical or acoustic, tactile, etc. symbols, according to minimal characters. Biologically, this is unequivocally purposive; it renders it unnecessary for the human being to deal with things in the possible, full ampleness of their qualities, and a stimulatability of the organism that is as many-sided and sensitive as possible is not the purpose of perception. If that were the case, human perception would have to be not merely symbolic. Rather, our chief and guiding mode of perception, the optical, is a means of providing ourselves with 'symbols' for expectations of success, resistances, reactions of things, and 'attainableness' in relation to our practical intervention, so that we can, with the aid of these symbols, begin and direct our movements and measure them out in a manner appropriate to achieving our goal, even prior to success or failure. (*ibid.*, p. 172)

In a symbolic structuration of his perceptual world that is in conformity with what he has learned through his manipulative commerce with things, the human being frees himself from the menacing abundance of stimuli, with which his organically unique situation ought in fact to confront him. But knowledge derived from experience that is social in the narrower sense – for example, mental presentations guided by desires or fears – is also considered by Gehlen as a reference factor of human perception that operates in this manner.

(c) The human capacity for voluntary motion is not innate; it must be learned in and through socialisation processes. The human being possesses an acquired, not an inherited capacity for voluntary motion. To the endangerment of the human individual by his lengthy learning period is counterposed the opportunity for the development of combinative capacities of the highest level on the part of his movements. The human capacity for voluntary motion set free from fixed patterns of movement tailored to organism-specific situations can approach closer to things' own proper structure in processes of refinement and co-ordination, attaining finally to the achievements of the handicrafts:

> Speaking positively, however, that means that they [human movements, A. H./H. J.] are developed, and are developed in accordance with experi-

ence; that is, they must be built up in relationship with the human being's experiential orientation and must themselves be experienced. (Gehlen, 1971, p. 42)

The human being can always co-ordinate anew his planned movements in relation to perceived states of affairs, until finally he has acquired a manner of movement that is superior to animals' capacity for voluntary motion, and that is suited to the objects in question. Gehlen has extended his analysis of human capacity for voluntary motion in several directions. From the results of his investigation of the human being's monitoring of his movements, he develops a non-substantialist concept of the 'human being's free will'. Under the rubric 'movement fantasy', he analyses the accomplishments of the anticipatory self-assessment of capabilities for movement. Lastly, with the notion of a 'symbolic structure of movement', he means the concentration of skill in movement 'on the elaboration of fruitful main and articulative phases' of human movements:

Skilful movements are, then, those symbolic movements that can be disposed over and applied using certain fruitful moments [of these movements, Trans.] which represent the entire movement sequence, inasmuch as the intermediary phases [of the movements, Trans.] have been attenuated or made automatic. (Gehlen, 1971, p. 191)

The basic idea of these anthropological definitions formulated by Gehlen is always the same: the human being's plastic impulsional system, his perception that is overwhelmed by stimuli, and his formless motility compel him, even from the standpoint of biology, to engage in action that gives form to his needs and wants, that structures his perception, and that guides his motility. The human being, therefore, frees himself in action from the dangers to his survival inherent in the organic starting situation of a deficient life form. From this theoretical leitmotiv of his anthropological theory Gehlen draws the conclusions expressed in his theory of institutions.

According to Gehlen, the human being can survive in the long term only if he re-establishes the lost link between instinct and response-triggering stimulus on the higher plane of behavioural patterns that have been so routinised that they have become analogous to instinctual behaviour. Man's dangerous openness to the world is counterbalanced by institutions that drastically restrict the latitude of action which he has in principle through firmly established interpretations of the world and generalised rules for behaviour. Institutions thus appear as historically conditioned ways of mastering tasks and circumstances that are critically important to human life, . . . as stabilising powers and as the forms that a being which is, by its nature, endangered and lacking in robustness, overburdened with affect, finds in order to tolerate itself both individually and reciprocally. (Gehlen, 1969, p. 97)[3]

It is no accident that Gehlen bases his concept of the institution on the supra-individual power relationship characteristic of archaic institutions. The objectivity and rigidity of the behaviour-governing regulations of those institutions, which were intended to persist, supply the institutional model according to which Gehlen conceives of the structure of institutions even in the present day (see Gehlen, 1964). The survival of the species is effectively safeguarded only by those systems of social order that force the human being's multifarious capacities for action into patterns of behaviour that are, to as great a degree as possible, proof against enquiry as to their foundation and justification. Gehlen thinks of institutions as 'guidance systems' that are analogous to instincts, and that fulfil their task of easing the strain due to an overtaxation from stimuli and drives that is specific to the human species all the more enduringly, the more rigidly they are protected against communicative scrutiny. This institutional ideal no longer permits at all the possibility of intersubjective communication regarding the reasonableness of institutionalised standards of behaviour, because such a reflexive distancing of the human actors from their activity would necessarily enter into conflict with the biological compulsion to act. The conservative institutionalism to which Gehlen's anthropology leads in this fashion, with a certain degree of inevitability, has its systemic basis in a deficiency of his premises from the standpoint of the theory of intersubjectivity.

Gehlen ties his anthropology so resolutely and exclusively to an individualist model of action that he is unable to become aware of the significance of intersubjective modes of action for socialisation as well as for the history of the human species. This criticism is not to be equated with the objection that Gehlen recognises only instrumental action. For his whole theory of institutions was aimed precisely at demonstrating the inability of instrumental action to bring forth viable institutions. This position leads him to identify ritual and presentative behaviour as a type of action and to make fruitful use of it in his studies of 'primitive cultures'. Although Gehlen is inclined in his discussion of these types of

---

[3] On Gehlen's concept of the institution, see, in addition to his chief work on this subject (Gehlen, 1964), the summary he gives (Gehlen, 1968a, pp. 69ff.).

behaviour, as in the case of the thesis of the deficient life form, to exaggerate antinomies, the substantive content of his analyses as well as of his social–psychological diagnoses of the present era must often be accorded a high value (Gehlen, 1964, 1980). His societal ideal and his personality ideal should not be understood as a totalising of instrumental action, but as the guiding image for an elite of ascetic individuals. Following the Second World War, the growing impossibility of speaking of the goals of this elite's action has caused Gehlen's theory to become tinged with resignation.

Action and intersubjectivity. The difference between Mead and Gehlen

In his anthropological studies, too, Gehlen is unable to resolve the residue of problems arising out of his solipsistic premises, the residue that makes his critique of classical epistemology so contradictory from the outset. In his early writings he no longer regards the human being's cognitive achievements as grounded in the constituting activity of a transcendental ego, but in the individual act of *Erlebnis*, without, however, taking into account the possibility of an intersubjective constitution of reality. Similarly, his anthropology grounds human beings' compensation for their inherent deficiencies, which is necessary for their survival, in the actions of a solitary actor. In a retrospective account of the basis of his work given in 1968, Gehlen clearly states the solipsistic character of the fundamental model of his anthropology:

> Whoever wanted to continue working in the field of anthropology had to achieve clarity about the form of the model. In order to make it simple and easy to grasp, it was advisable to adhere to the abstract model of an imaginary solitary human being, a Robinson Crusoe, for then all further-reaching questions concerning society, social life, even sex could, so to speak, be put aside, leaving behind only a note as a reminder of them. (Gehlen, 1968b, p. 6)

The theoretically far-reaching consequences that this individualistic model of action carries with itself into the very heart of Gehlen's anthropology can be adequately presented only in the confrontation of that anthropology with a theory that Gehlen himself introduced into Germany, albeit in a restricted form. Since the revision of his principal work *Der Mensch* (Man) after the end of the Third Reich, Gehlen has drawn on the pragmatism of George Herbert Mead (for additional contributions to the following discussion, see Joas, 1978a, 1979, 1985). He praises the American philosopher and social psychologist for his masterful analysis of the genesis of the significant symbol and of role-taking; Gehlen draws upon Mead's work in the central parts of his anthropological theory of language, as well as in his development of the notion of 'reciprocity', in his theory of archaic cultures, and in his ethics. It is true that Gehlen thereby made a beginning in the critical exam-ination and appropriation of Mead's ideas in Germany; on the other hand, though, he took notice only of a fragment of Mead's theory. In doing so, Gehlen was following his usual practice of working into the fundamental conceptual framework of his anthropology approaches that appeared useful to him, proceeding in a consciously selective fashion rather than using the method of 'understanding'. This fact went un-remarked, however, primarily because for a long time the reception of Mead's work in Germany scarcely went beyond the level attained by Gehlen. If he was known at all, Mead was known as the author of a posthumously published book composed solely from his students' notes on his lectures, *Mind, Self, and Society* (1934). His name stood for a theory of 'intersubjectivity' that had not been pursued further in all its implications. To be sure, as symbolic interactionism became more widely diffused within sociology, Mead became ever better known. Yet this did not lead to study and utilisation of Mead's intersubjectivist pragmatism in its entirety.

In the theoretical discussions of the social sciences, Mead has been treated chiefly as a 'social behaviourist' or a 'symbolic interactionist', terms that have become firmly established in the history of social science. The epithet 'social behaviourist' has its origin in Mead's own claim that he provides a 'behaviourist' explanation of 'mind' or 'spirit' and of the 'self'. The application of this designation to Mead is, ad-mittedly, misleading, inasmuch as a reduction of human action to stimulus-response schemata was precisely what Mead, unlike Watson, the founder of behaviourism, was not interested in. Rather, Mead's goal was to ascertain the fundamental difference between human action and animal behaviour. Mead not only accepted, as did the later, liberalised versions of behaviourism, the existence of inner experience; he also made a point of seeking to determine the genesis and function of that experience. With the expression 'behaviourist', Mead wanted to charac-terise his own attempt to abandon entirely the primacy of this inner experience, as well as the derivation of human behaviour and of the external world from the self-certainty of an ego that is ontologically prior to them. The fundamental model according to which Mead conceived of this surpassing of the Cartesian perspective was the organism that secures its survival in its environment through its behaviour. All that was psychical in nature was to be investigated from the standpoint of its function in behaviour; all behaviour was to be examined with respect to its functionality for the reproduction of the individual and of the species:

> Social psychology is behaviouristic in the sense of starting off with an observable activity – the dynamic, on-going social process, and the social acts which are its component elements – to be studied and analyzed scientifically. But it is not behaviouristic in the sense of ignoring the inner experience of the individual – the inner phase of that process or activity. On the contrary, it is particularly concerned with the rise of such experience within the process as a whole. It simply works from the outside to the inside instead of from the inside to the outside, so to speak, in its endeavour to determine how such experience does arise within the process. *The act, then, and not the tract, is the fundamental datum in both social and individual psychology when behaviouristically conceived*, and it has both an inner and an outer phase, an internal and an external aspect. (Mead, 1934, pp. 7–8)

The misunderstanding of Mead as a behaviourist posed a considerable obstacle to the reception of his writings, and was diminished only by the popularity he gained owing to the spread of interest in symbolic interactionism. However, his association with this school gave rise to new misunderstandings. Unavoidably, it gave the impression that Mead shared symbolic interactionism's restriction of action to interaction, that he too considered the natural foundations of action to be of only trivial importance, whether these were the human being's bodily endowment with needs, or an environment necessary to life, and that he also assumed, illusorily, that a society had been achieved which was free of domination, and in which there was self-determination by its members. Mead, however, in keeping with the model 'organism–environment' that is the premise of his reflections, assumes precisely the opposite: he does not at all accord central importance to the form of action termed interaction, but rather to human beings' manipulation of physical objects. 'The mechanism of human society', asserts Mead, 'is that of bodily selves who assist or hinder each other in their co-operative acts by the manipulation of physical things' (Mead, 1932, p. 169).

Mead's goal is, then, not a theory of interaction, or of instrumental action, but the linking together of both of these theories through enquiry into the function of communication and self-consciousness for co-operation. As his historical study of nineteenth-century philosophy, for example, shows, Mead takes over from German idealism the question of the constitution of self-consciousness. He does not, though, undertake to answer this question within the framework of speculative philosophy, but under the conditions of social theory created by the developed natural sciences and industrial production at the beginning of the twentieth century. A close examination of Mead's intellectual history shows that three fundamental themes are prominent in his work: confidence in the emancipatory prospects of scientific rationality; the effort to root 'mind' or 'spirit' in the organism; and the attempt to elaborate a theory of intersubjectivity that would conceive of the self as socially originated. These themes led him along a tortuous path of intellectual development that took him first through an Hegelian phase, then through a concentration of his efforts on the elaboration of a non-reductive definition of the psychical, and on to the development of his basic notion of symbolic interaction and its application to several substantial fields. In the works of his final period, he attempts to refute the objectivistic conception of science then prevalent among scientists in order to safeguard the susceptibility of ethical and aesthetic values to being rationally grounded (see Joas, 1985, chapter 9).

Gehlen shares with Mead his interest in making use of themes of pragmatism and *Lebensphilosophie* in dealing with central problems of German idealism. Common to both of them is the intention to transform transcendentalism into a 'scientific' or 'empirical' philosophy. The key concept in the theoretical frameworks of both is the category of 'action', which is intended to render definitively ineffectual the anthropological tradition of body–soul dualism. However, it is also with respect to the concept of action that the two theoretical models differ from each other. Whereas Gehlen constructs his anthropology on the basis of the action of the solitary subject, Mead, as a matter of theoretical principle, takes the 'social act' as the starting point of his investigations. This expression does not mean, as it does in Max Weber's writings, the social action of an individual from which social relations first arise, but rather the opposite, namely the collective behaviour of a group of organisms belonging to the same species. The individual action is then only part of an encompassing societal plexus of action:

> Social psychology studies the activity or behavior of the individual as it lies within the social process; the behavior of an individual can be understood only in terms of the behavior of the whole social group of which he is a

member, since his individual acts are involved in larger, social acts which go beyond himself and which implicate the other members of that group.

We are not, in social psychology, building up the behavior of the social group in terms of the behavior of the separate individuals composing it; rather, we are starting out with a given social whole of complex group activity, into which we analyze (as elements) the behavior of each of the separate individuals composing it. (Mead, 1934, p. 7)

Mead's anthropological interest is directed to comparison of animal and human forms of sociality. Groups of human organisms live under conditions that are essentially different from those of the pre-human stage of evolution. In contrast to the highly developed social forms of insect colonies, for example, in human societies a system of rigorous division of labour is no longer guaranteed by biological specialisation in bodily structure and by differentiation of innate modes of behaviour. The principle governing the social life of vertebrate animals, namely the regulation of group life through instinctually rigid forms of behaviour that are modified solely through the acquisition of a particular status in a unilinear hierarchy of dominance and submission, is impossible in human society given the organic preconditions inherent in the human species. Admittedly, even in the case of social groups of primates traditions occur; however, they remain narrowly limited, as they do not assume an objectified form. For human societies, in contrast with those of primates and other vertebrates, there exists the problem of how individual behaviour that is not fixed by nature can be differentiated over a wide range of variation and at the same time integrated by means of mutual behavioural expectations to become group activity.

With his anthropological theory of the origin of specifically human communication, Mead undertakes to uncover the mechanism making possible such differentiation and integration. Only the human being can orient his own behaviour according to the potential reactions of his partners in interactions, for only the human being is capable of anticipatory representation of the behaviour of the other. Through the gesture that he can himself perceive, he can trigger in himself the very reaction that he is seeking to call forth in his partner. Now it is possible consciously and purposefully to join together individual actions. Human action is oriented according to behavioural expectations; inasmuch as a human being's partner in an interaction necessarily also possesses this same capability, a collectively binding pattern of mutual behavioural expectations is the precondition of collective action. This anthropological analysis provides Mead with the fundamental concepts of his social psychology. The concept of 'role' refers precisely to the pattern made up of behavioural expectations; 'taking the role of the other' is the anticipation of the other's behaviour, not the taking over of his position in an organised social situation. As a result of this internal representation of the behaviour of the other, different agencies are developed in the human individual. For now the individual human being makes his own behaviour an object of his consideration in a similar fashion to the behaviour of his partner; he sees himself from the perspective of the other. The drive-impulses are now joined by an agency that serves to assess them; this agency consists in the expectations of the other's reactions to the expression of the impulses in action.

In this connection, Mead speaks of 'I' and 'me'. In philosophical tradition, the concept 'I' refers to the principle of creativity and spontaneity; for Mead, though, it also has a biological meaning, and refers to the human being's endowment with drives. 'Me' refers to my mental representation of the image that the other has of me, or, on a more primitive level, to my internalisation of his expectations of me. The 'me' as the precipitate in me of an attachment figure or any interaction partner is an assessing agency that guides the structuration of the spontaneous impulses and is an element of an emerging self-image. If I confront several interaction partners that are important to me, then I acquire several different 'me's' which must be synthesised into a unitary and coherent self-image, if self-consistent behaviour on my part is to be possible. If this synthesis is successful, then there emerges the 'self': a coherent self-assessment and orientation of action that is, however, flexible and open to communication with a gradually increasing number of partners in interaction; conjointly, a stable personality structure that is certain about its needs and wants is developed.

These reflections of Mead clearly show the central importance given in his theory to the intersubjective structure of action and reflexivity. Mead regards the ability to communicate and the capacity for reflection made possible by it as the crucially important achievements of human sociality. As a philosopher of history, Mead hopes for a process of socio-cultural progress that will dismantle the barriers to social communication, while simultaneously heightening the species' self-reflection. In contrast, in his theory Gehlen places discussion and reflection in an essentially necessary opposition to action; indeed, in his eyes the intersubjective readiness to discuss the always new and unforeseeable requirements of situations with a view to finding rational ways of satisfying them does not constitute a step forward in social progress, but instead a species-threatening danger that must be seen as opposed to the anthropological necessity of firmly established interpretations of the world that have not been called into question, and to the social ideal of behavioural patterns that have become so routinised that they have become analogous to instincts. Thus Gehlen's anthropology clearly causes the intersubjective structure of human action to disappear behind its instrumental relationship to its object; a central position in his theory is occupied by the 'grasping hold', i.e., the appropriation of reality in action, because only thereby is relief from the human being's constitutionally dangerous openness to the world assured. However, the criticism that Gehlen ignores the communicative character of human action seems to be disproved by the fact that Gehlen frequently, and in the context of references to Mead or Dewey, speaks of the communicative structure of all psychical processes and of all sensory experience. In *Der Mensch*, we read:

> Sensory experience is not a 'solitary' process, since 'action with regard to a "you"' is the fundamental structure of everything psychical. We can say that everything, no matter what, takes the role of this 'you' whenever we make it the object of sensory experience! (Gehlen, 1971, p. 166)

This passage shows that Gehlen applies his concept of communication also to the handling of things and thereby conceals the original intersubjective sense of the notion of the communicative character of sensory experience. The substantive problem implicit in this procedure cannot, as far as Gehlen is concerned, be disposed of through the simple expedient of a clear-cut definitional distinction between instrumental and communicative action. It should be stressed, however, that Gehlen deserves credit for establishing, using the notion of communicative commerce with things, that instrumental action is not an external and static guiding of objects, but that all action has, rather, the character of a response to situations, that human perception and motion, while they are altering an object, become charged with experiential knowledge in a circular process that leads to productive results with respect to their objects. However, the problem acquires substantive content only when Gehlen's downplaying of the importance of the concept of communication prevents him from investigating the intersubjective structure of conditions that is proper to specifically human capabilities in an appropriate manner; this is a significant shortcoming in Gehlen's anthropology, especially if it can be shown that his own explanations of centrally important phenomena come to grief on just this point. The validity of this contention can be demonstrated for Gehlen's theory of language.

There can be no doubt that Gehlen's work is one of the most

ambitious and most impressive attempts to elaborate a theory of language that is founded on the theory of action and is non-intellectualist. In this theory, speech is not conceived of as the expression of a consciousness that has achieved finished form prior to language, but as a possibility of acting without acting, that is, of varying the givens of situations fictitiously and experimentally, without altering the situation in actual fact. Furthermore, human speech assures both the transferability of experiential knowledge and an enormous increase of the independence of the achievements of human intelligence from particular situations. But, no matter how much Gehlen, in his theory of language, turns the old sequential schema relating thought and speech upside down in a pragmatist fashion, he does not succeed in doing this for the intersubjective dimension of the relationship between expression and communication. For him, the cry is only one root of language among many others; he explicitly asserts the possibility that the word does not 'become a constant quantity only owing to its effective functioning within the community' (*ibid.*, p. 204). The problem is clear: if one begins, as Gehlen does, with the single actor, then one becomes aware, certainly, of speech as a highly developed form of sensorimotor behaviour, but its dialogical character appears to be of secondary importance. As far as the voluntary articulative movements and speech perception are concerned, speech is indisputably a sensorimotor process; as Gehlen correctly observes, speech acquires important functions in the enhancement of cognitive achievements in virtue of the fact that linguistic symbols can be made use of independently of particular situations. However, Gehlen consistently evades the question of where these symbols themselves originate. While it can be surmised that they constitute a continuation of the cognitive achievements, they do not simply arise out of the latter. At this point Gehlen's evolutionary model, according to which language has its origin in the co-operating group, is of no help, inasmuch as it merely describes the function, but not the genesis of those actions consisting in speaking – a distinction to which Gehlen himself, in his analysis of archaic forms of sociality, attaches the greatest importance. In this context, the consequences of the neglect of pre-human forms of sociality, which ensue from Gehlen's individualist model of action, become evident, for only within the framework of pre-human forms of sociality can the genesis of the symbol that always carries the same meaning be understood.[4]

---

[4] This insight unites such different approaches as those of Jürgen Habermas, who draws on the work of Earl Count, and of Volker Schurig (see Schurig, 1976; Count, 1973).

From the standpoint of the theory of socialisation, too, Gehlen's linguistic theory leads him to a strikingly mistaken proposition. For along with the possibility of an independent development of speech by the child, Gehlen assumes that the infant's lalling monologues can lead to a development of the capacity for articulation by means of the playing through of articulative possibilities, without communication between the child and a competent speaker. In making this claim, he overlooks the fact that such a development would be undirected, since the direction in which the child's phonological repertoire would be developed would be entirely undetermined. The sounds that a child makes himself and also perceives do not after all have the same kind of self-founded pre-givenness of things as the objects which the child touches and fingers; without the norm-setting demonstration by an attachment figure of how words should be pronounced and their corrective utterance following the child's attempt to imitate them, the development of the child's ability to speak would be impossible.

The theory of language is, certainly, not the only area in which an inadequate elucidation of the intersubjective structure of human action also leads Gehlen to make factual assertions that are anthropologically inadequate. His undifferentiated concept of communication, which first subsumes instrumental commerce with things under communication, then equates this instrumental commerce with things in its entirety with human action, also leads Gehlen to explain insufficiently the relation between the development of the capability for instrumental action and the development of the capability for communicative action. Gehlen's theoretical account of the cognitive constitution of the physical thing, which is for him 'the conclusion, the end of all the achievements of the immediate, sensorimotor orientation to the world and experience of it' (Gehlen, 1971, p. 195), differs from that of Mead through its omission to show that there are social, that is, communicative conditions of the constitution of permanent objects. Mead's little-known theory, contained in parts of *Philosophy of the Act* (1938) and in other posthumously published writings (1932, pp. 119ff.), makes it clear that Gehlen's anthropology, even in this central portion of his theory, suffers from the deficiencies of his concept of intersubjectivity.

At first glance, Gehlen's and Mead's explanations appear to be identical. Both of them accept the premise that the constitution of permanent objects presupposes two processes: first, the transference of the sensory experiences of the contact senses to the distance senses, chiefly the co-operation of hand and eye; second, the capability to change one's perspective in relation to one and the same object, during which change the abandoned perspective must be mentally retained. This second process consists, on the one hand, in the elementary 'decentring', using Piaget's term, of individual modes of perception and of their combination with one another, and, on the other hand, in the internalised co-ordination of one's own perspective with that of other subjects and hence in the overcoming of a fixation on one's own body-centric possibilities. Gehlen considers the capability for co-operation between hand and eye, which lies beyond the limits of what animals can accomplish, to be grounded in the fact that owing to the reduction of instincts in the human being, human needs and wants can be uncoupled from manipulative actions. This idea appears in a very similar form in Mead's emphasis on the freeing of the human hand from use in locomotive movements. The capability to change perspective is derived by Gehlen from the unrestricted reproducibility of human sounds, which make possible the replication of any and every point of view, independent of the particular situation and the particular circumstances. Both of these explanations are by no means wrong, but they lack precisely the component that is most important. The reduction of instincts in the human being and the freeing of the human hand from employment in locomotion constitute only a necessary, not a sufficient condition for the co-operation of hand and eye; accounting for the human ability to change perspectives with the independence of symbols from particular situations does not posit the cognitive use of linguistic symbols as the precipitate of a dialogical phase of the development of speech, of which that use is merely the internalisation. However, it then remains inexplicable how the percipient subject is able to identify different sensory experiences as his own in each instance and to compare them, if one is not willing to assume, in the manner of transcendental philosophy, the original givenness of an ego.

Mead's explanation of the constitution of permanent objects is more logically rigorous. In his reconstruction of both the capability for co-operation between hand and eye and the capability for changing perspectives, he has recourse to the intersubjective structure of human action. Mead founds the ability to change perspectives that is proper to the human being in role-taking, that is, in the capability to adopt the perspective of others. In every taking of a role two perspectives from which objects are viewed are represented in me, namely my own original perspective and that of my partner whose role I enter into. I must and can succeed in integrating both of these perspectives into a many-sided image of the object, similarly to the way in which different 'me's' must be synthesised. By taking the standpoints of imaginary others and ultimately by adopting the perspective of Mead's 'generalised other', I can attain to a comprehensive image of the object.

The insight that subjective perspectives exist objectively leads finally to the reconstruction of the structure of relationships encompassing me and my perspective. Following this path, Mead can take the organism–environment model as the starting point of his epistemological investigations without naturalising human cognition in any reductionist fashion or depriving it of its universal claim to truth.

Now, it is easier to account for the development of human capabilities using the theory of intersubjectivity on this level than on the still more fundamental level of the co-operation between hand and eye. At this elementary stage of sensorimotor development, linguistic symbols do not yet play a role; however, since Mead assumes that intersubjectivity develops first in gestural communication, thus by no means in merely vocal communication, he can undertake to ground even the early co-operation between hand and eye in a still more fundamental and temporally prior stratum of intersubjective action. Like Gehlen, Mead assumes that the constitution of permanent objects requires the transference of data from the distance senses to the contact senses; the capability to make this transference, however, necessarily presupposes, according to Mead, the capability for role-taking. This he explains in the following way: we perceive a thing as a thing only when we impute to it an interior that exerts pressure on us as soon as we touch it. This interior that is able to exert pressure can never be found by dismembering or cutting up the object, for that only results in ever more new surfaces. This interior must always be imputed to an object. I do this in accordance with the scheme of pressure and counterpressure which I learn of experientially in the perception of a pressure exerted on myself by myself, for example, in the play of my two hands with each other. I can transfer this experiential knowledge to things by representing in myself, as emanating from the object, a pressure equal to the pressure exerted by me, but that pushes in the opposite direction. This transference Mead calls the role of the object. If I succeed also in doing this anticipatorily, then I can thereby handle things consciously, with full awareness of what I am doing, and acquire experiential knowledge through manipulative action. Considered together with the co-operation between hand and eye, this fact means that the distance senses can of themselves trigger in the human organism the reaction of the sensation of resistance corresponding to the manipulation of things, and in point of fact do trigger that reaction. The object is then perceived as an anticipated datum of contact sensation: we 'see' the heaviness, the hardness, or the warmth of an object from its appearance.

Now, within Mead's theoretical framework no conscious perception by me of the pressure I exert upon myself may be postulated as primary. It is a matter here of a perception analogous to the perception of the sounds that I produce. In order that this perception can be transferred to objects, and that a counterpressure can be anticipated, the fundamental form of the capability for role-taking, Mead maintains, must already have been acquired. Only experiential knowledge gained from interaction allows that with which I am dealing to appear to me as something that is acting, i.e., that is 'exerting pressure'. If this thesis is correct, then knowledge gained from social experience is a precondition for the synthesis of 'things' out of the chaos of sense perceptions. Mead also thereby explains why initially – that is, in the consciousness of the small child and of primitive cultures – all things are perceived as animate partners according to the schema of interaction, and why it is only later that the social object becomes distinguished from the physical object. In turn, the constitution of permanent objects is a prerequisite for the human organism's delimiting of itself from the other objects and its self-reflexive acquisition of a sense of itself as a unitary body. The self develops, then, in a process that is continuous with the formation of 'things' for the actor.[5]

The concept of practical intersubjectivity that Mead elaborates in such trains of reasoning supplies the fundamental prerequisite for an anthropology of social action. In the following steps of our argumentation, this concept will be the common point of reference of the questions posed and of the criticisms that will be made.

Human expressiveness. Helmuth Plessner's anthropological hermeneutics

In his book *Die Stufen des Organischen und der Mensch* (The Grades of Organismal Being and Man), first published in 1928, Helmuth Plessner presented the fundamental theoretical framework of his philosophical anthropology, which shares with the later theory of Gehlen a naturalistic

---

[5] Empirical evidence supporting the validity of this thesis and further implications of Mead's work for the theory of socialisation are not discussed here. For treatments of these topics, see the bibliographical references given in Joas, 1985.

basic orientation and a point of departure in the critiquing of meta-physics. In all his anthropological writings, Plessner begins with the findings of research in human biology; he numbers the human being's weakness of instincts, the primitiveness of his organs, and his drive surplus among the biological peculiarities that make the human capable of developing and using language and of acting. Like Gehlen after him, Plessner pursues from this biological perspective the goal of overcoming the metaphysical dualism of the philosophical theory of man: the human being is to be philosophically understood no longer through the consti-tutional breach between body and soul or consciousness, but rather through the total organic structure that is proper to man alone. The nature of the human organism's position, in Plessner's sense of the term, the relationship of the organic body to its environment – Plessner makes the investigation of these the cardinal principle of his anthropology.

To be sure, Plessner's anthropological theory stands in a different relationship to scientific experience than does that of Gehlen. Whereas the latter constructs his anthropology as an empirically scientific philos-ophy, hence a philosophy that is founded on empirical evidence, Plessner is guided by a phenomenological concept of experience. His anthropology obtains its primary material for investigation not from the results of empirical science which can be subjected to intersubjective scrutiny, but from the data of immediate self-experience that are initially accessible only subjectively. It 'is a question here of the strata of immediacy, of data or phenomena that are reserved to conscious experi-ence, to intuition, or to the discernment of essences' (*ibid.*, p. 29). This subjective mode of experience is intended to secure and preserve the freedom of anthropological theory from the methodological imperatives of a strictly empirical science. Plessner's use of phenomenological methods follows systematically from the *Lebensphilosophie* that is the foundation upon which he erects his anthropology. For unlike Gehlen, Plessner does not strip away the conceptual limits of *Lebensphilosophie* in a theory of action. Rather, he takes as the basis of his investigation of behavioural possibilities specific to human beings precisely the peculiarly fractured, discontinuous structure of human life. Plessner intends his anthropology to be nothing less than a naturalistic radical-isation of Dilthey's *Lebensphilosophie*. Correspondingly, from his anthro-pological standpoint an intermediary domain becomes the focus of theoretical interest, one that Gehlen, in his opposition of action to reflection, seems more to neglect. In his study *Laughing and Crying: A*

Study of the Limits of Human Behavior, Plessner examines and describes
the exceptional position of the human being in comparison with other
life forms, as manifested in the structure of some possibilities of expression at the disposal only of the human being, and that allow the specific
relationship of the objectual and instrumental body to the organismal
body,[6] and thus the structure of human life, to become clearly and
strikingly perceptible in, say, the expressive forms of laughing and
weeping. The theory of human expressiveness, to which Plessner's
anthropology is led in this fashion, can be meaningfully developed only
from the programme of a biologically grounded 'philosophy of life' or
Lebensphilosophie.

Plessner conceives of his anthropology as a continuation of the hermeneutics of Dilthey's *Lebensphilosophie.* The latter sought to reconcile
neo-Kantianism's rigour from the standpoint of the theory of science
with the subjectivism of *Lebensphilosophie* in a theory of the socio-
cultural sciences ('Geisteswissenschaften') (see Misch, 1947, pp. 37ff.;
Habermas, 1971a, ch. II, 7 and 8; Plessner, 1979, pp. 276ff., and esp.
chapter 5). Dilthey regards the structure of everyday understanding, in
which the individual life closes itself into a continuous circle of conscious experience, expression of that experience, and understanding of
this expression, as the pre-scientific model of the method of the socio-
cultural sciences. In the hermeneutic mode of attending that is proper to
the socio-cultural sciences, we attempt to decipher in cultural objectivations the expressions of conscious experience that converge with
our own life experience in the manner in which, in everyday life, we seek
to understand, on the basis of our own life situation, intentions manifested in others' expressions of their life. Plessner takes over this method-

---

[6] In the German, Plessner makes the distinction between these two aspects under which
the human body can be regarded with the terms *Leib* and *Körper.* The article in
Historisches Wörterbuch der Philosophie (eds. Joachim Ritter and Karlfried Gründer, vol.
5, Darmstadt, 1980) that discusses this pair of terms begins: 'The term *Leib* is a
distinction peculiar to the German language which sets off a body [*Körper*], insofar as it is
conceived as animate, from the multitude of the other bodies by means of a special
word.' Dorion Cairns (*Guide for Translating Husserl,* The Hague, 1973) suggests that
Leib be rendered into English as 'animate organismal body'. I gratefully followed
Cairns's suggestion, but judged that the qualifier 'animate' was superfluous in most
instances in the present context. Also guided by the context of the present chapter, I
judged that the second term of the pair would best be rendered into English as
'objectual–instrumental body', that the use of this compound qualifier was necessary to
express in English the distinction Plessner is making.

Since the distinction is made in English by the modifiers rather than by two different
nouns, the unadorned term 'body' is made available for use in referring to the human
body under neither of the two contrasted aspects. Trans.

ological foundation of the socio-cultural sciences, while giving it a decisively important naturalistic turn: a hermeneutics of human expressions of life can do theoretical justice to its object only if it also systematically takes into consideration the human being's organismal constitution. The individual modes of expression, to which hermeneutics directs itself for the purpose of understanding them, are tied to the organismal bodiliness of the human being:

> Consequently, the idea of laying the foundation for sensory experience of the kind appropriate to the socio-cultural sciences necessitates reflection upon problems that reach into the sensual–material sphere of 'life', the sphere of the objectual–instrumental body; it necessitates, therefore, a philosophy of nature, understood in its broadest and most original sense. (Plessner, 1975, p. 24)

Plessner criticises both Dilthey's theory of the socio-cultural sciences and Heidegger's analysis of *Dasein*, 'being-there' (Plessner, 1976, pp. 180ff.), for their pervasive abstraction from man's organismal bodiliness; according to Plessner, the claim to offer a philosophical interpretation of human life, which both Dilthey and Heidegger make within different theoretical frameworks, can therefore be realised only in the form of an anthropology that incorporates the findings of biology. Methodologically, this anthropology makes use of phenomenological description. Plessner frees phenomenology from all ontological presuppositions, as well as those required by phenomenology as a transcendental philosophy, in order to be able to make use of the descriptive procedure for recording processes of consciousness, by means of which Husserl sought to grasp only the acts that are immanent in consciousness, as the foundation of a theory directing its anthropological interest to all of man's expressions of his life that are oriented to his environment (see Hammer, 1967, chapter II, 3; also Plessner, 1979, pp. 43ff.). The 'most intense and most immediate possible intercourse with the world itself in experiences of consciousness' will assure the validity of the theoretical data in which Plessner considers his anthropology to be grounded. Thus he conceives of this anthropology as a hermeneutics that undertakes, in the fundamental phenomenological attitude, to decipher the life expressions of the human being in his organismal bodiliness.

This naturalistically radicalised hermeneutics presupposes a theory that helps to relate the different forms of human expression back to the one single fundamental organismal structure of human life. Plessner pursues the elaboration of such a fundamental biological theoretical framework with the aid of a hierarchical schema that works out the organic peculiarities of plants, animals and human beings on the basis of the relationship to its own environment that is specific to each kind of life form:

> An idea of the mode of existence of the human being as a natural occurrence and as a product of the history of his mode of existence can only be obtained by contrasting it with the other modes of existence of animate nature that are known to us. To do that a guiding thread is necessary; as such a guiding thread I have chosen the notion of positionality, a fundamental character by which animate products of nature differ from inanimate ones. (Plessner, 1975, p. xix)

The notion of 'positionality' is of central importance for the biological basis of Plessner's anthropological hermeneutics. By means of this notion, the metaphysical dualism is to be overcome in which, in the Cartesian tradition, the human being was divided into an objectual and instrumental body, on the one hand, and consciousness on the other. No longer is man to be distinguished from lower levels of organic life through a particular substance, for example, the classical anthropological entity of 'mind' or 'spirit', but by the structure of his vital relation to his environment, which is proper only to him. Organisms are not closed upon themselves, do not repose in themselves, but stand in an active relationship with the environing world. For their development and their survival, they require exchange with an environment with which they are, structurally, in a reciprocal relation. All this is expressed by the concept of 'positionality': 'A life form appears set over against its environment. From it there goes forth the relation to the field in which it is situated, and the relation comes back to it in the opposite direction' (*ibid.*, p. 131). The position of an organism in the world, that is, the specific relationship in which its animate organismal body stands to its environment, determines its organisation, as much in the sphere of the objectual–instrumental body, as in the spheres of cognition and of the vegetative nervous system. Therefore, the organic peculiarity of a life form is, in the psychophysical sense, neutrally characterised with the concept of 'positionality'; the biological description using this notion is neutral with regard to the traditional distinction among that which appertains to the body, what is mental, and what is psychical. Under these presuppositions, Plessner characterises the animal organism as a centric form of life: the animal lives outward from a life centre and into this life centre. It reproduces itself as a system of organs, the organisation of which is directed inward towards a centre; unlike the plant, which is, by virtue of its entire structure, integrated into its natural life sphere in a non-independent manner, the animal is compelled to engage in behaviour directed outward from itself that reacts to environmental stimuli. However, as this centre of behaviour, it cannot experience itself in its environment:

> Insofar as the animal is itself, it lives wholly in the here and now. The here and now does not become an object for it, does not become distinct from it, remains a state or condition, a mediating 'passing through' of concretely living effectuation. The life of the animal is a living outward from its centre, into its centre; but it does not live as a centre. The animal has experience of contents in the perceptual field surrounding it, of what is other than it and of what is properly its own; it can also gain mastery over its own organismal body. It forms a system that is reflexive upon itself; it constitutes an 'itself', but it does not consciously experience itself. (*ibid.*, p. 288)

The human being is a different matter. Whereas the position of the animal vis-à-vis its environment is centric, man is always beyond, outside of the centred life sphere, without, however, being able, in virtue of that fact, to burst asunder the centring of his environment upon himself. Plessner begins with the premise that the human being is naturally underprivileged, that man is forced constantly to effect a balance between a form of existence that is 'referred to a centre' and a form of existence that is not 'referred to a centre':

> In this respect man is inferior to the animal since the animal does not experience itself as shut off from its physical existence, as an inner self or I, and in consequence does not have to overcome a break between itself and itself, itself and its physical existence. The fact of an animal's being a body does not cut it off from its having one. (Plessner, 1970a, p. 37)

In contrast, the brackets around all human expressions of life are the organically based discontinuity in which the human being, in his agency as a body, simultaneously also experiences himself as an acting body. In the human form of existence, the centred behaviour, out of which the animal solely lives, becomes conscious of itself. Thus the human being lives in unceasing discontinuity between the state or condition which is his existence as an animate organismal body and his objectual existence as an instrumental body:

> For the human being, the sudden shift from his being within his own

organismal body to his being outside of his organismal body is a twofold character of his existence that cannot be abolished; it is a true rupture of his nature. He lives both on the near side and on the far side of the break, as a soul and as an objectual, instrumental body, and as the psychophysically neutral unity of these spheres. The unity does not, however, cover over the twofold character of his existence, does not permit it to arise out of itself; the unity is not the third term that reconciles the two opposed terms, that effects a transition into the opposed spheres; it does not constitute an autonomous sphere. It is the rupture, the hiatus, the empty 'passage through' of the mediation [of the two opposed spheres, Trans.] that is equivalent for the human being himself to the absolute double character and twofold aspect of body, considered as both organismal and objectual–instrumental, and soul, in which 'passage through' of mediation the human being experiences that twofold character and aspect. (Plessner, 1975, p. 292)

This structure of the human mode of life is expressed by Plessner in the concept of 'excentric positionality'. It describes a behaviour with respect to an environment that is tied to a body, and that is constantly required to balance between being an organismal body and having an objectual–instrumental body. In all of his expressions of his existence, man is compelled to live out of his organismal body and at the same time to dispose over his objectual–instrumental body. From the standpoint of natural history, Plessner, like Gehlen, accounts for this excentric position of the human being by means of the organic results of an ontogenetically premature birth. Weakness of instincts, and primitiveness of his organs, these results of a determination of the organism that has, so to speak, not been brought to its conclusion, leave man in a constant tension arising from the necessity of learning to have mastery over his objectual–instrumental body with growing ease of control, while never being able to overleap his original condition of being an organismal body (see Plessner, 1976, pp. 7–81; the discussion summarised here is to be found on pp. 56ff.). Plessner bases his understanding of the specifically human capacities directly on this distinction and this relationship between the organismal body and the objectual–instrumental body; speech, interaction and work, for Plessner the human being's supreme monopolies, are the capabilities in which man, on the basis of his given organic constitution, has been able with time to instrumentalise his objectual body:

Speaking, acting, the fashioning of materials in various ways imply the human being's control of his own objectual–instrumental body, which had to be learned, and which requires constant monitoring. This distance within

myself and from myself is precisely what gives me the possibility of surmounting that distance. It does not mean a cleavage and splitting in two of my
fundamentally undivided self, but rather is the very prerequisite for being
autonomous. (*ibid.*, p. 56)

The capabilities for speech and action that are specific to the human
being can be accounted for in this manner by means of the human
being's excentric position, from which man must learn to dispose over
his objectual–instrumental body in order to be able to survive as an
organismal body.

Now, Plessner distinguishes between the instrumentality and the
expressiveness of the human body in order further to differentiate the
human being's experience of his body as an object, that is, his having an
objectual–instrumental body, through examination of the human
being's hybrid condition (Plessner, 1970a, p. 51). The human being
either employs his objectual–instrumental body as the instrument of his
interactions, in communicative and instrumental action, or he makes it
available to serve as the means of expressing his feelings and intentions,
in gesture, in mimic expressive behaviour, and in speech. The expressiveness of the organismal body, which is what this distinction is intended
to grasp, is the key concept for achieving the goal of a naturalised
hermeneutics which Plessner's philosophical anthropology, on the
whole, pursues. For, on the basis of the human being's positionality, the
forms of expression of his organismal body can be classified according to
the role they play functionally in the balancing between being an organismal body and having an objectual–instrumental body that is proper
only to the human being. Plessner's hermeneutics recognises three
classes of expressions, specific to the human being, each of which stands
in a different relationship to the structure of the human being's bodily
existence in its two aspects (*ibid.*, pp. 56ff.): the already-named forms of
expression, speech and gesture; mimic expressive behaviour; and lastly
the expressive reactions of laughing and weeping that lie between the
first two kinds of expression. Speech and gesture have in common the
instrumental role that they assume in the domain of the human being's
expression of his life; the human being can freely make use of linguistic
or gestural means in order to give expression to the intent of an action or
to an emotion – in speech and in gesture I am able to dispose over my
objectual–instrumental body. Both means of expression possess, therefore, a propositional content: with their aid I communicate a state of
affairs. However, propositional contents can only be communicated if I

address myself to a co-subject with communicative intent. Thus, in addition to the matters they are used to refer to, speech and gesture have in common their intersubjective structure: in them human beings establish a dialogical relation with one another. With language, states of affairs can be communicated independently of particular situations; in speech, man makes use of phonic material in order to make meanings communicable in a manner that has been freed from a particular situational context:

> Language makes use of articulate sounds as signs for meanings that can express states of affairs without being tied to the affect and the situation of the speaker. (*ibid.*, p. 47)

Language is the centrally important medium of communicative experience; it is only in linguistic utterances that man becomes conscious of the intersubjectivity of the plexus of relations in which he lives:

> Although I can mentally experience myself as the middle point of an interior that is closed about by my organismal body, as if I were in a sheath, opaque for others with respect to what is happening within me; although I can experience myself as a prisoner of my consciousness, encompassed by a horizon that, unsurmountable, unbreachable, goes wherever I go along with my perceptions and actions, I am released from this immanence by language. In language there is no *solus ipse*. (Plessner, 1976, p. 45)

The human being can also communicate something to another subject in the non-linguistic expressive form of the gesture; it is not for nothing that we speak of the 'language of gestures' when referring to gestures such as the nodding of the head or the raising of the arm:

> Words are lacking in this language; the body alone speaks, and that it speaks is attested, not only by the success of mutual understanding, but also by the representative nature of the gestures. (Plessner, 1970a, p. 58)

The gestural utterance is just as much a form of communication as the speech act; the meaning content of sentences can be translated into the extraverbal medium of gesture. Plessner interprets the gesture as a sign established by intersubjective practice that expresses meanings in mimic movements of the body:

> To be sure, gesticulatory language does not make use of articulated sound complexes as vehicles of meaning, but of bodily, and occasionally also acoustical, movements; but by means of such movements it conveys information and, indeed, in a manner analogous to speech, since it invests them with a symbolic character. This wordless speech often takes the place of

spoken words. (Gestures of command, pointing, attestation, entreaty, submission, gestures indicating 'perhaps', 'yes', 'no', 'thanks', 'delighted', etc., play an important role in social intercourse.) And occasionally, such gestures serve to weaken or strengthen verbal discourse. In every case they have a meaning which they convey through signs and thereby qualify as language, not as mime. (*ibid.*, p. 51)

In contrast, mimic expressive behaviour, which we employ, as it were, only in stylised form in the socially conventionalised gesture, possesses an immediacy that is incomparably more closely tied to the organismal body. The various kinds of this behaviour constitute the second class of expressive forms which Plessner distinguishes in his anthropological hermeneutics. Mimic expressive behaviour, for example, the reactions of turning pale and of blushing, of becoming rigid, or of relaxation, do not have the very two fundamental properties that link language with gesture. With mimic expressive behaviour, the human being cannot express an intentionally meant state of affairs; in such behaviour, rather, an emotional state expresses itself independently of the individual's volition:

If gesture expresses something because we mean something *by* it, mimic expression . . . *has* a significance because an agitation (a condition or a welling-up emotion of the internal state) is externally reflected *in* it. (*ibid.*, p. 53)

In this case, a hermeneutic interpretation cannot be directed at a meaning to which a subject has given linguistic or gestural expression, but instead must decipher an affect that procures expression of itself at a level below that of subjective intentions; therefore mimic expressive behaviour does not possess, in the strict sense, a propositional content. Further, it is also not tied into an intersubjective communication nexus; in the mimicry of the face or of the expressive behaviour of the entire body, a subject does not communicate something to his partner, but is marked by an affect without purposing to be so. The expressive content of the mimic expression lies beyond all individual intentions, hence also beyond interactive orientations:

Expressive movements as such are immediate, spontaneous, and intrinsically unrelated to others, i.e., are without intentional character, even when the presence of others is necessary for the release of the expression. (*ibid.*, p. 52)

Moreover, the mimic expressive movement of the body is also immediate in virtue of the fact that the expressive content uttered in that movement cannot be represented by any other expressive utterance. The meaning that is meant in linguistic or gestural communication can be detached from the concrete happening in a given situation to such a degree that ultimately it lives by means of a different word in each different instance, or can be replaced in each different instance by a different gesture from the linguistic and gestural repertoire that has been established by social practice; in contrast, the expressive content of an affect cannot be objectivated to such a degree that it becomes presentable independently of the organically determined physical appearance or state.

The mimic expressive physical appearance or state has no cognitive content that could be reproduced accurately in propositions or in gestures, inasmuch as its expressive content is immediately fused with the expressive activity or state manifested by the objectual–instrumental body:

> In expressive mime, psychological content and physical form are related to each other as poles of a unity, which cannot be separated and reduced to the relation of sign and thing signified, . . . without destroying their organic, immediate, and spontaneous living unity. (*ibid.*, p. 55)

Thus, mimic expressive behaviour is the type of the forms of human expression in which it is not the subject that embodies himself, hence disposes over his objectual–instrumental body in free expressive purposiveness, but in which rather the human organismal body obtains expression for itself by means of the objectual–instrumental body; in mimic expression, the human being makes his objectual–instrumental body available to serve as the sounding-board of his feelings.

A third class of human forms of expression to which Plessner's hermeneutics is directed refers to the dimension in which the subject can no longer maintain a balance between being an organismal body and having an objectual–instrumental body, a balance he has to maintain as a human being. It is a question here of the forms of expression laughing and weeping. In his theory, Plessner concentrated his efforts at an early stage on the anthropological interpretation of their significance. With this intent he was aiming far beyond the explanatory claims that are made, say, by a phylogenetic derivation of these two kinds of expressive behaviour from visual signals in animals (see van Hooff, 1972). Plessner's hermeneutic interpretation of the expressive content of these forms of expression is supposed to make immediately comprehensible the determination of the human being's position which had been elab-

orated only categorically in his biologically oriented theory of the hierarchical ordering of life forms. Laughing and weeping are regarded by
Plessner as forms of expressive behaviour that are proper only to the
human being, and that occupy a clearly peculiar intermediary locus
between, on the one side, linguistic and gestural forms of expression,
and, on the other side, mimic expressive behaviour. Laughing and
weeping are distinguished from the expressive means of speech and
gesture primarily by their reactive character as expression: the human
being cannot employ laughing and weeping as a means of expression
with conscious intent; rather, man is involuntarily overwhelmed by these
forms of expression. Furthermore, they both lack all cognitive meaning,
precisely that by which speech and gesture set themselves off among the
possible forms of human expression. A state of affairs cannot be communicated to another human being through laughing and weeping;
instead, in them a psychical excitation procures for itself immediate
expression in an expressive physical state or activity. Hence, in laughing
and weeping as forms of expression, emotional content and the expressive appearance or state manifested by the objectual–instrumental body
are directly fused with one another, as in the case of mimic expressive
behaviour:

> Irreplaceability, immediacy, and involuntariness give laughing and crying the
> character of true expressive movements. Their original link with the emo-
> tions – never mind for now with which – forces itself upon our eyes and ears
> with irresistible authority. With scarcely any other expression is it easier for
> us to distinguish the authentic from the inauthentic. (Plessner, 1970a, p. 56)

However, a comparison of laughing and weeping with the forms of
mimic expressive behaviour also encounters limits. In the latter kinds of
expression, an emotion attains to appearance by means of the objectual–
instrumental body in such a manner that, on the one hand, the individual's intentionality is rendered inoperative, while on the other hand the
individual organismal body is put into operation as a field of emotional
expression; in laughing and weeping, however, the human being loses
every relation whatsoever to his physical existence. In laughing and
weeping, the objectual–instrumental body emancipates itself entirely
from the human being's experience of himself as an organismal body in
an eruptive expressive event that overwhelms the subject, so that it is not
the ego, which monitors and makes use of the processes of its objectual–
instrumental body, but the very unity of the person as an animate
organismal body that becomes incapable of action:

> The living transparency of the body reaches its lowest point in them [laugh-

ing and crying]. Bodily reactions emancipate themselves; man is shaken by
them, buffeted, made breathless. He has lost the relation to his physical
existence; it withdraws from him and does with him more or less what it will.
(*ibid.*, p. 66)

In contrast to mimic expressive behaviour, laughing and weeping are
human modes of expression in which the loss of a balance between the
organismal body and the objectual–instrumental body itself has expressive value. At this point, a hermeneutics of human expressiveness
no longer encounters expressive manifestations that allow subjective
intents or affects to become clearly apparent; it encounters, rather,
expressive movements indicating the dissolution of the subjective capability for reaction itself. Plessner, therefore, understands the expressive
forms of laughing and weeping as expressive manifestations signalling
personal crisis. The first two classes of expressions specific to the
human being correspond to the normal case in action situations to which
the subject responds either by instrumentalising his objectual–instrumental body in gesture or speech, or by making his organismal body
available as a field of emotional expression (mimicry). In contrast, the
last class of expression corresponds to the exceptional case among
action situations, to the plurisignificance of which the subject is no
longer able to find a univocal relation. The subject reacts to the confused action situation with the disorganisation of his normal equilibrium
between his organismal body and his objectual–instrumental body:

> If, however, the situation cannot be brought to fulfillment, if it becomes
> unanswerable in itself, then speech and gesture, action and expressive
> movement, break down. Then there is nothing more to be done with the
> situation; we have no more to say to it, we don't know where we are with it. In
> such defective circumstances that point of reference must also vanish which
> man needs if he is to find a relation to his physical existence. (*ibid.*, p. 67)

In the forms of expression of speech and gesture, the human being
disposes over his objectual–instrumental body in order to communicate
something; in mimic expressive behaviour, he, as an intentionally acting
subject, steps back behind his organismal body, which gives expression
for him to psychical excitations by means of the objectual–instrumental
body. However, in the expressive modes of laughing and weeping, the
human being no longer finds any meaningful relationship whatever to
his objectual–instrumental bodiliness; in his acute disorientation, he
loses control of this bodiliness to such an extent that his objectual–

instrumental body reacts independently in eruptions that have the character of automatic mechanisms. Plessner distinguishes between the two forms of expression according to the manner in which the ego is involved in the situation to which no response is possible.

In laughter, the objectual–instrumental body reacts for the subject to a situational structure in which an unequivocally meaningful relation can no longer be established to the ambivalent, self-contradictory meaning-relations of one and the same sequence of action or linguistic utterance. The matters in response to which the human being, in the confusion into which he has been forced by the paradoxes of excitation and meaning of a given situation, can no longer do anything but abandon himself to the automatic mechanisms of laughter appertaining to the objectual–instrumental body include, at one end of their range, jubilation and tickling, which are still very similar to mimic expressive behaviour, as well as comicalness and jokes, and at the other extreme the existential boundary situations of embarrassment and despair. In laughter, then, the tension is discharged that results from a human individual's momentary entanglement in ambivalences of sense that are by their nature unresolvable:

> Unanswerableness, through (various) mutually exclusive possibilities of response, sets up resistance against a rebuff by the problematical situation, i.e., the tension which is released in laughter. Thus we respond to the unanswerable in its multiplicity of sense. Thus we put 'paid' to a situation which is vitally, spiritually, and existentially 'contrary' to sense . . . with a reaction which betrays at one and the same time both self-assertion and self-abandonment. When a man laughs, he gives way to his own body and thus foregoes unity with it and control over it. With this capitulation as a unity of ensouled body and mind, he asserts himself as a person. (*ibid.*, p. 142)

In contrast, the range of the situational causes or occasions of the expressive form of weeping is incomparably narrower. Here, too, the human being must give himself over to an automatic mechanism appertaining to the objectual–instrumental body, because he can no longer respond to a situational structure in the accustomed manner with a meaningful action, a linguistic utterance, an adroit gesture, or mimic expressive behaviour. Whereas the inability to react that precedes laughter arises from the simultaneity in a situation of self-contradictory meaning-relations, weeping has its origin in a situation in which every meaningful response whatsoever to the content of a deeply felt mental–emotional experience is impossible owing to the subject's lack of emotional distance from that content. In pain, in rage, in pity, or in devotion, all of which Plessner includes among the affective causes or occasions of weeping, we are deprived of all possibility of a motivated response to a state of affairs to such a degree that we are unable to place ourselves in any kind of a relationship to that state of affairs. In these circumstances also, the body then answers for us, as we abandon ourselves to the anonymous and compulsive expressive movement that we call weeping:

> With crying on the other hand, the helplessness results from a curious immediacy in the exposure to pain, in the sudden shift from tenseness to relaxation, and in being deeply moved. Now 'helplessness', by its very meaning, can have the appearance of being only a matter of the inability to resist a force. Such may seem to be the case in situations involving physical and mental pain. On the other hand, in peripeteia, in remorse, overpowering joy, conversion, and in the various forms of being deeply moved, helplessness appears as an absence of distance – not from the actual feeling but from the content which engrosses me in the feeling, which rouses and shakes me. (*ibid.*, p. 143)

Plessner accounts for the two forms of expression, laughing and weeping, with the fundamentally monological situation of the subject who can no longer find, in his experience of himself as an organismal body, a proper relation to the fact of his objectual–instrumental bodiliness. Although the causes of laughing and weeping are situationally bound up with interactions, the reason why the two forms of expression are possible is to be found solely in the internal tension of the solitary subject. In the mimic expressive activities of laughing and weeping, the human being does not react to a perturbation of the structure of intersubjective action, but to a perturbation of the balance between his organismal body and his objectual–instrumental body. In this manner, Plessner makes the tension within the human being between the organismal body and the objectual–instrumental body, thus man's excentric position, the constitutional root of all capabilities that are specific to the human being. This solipsistic fundamental premise of Plessner's anthropology has led Habermas to pose a question that is, in contrast, directed to the conditions of such an experience by the human being of himself as an objectual–instrumental body, conditions which are themselves intersubjective:

> Would it not be more plausible . . . to derive the structure of the mirror–I . . . directly from the structure of linguistic communication – and the formation of the self from the acquisition of linguistic competence, in particular from the practical acquisition of an understanding of the system of personal

pronouns? Then the twofold structure of language would merely be copied in the twofold character [of human bodiliness, Trans.] of the organismal body and the objectual–instrumental body. The twofold structure of language consists in the fact that speakers and actors encounter one another intersubjectively only when they are also communicating about objects or states of affairs, and that, in contrast, they can only exchange propositional contents if they also enter into an intersubjective, that is, a non-objectified relation with one another. (Habermas, 1973a, pp. 232–5; the passage quoted appears on pp. 234f.)

This criticism is as much right as it is wrong. Habermas has put his finger on the weakest point in Plessner's analysis: the fact that the human subject can perceive his own objectual–instrumental body is not accounted for in Plessner's theory by the structure of the subject's capability to do so, which is in and of itself already intersubjective; for the ability to identify something as one's own requires, after all, an anticipatory apprehension of the unity of one's own objectual–instrumental body, which unity is never perceptible as such. But Habermas is mistaken when he too hastily identifies the fundamental structure of intersubjectivity with speech. It is, ontogenetically speaking, beyond all doubt that the acquisition of the ability to identify one's objectual–instrumental body as properly one's own clearly precedes the 'practical acquisition of an understanding of the system of personal pronouns'. Similarly, it cannot be maintained that the demarcation from each other of communicative and propositional content of utterances is prerequisite for the human being's consciousness of his bodiliness under the twofold aspect of his organismal bodiliness and his objectual–instrumental bodiliness. A critique of Plessner's anthropology from the standpoint of the theory of intersubjectivity must avoid narrowing a theory directed at the basic structures of intersubjectivity down to a theory of language and must develop its criticism ontogenetically, drawing perhaps upon the germinal ideas presented in Mead's writings of his late period.[7]

To be sure, the solipsistic foundation on which Plessner thus erects his hermeneutics of non-linguistic forms of expression only exhibits its problematical features fully in the politically oriented parts of his anthropology. From the outset, Plessner mistrusts, as a normative guiding idea, the notion of communication that is free of domination, such as pervasively influences the writings of, say, Mead and Habermas. In its

---

[7] Most explicit in this regard is the manuscript in Mead's literary estate beginning with the words: 'The human individual has as a part of his self the physical organism'; see also some passages in *Philosophy of the Act* (1938, pp. 120, 431).

stead he puts the idea of a society that creates social distance among its members, and institutionally guarantees the psychophysical self-preservation of the individual subject. In the grounding of this conception of society, which is central to all Plessner's politico-sociological writings, the anthropological premise of an egotism on the part of the human being that is conditioned by his organismal bodiliness plays a crucially important role in the argumentation. The study entitled *Grenzen der Gemeinschaft* (The Limits of Community), which was published in 1924, explicitly presents this idea for the first time in a kind of critical socio-philosophical scrutiny of the present historical period; in contrast, Plessner's later contributions to a 'political anthropology' moderate this line of thought in their implicit theory of society.

Plessner intended the aforementioned study to be an anthropologically oriented critique of the notion of community that holds fast to the ideal of a social group grounded in direct interaction among its members and in their personal intimacy with one another. He distinguished between the 'racially nationalistic' ('national–völkisch') idea of the *Blutsgemeinschaft*, of the community founded upon the blood-ties of race, and the 'communistic' idea of the *Sachgemeinschaft*, of the community founded upon rational discussion of, and decisions about, common interests and enterprises and upon their co-operative pursuit, as two complementary versions of a social radicalism seeking to politicise in a *Gemeinschaftsethos*, a communitarian ethos, the widespread reserve regarding the growing anonymity and interpersonal remoteness in social life. Although Plessner names neither the intellectual authors nor the political and social bearers of the radical communitarian ethos which he is criticising, he obviously has in mind, on the one hand, the communist and socialist critique of capitalism, and on the other the right-wing conservative and pre-fascist critique of culture. In his study, the two types of societal critiques become fused together as two sides of one and the same central, guiding idea. For both these attempts to radicalise the concept of cummunity are, in Plessner's view, complementary for the very reason that each of them made only one moment of the human being's twofold psychophysical existence the unifying principle of a community life that is opposed to a society which has become abstract. In its notion of a people united through membership in a single race, the ideology of a *Blutsgemeinschaft* is aimed solely at the physical dimension of human life, from which the communist idea of a *Sachgemeinschaft*, constituted by processes of rational agreement, abstracts. Now, Plessner shows that for the two versions of the communitarian ethos to reach the limits of their applicability, it suffices to take into consideration the dimension of the human being's hybrid psychophysical existence that has been excluded in each case. For if one has a clear view of this state of affairs from which anthropology begins, then it becomes evident that the communitarian constructions which are based on complementarily one-sided conceptions of the human being, can satisfy neither the totality of tasks of a relatively large social group, nor the requirements arising out of the nature of such a group. The racially nationalistic communitarian ethos must come to grief on the necessity, which is inherent in civilisation, of settling all human affairs publicly and rationally, just as the communistic communitarian ethos is finally frustrated by the socially unbridgeable chasm between rational decision-making and normatively open life in a society. It is at this point, in connection with his critique of the 'communist' idea of free and open negotiation, bound to follow rational argument, in order to settle all socially relevant matters, that Plessner explains his critique of the notion of communication that is free of domination as a normative leading idea:

> If our actual behaviour is scrutinised through the magnifying glass of discussion – after all, according to the idea of a communism carried through with logical rigour, our behaviour would have to accept that in a *Sachgemeinschaft* – it can turn out to be correct, but it might just as well turn out to be wrong . . . The mind that is always organic, systematic and unequivocal, comes to grief on the fragmentary character of human existence, on the impenetrable ambiguity of situations. (Plessner, 1972, p. 50)

The imbalance, peculiar to man, between his existence as an organismal body and the purposive attitude of command that he can adopt in relation to his own body – between his being an organismal body and his having an objectual–instrumental body, as Plessner says later – does not allow of a rational community that intersubjectively comes to an understanding about goals of action; despite all interpretative efforts and all compulsive strivings to achieve unequivocalness, the human being's physical existence retains a moment of perpetual openness, and this openness is a matter that the individual subject must settle with himself alone. This fundamental idea, tinged by *Lebensphilosophie*, now serves Plessner also as the foundation of a 'defence of society' going beyond his critique of the communitarian ethos.

In these constructive portions of his study of the limits of community, Plessner speculatively anticipates the fundamental anthropological ideas which he will later make the biological basis of his hermeneutics of the non-linguistic forms of expression. He accounts for the socio-cultural primordiality of social relationships of distanciation, i.e., those in which the members of a society encounter each other not in direct communication related to their practical affairs, but in ceremonially defined interactions, by the peculiarity of the human form of existence. He maintains that the human being is first of all an individual subject, not by the very nature of his bodily, physiological endowment, but in virtue of his permanent psychical distance from everything that in fact happens:

> What truly first makes an individual of him, makes him indivisible and unique from the inside outward, is the awareness that he possesses a soul, is his living in the centre of an interior that feels, wills and thinks, that has a will of its own in relation to the environment and to its own organismal body, that is incomparable in its depth and its inner wealth of qualities. (*ibid.*, p. 56)

Because the human being, in his psychical individuality, encounters an unceasing stream of ever new sensory experiences and emotions, so that he can never become wholly and definitively unequivocal even to himself, he must also safeguard himself against all social compulsion to present himself in a definitive manner, against all pressure restrictively to define himself. On the other hand, though, because he cannot renounce the social presentation of his ever new individuality, which objectivation of himself is necessary if he is to remain continuously comprehensible to himself, he is also, anthropologically speaking, dependent just as much on the sphere of social unequivocalnesses. The structure of his mode of living therefore forces the human being to balance continuously his personal and experimental openness and his intersubjectively binding self-definition. However, Plessner concludes, only the social framework of 'society' guarantees to the isolated individuals both the possibility of carrying out such a psychophysically constantly necessitated balancing act and the subjects' safety while they are engaged in this balancing act.

Now, against the background of this speculative anthropological line of thought, Plessner conceives of 'society' as a broad system of socially established and regulated forms of interactions that mediate between the family as a private place of safety and the institutionalised system of publicly obtaining norms. Only in a network of rules governing communication which give to social intercourse a form that is both distancing and playful, can the individual subject present himself without danger and without incurring obligation, and in a way that can be revised over and over again. In the interaction forms of ceremonials, of prestige-related behaviour, of diplomacy and of tact, the 'intermediary domain' of society continuously provides the opportunity for precisely this kind of behaviour. For Plessner, proof of human beings' inescapable and ineradicable compulsion to form societies is given by the 'ethos of gracefulness':

> social behaviour, mastery not just of written and enacted conventions, the virtuoso use of the forms of play with which men approach close to one another without colliding, with which they distance themselves from one another without hurting each other by indifference. Amiability is the atmosphere [of this gracefulness], not forcefulness in interaction; play and the observance of its rules, not gravity, is its moral law. The forced remoteness between one human being and another is ennobled to detachment; the offensive indifference, coldness and rudeness of individuals' living-past-each-other is rendered ineffectual by the forms of courtesy, deference and attentiveness, and a too great intimacy is counteracted by reservedness. (*ibid.*, p. 73)

Plessner can interpret these abstractive forms of social activity as a gain of freedom only because he understands them as assuring the individual's self-preservation; in his view, 'human dignity' is realised in the social behaviour of a subject who playfully envelops his own individuality in highly formalised communicative forms, but also learns something new about himself in the stylised presentation of his individuality. It is, however, only due to Plessner's anthropological anticipatory interpretation of the human being as an isolated subject by his essential nature, as a subject individually effecting a balance between his vital openness and his restrictive social definition, that he must allow the nexus of social life to shrink down to the dimension of strategic action carried out among subjects intent on sustaining themselves.

This line of argument is also Plessner's answer to the question he poses to himself: in which dimension is social progress possible under the conditions of the human being's natural endowment? For if the human being's inceptive organic state forces him, of itself, to engage in playful and individual self-sustentation, then the self-unfolding of the human being in the course of history must be co-extensive with the expansion of the social relationships of detachment upon the economic base of the domination of nature:

> Affirming society for the sake of society, which has its own ethos, its own

greatness that is superior to that of community, and learning to comprehend that an exertion of the intellect which must be increased endlessly is required for the advancing perfection of social life, for ever greater sovereignty over nature; affirming the machines from whose social consequences the present era is suffering; to take upon oneself the whole burden of obligations of the civilisation which the West has invented and elaborated, for the sake of the growing possibilities for play offered by that civilisation – that is the true strength upon which everything depends. Not conceived as the virtue of all, but as the ethos of the rulers and leaders. (*ibid.*, pp. 35f.)

Self-confidently, Plessner believes he can still ascribe the societal ethos that his study seeks to describe and define from the perspective of social philosophy to a bourgeois elite that is not led by the proletarian critique of capitalism, on the one hand, or by the aristocratic masters' code of morality on the other, to lose sight of its goal of refining the social forms of style and the social techniques of self-presentation. It is true that as early as his *Grenzen der Gemeinschaft* doubts can be heard in Plessner's writings that a mere decade later, after he had witnessed and lived through the seizure of power by the National Socialists, became radicalised into a general suspicion of ideology:

The historical purpose of modern society, the Western world's conception of its mission: the expansion of technical–scientific civilisation founded upon subjection of the forces of nature, an expansion that shrinks back from no external obstacle, that can be stopped by nothing, is starting to come into conflict with Western man's cultural consciousness. (*ibid.*, pp. 39f.)

In 1934–5, Plessner gave a lecture in Holland expressing the views of the half-Jewish émigré on the cultural and political developments in Germany. In this lecture, which was republished in 1959 with the title *Die verspätete Nation* (The Belated Nation), Plessner examined and attempted to explain the shattering of the bourgeois societal ethos by German Fascism. He adopted the increased mistrust of the ideals of European civilisation and reconstructed the stages of German intellectual history as those of a progressive philosophical understanding of the ideological character of all ethical norms. However, he makes no factual objections to the result of this process of disillusionment, namely philosophical nihilism, but can oppose to it only a postulate of humanism that is in itself theoretically unfounded (cf. Habermas, 1971d, pp. 222ff.).

Instinct and need. Agnes Heller's social anthropology

Like the other members of the now-dissolved 'Budapest School' of Marxism, Agnes Heller is no longer unknown in the West. In recent years, a number of works by her and other students of Lukács during the philosopher's late period, namely György Márkus, Mihály Vajda and Ferenc Fehér, have been published in German and English. These writings originally responded to the contradiction between nationalised economies and absence of political democratisation, which is the central contradiction for the socialist countries of Eastern Europe, by undertaking to elaborate a theoretically oppositional interpretation of Marxism. Thus the political significance of these studies lies in their authors' enterprise of making the bureaucratic forms of domination of Eastern European socialism indirectly transparent by showing that the core of historical materialism consists of an ethics and of the philosophy of praxis (cf. Rovatti, 1976; Breccia-Boella, 1974; Joas, 1978b). Agnes Heller has sought to clothe this theoretical intent in the systematic form of a social anthropology. In the volumes that have been published so far, she has set herself the task of filling the normative anthropological basic framework of Marxism that György Márkus has ascertained in his interpretation of Marx's writings (see above, pages 36–40) with a substantive theory of the specifically human capacities for action. So far, the centre of this broadly conceived social anthropology consists of two studies that seek to establish the peculiarity of the structure of human needs in contrast to the animal system of instincts. A third investigation that treats of the psychical structure of human feelings has also been published (Heller, 1979b). Heller's studies on the theory of needs offer outlines of that theory which give an overview of the competing anthropological theories of needs for the purpose of working out a theoretical system. In that overview are contained the possibilities and the limitations of an attempt to present this key concept of anthropology through an examination of her investigations. Further, a book chapter aimed at interpreting Heller's work cannot do justice to the abundance of empirical information and the nuances of theoretical differences in which ethology, behaviourism, and above all psychoanalysis, pose this crucially important problem today.

In her book *Instinkt, Aggression, Charakter* (1977), in which a critique of Erich Fromm's theory of personality is combined with a study of the concept of instinct, and the second part of which has been published in English as *On Instincts* (1979), Heller deals with a wealth of findings of anthropological and ethological research in order to present evidence of the plasticity of the specifically human structure of needs. In contrast, her book *The Theory of Need in Marx* (1976) is a more philologically oriented attempt to demonstrate the significance of the category of need for the total architectonics of Marx's theory. The first-mentioned work is based throughout on the fundamental anthropological framework provided by Arnold Gehlen's theory; however, it gives that framework a decisively different interpretation from the standpoint of social philosophy. For Gehlen, the plasticity of the structure of human instincts is accounted for by the organically unique situation in which a defective life form initially finds itself:

> the potential instinctual investment of absolutely all kinds of human activities, from philosophy all the way to head-hunting, which are, certainly, learned in each case, and the variations of which remain always just as conceivable as their complete cessation, is of great importance. It must be explained by the same reduction of instincts that obviously includes the receding of authentically instinctual behaviour. The dismantling of authentic instinctual actions apparently takes place in a complementary relationship to the morphological fetalisation [of the human being, Trans.] and the development of the cerebrum; but it means on the other hand a de-differentiation of the instinct structure such that now all modes of behaviour, be they ever so highly mediated and accidental, with whatever character of work or play, can appear as instinct-invested and with the capacity to satiate. (Gehlen, 1971, pp. 329f.)

Agnes Heller makes this recognition her own. She criticises all naturalistic theories of instinct that restrict human instinct to some organically rooted tendencies, the nature or goal of which is rigidly fixed. The latter appear frequently in the categorially unclear assertion that the human being reacts to critically important situations with his basic instincts. However, the human being, as Heller seeks to show, is not a behavioural organism directed by instincts. Instincts are highly specific patterns of movement that are triggered by innate automatic mechanisms in response to species-specific crucial stimuli on the organic basis of an internal production of stimuli:

> by instinct I mean those compulsory behaviour mechanisms or movement coordinations which are species-specific, and at the same time are action-specific, [which are] inherited through the genetic code [and] elicited [i.e., triggered] by internal and external stimuli [,] which play a leading role in the preservation of the species within a certain stage of the development of the

organism [,] and which surpass the intelligence of the given species from the point of view of [their] positive selective value. (Heller, 1979a, p. 22)[8]

The external stimuli, in response to which the species-specific in-stinctual movements are triggered, are composed of chemical signals and acoustic or optical signs that have a functional significance in the animal organism's behaviour for the reproduction of itself and its spe-cies. As a prime example for an instinct-directed kind of animal, Heller names insects. In addition to instincts, vertebrates also possess the capability of learning – in processes similar to human experience – to perceive events in their environment as signals important for their survival and thus as instinct-triggering stimuli. The human being, though, still possesses such an organically rooted system of instincts only vestigially. At this point in the exposition of her argument, Heller cites Konrad Lorenz:

> Apart from certain motor forms of food-uptake (seizing, placing-in-the-mouth, chewing and swallowing), mating (frictional movements) and poss-ibly certain automatic elements in walking and running, an adult human being appears to have no centrally coordinated motor patterns, based on endogenous automatisms. (Lorenz, vol. 2, 1971, p. 162)

Here actions have freed themselves from firm attachment to the system of instincts. In the human being, the organic instinctual energies do not discharge themselves in rigidly structured patterns of behaviour that are automatically triggered by external stimuli, but rather constitute a per-manent instinctual potential that can enter into different socio-cultur-ally informed modes of behaviour. In order to describe the nature of the uncoupling of the structure of action from the instinct structure that is characteristic of the human being, Heller has recourse to Gehlen's notion of 'hiatus':

> The inner stimulus subsists in humans as well (hormonal processes in the form of stimuli released by the central nervous system), but the action resulting from them is not biologically determined. (Heller, 1979a, p. 16)[9]

[8] The English translation of Heller's *On Instincts* was made from the Hungarian version of that work. I have emended the passage quoted here in accordance with the correspond-ing passage in the German version of Heller's study; cf. Heller, 1977, p. 81. Trans.

[9] As the passage quoted from the German version differs quite a bit from the passage in English, I give here a rendering of the German: 'The human being, too, has inner stimuli. They appear in the form of hormonal processes, of stimuli released by the central nervous system. However, the action through which these are abreacted is not biologically determined' (Heller, 1977, p. 73). Trans.

The human being's system of organic impulsion cannot, therefore, be analysed into basic instincts, to each of which a set of actions aimed at satisfying the particular instinct can be positively assigned. The natural-istic theories of instinct do not do justice to the plasticity of the im-pulsional potential of human beings. The human being's instinctual energies are capable of development and are susceptible to being shaped. They are capable, with time, of becoming the bearers of all modes of action occurring in the course of human history. Today this fundamental understanding of human instincts, to which Agnes Heller was led by her critique of the naturalistic instinct theories, constitutes the framework of all theories of motivation that investigate the ontogen-etic process of the forming of human drives. These theories differ from one another principally in virtue of the fact that they locate the process of the structuration of the unformed instinctual potential in very different zones of experiential learning during socialisation.

At present, three types of such motivation theories can usefully be distinguished: first, a broad array of psychoanalytical approaches having in common the assumption that the human being has a libidinous potential of drives that is shaped in the interactions between a child and its mother and father which are highly cathected, that is, in direct interaction within the family; second, various theoretical models pro-posed by developmental psychology and symbolic interactionism, which embed the process of the formation of motivation in a whole network of interactional experiences that may also be less invested from the stand-point of the dynamics of the instincts, and on the basis of which the child structures his own impulses in learning processes; and last, the theoreti-cal models, such as that proposed by Critical Psychology (see below, pp. 102ff), according to which the process of the formation of motivation is a gradual shaping of the productive instinctual potential that advances step by step by means of practical experiences with things.

A second question to which the various interpretations of the theory of drives today give different answers has to do with the relationship between the drives and language, between the unconscious and con-sciousness. There are two opposed conceptions of this relationship, which can be formulated as ideal types. On the one hand, it is assumed that the unconscious is that part of the psyche consisting of the drives which are, in the socialisation process, excluded by the subject from his individual use of language and thus repressed; because they no longer have the possibility of linguistic expression, such 'excommunicated' portions of human needs manifest themselves as symptoms in the subject's actions. From the standpoint of this conception, the normative goal of every process of individualisation is a condition in which the most complete linguistic expression possible of all needs is achieved (see, e.g., Lorenzer, 1970; Habermas, 1971a, part III). This view is, however, decidedly contradicted by a second linguistic interpretation of the theory of drives that has developed in the train of Jacques Lacan's studies (see Lacan, 1977; Lang, 1973). According to this second conception, the unconscious does indeed consist of the portions of human needs lying beyond the conscious use of language; however, taken together, these portions of human needs make up a language of their own, an unconscious language, that is constantly obtruding itself uncontrolledly into all human actions; a human subject's intentional linguistic utterances are always accompanied by symbolisations that he is not aware of, and that go beyond his intentions. According to the first conception, then, the unconscious is the socialisation product of a process of exclusion from linguistic expression, while the second conception views the unconscious as nothing less than the medium of the true essence of language. Consequently, for the latter conception the normative goal of the process of human socialisation cannot be understood as a state in which all instincts are given linguistic expression. In all likelihood, only a further clarification of the relationship between the development of needs and their linguistic expression will be able to resolve the problems raised by this controversy (as a beginning, see Brede, 1976).

Agnes Heller makes use of her fundamental considerations in a critique of the theories of aggression that are current at the present time. In her critique, she distinguishes a naturalistic strategy, a behaviourist strategy, and a strategy employed by the theory of personality for accounting for aggression. These strategies maintain either that aggressivity is an organically rooted or that it is a socio-culturally necessary type of human behaviour. The naturalistic theories of aggression (see Heller, 1979a, pp. 26ff.) postulate an instinct of aggression occurring in all developed species of animals, and hence also in the human being, or else that is peculiar to the human species alone. According to this account, aggressive behaviour, which is supposed to be at the bottom of such diverse social phenomena as war and criminality, is explained by a specifically aggressive instinctual potential which can, so to say, discharge itself in appropriate socially significant situations. Heller opposes both versions of this biological theory of aggression. The theory that explains human aggressivity as merely the derivative, produced by the phylum's history, of an instinct of aggression that is organically rooted in the animal, overlooks the impossibility of describing forms of animal behaviour as such according to the pattern of socially defined modes of action:

> Thus the [so-called] basic instincts, I repeat, are constructed on the basis of the ideological image of contemporary man and retrospectively built into animal behaviour as [its] 'motives'. (Heller, 1979a, p. 30)[10]

Recent ethological research has been able to show that aggression among animals serves to balance out organically based individual differences in hierarchically structured animal societies:

> It seldom encounters serious resistance, that is, it must seldom change into destructive behaviour, on the one hand because superiority and inferiority as an animal's primary status are manifested to a great extent in innate and acquired attributes (symbols) which as a rule signal – in part as innate triggering stimuli – the outcome of a possible confrontation and, when it is a matter of inferiority, serve to inhibit aggression or destruction, and second because primary inhibitory mechanisms provide a guarantee that the claims associated with privilege do not place in question the minimal claims associated with the inferior primary status. (Nolte, 1971, p. 132)

An interpretation of these results within the framework of the concept of aggression advanced by the theory of society is impermissible because it would tacitly and falsely apply the criterion of intentional action to the instinctual, relatively fixed behavioural repertoire of animals.

The several versions of the biologistic theory of aggression that regard the instinct of aggression as a motivational element proper solely to the human being utilise a 'bio-psychical' connecting link in their argumentation. According to this step in their argument, it is a specifically human rage affect that in response to particular stimuli causes the aggressive instinctual potential to be discharged. Heller counters this argument by pointing out the fundamental theoretical contingency in our assigning of specific actions to the various affects. Inasmuch as an individually perceived, potentially rage-triggering stimulus can become a motive of action only by means of 'socio-culturally' mediated interpretation, it cannot be maintained that there is a general natural nexus of stimulus, affectual reaction and action (Heller, 1979a, pp.

---

[10] Emended in accordance with the corresponding passage in the German version of Heller's study; cf. Heller, 1977, p. 89. Trans.

35ff.). Instincts and actions are linked with each other only in and through socially binding patterns of interpretation. This account can be generalised, for social phenomena of aggression do not have to be explained by an aggressive instinctual potential of the human being, but can be explained just as plausibly by the thesis according to which the human being's organic instinctual potentialities develop only after, and in accordance with, forms of action having historically and socially different traits from instance to instance; human instincts are plastic enough to become the organic bearers of the aggressive activities that are traits of a given social structure (e.g., war, envy, hate) (*ibid*., p. 51). The naturalistic theories of aggression, then, constitute a theoretical retroprojection on to the human being's inceptive organic condition of what has been observed in the given contemporary historical period:

> Undoubtedly, every so-called basic instinct is a philosophical abstraction, and the source of this philosophical abstraction is the historical and ideological 'basic experience' of the ever given present. (*ibid*., p. 6)

Against the behaviourist version of the theory of aggression, Heller advances in principle the same criticism that she also makes of its naturalistic version. In its rigorous form, behaviourism analyses both animal and human behaviour without reference to inner, that is, mental or psychical states; nor may organic motivational states enter into the behaviourist explanation of courses of behaviour, because behaviourism's scientific logic admits only objectively observable states of affairs. The behaviourist theory of aggression, therefore, argues below the level of any theory of instinct or drive:

> According to the behaviourist interpretation instinct does not exist – or at least cannot become the object of scientific investigation – (nor does internal stimulus exist), but man and animal alike are characterised by movement co-ordinations or types of reaction that are independent of each other and are elicited by external stimuli. (Heller, 1979a, p. 68)

The behaviour of the human organism is guided by external stimuli, to which it learns to react functionally, that is, in a way that assures its survival. Thus behaviourism explains aggressive forms of behaviour environmentalistically; the version of this explanation that is most widespread today is the frustration–aggression hypothesis. According to this hypothesis, the human being reacts with aggressive forms of behaviour to events in his environment that are frustrating to him in some way.

However, the socio-cultural processes of interpretation by means of which human subjects first perceive events in their environment, no matter what they may be, as frustrating experiences are ignored in this line of argument just as much as in the naturalistic theory of aggression:

> The same individuals may react differently to the same 'frustration' depending on [the person] from whom it originates (do they like him, do they trust [him], is he an authority figure to them, what is the source of this authority, etc.). Furthermore, their reaction varies according to whether or not they know the cause of [i.e., the reason for] the 'act of frustration', whether they consider this cause sensible or senseless, or on how they evaluate the cause as motive. (Heller, 1979a, p. 73)[11]

Human impulses cannot be presupposed, in the manner of behaviourism, as a bundle of energy that can be given any form whatsoever, and into which socio-structural imperatives are merely impressed; rather, they must be taken into account from the standpoint of social anthropology as an impulsional potential that is always socio-culturally already fully formed, so that frustrating experiences can be translated into aggressive actions only via the second nature of the individual personality structure.

The naturalistic theories of personality (in particular that of A. P. Maslow) make up the third class of theories of aggression that Agnes Heller examines. In these theories, the human species' organically rooted capabilities for action are projected directly on to the endowment of the individual personality; every subject of action possesses from the very beginning the potentialities for development that can be ascribed anthropologically to the species as a whole. From the standpoint of these theories, the social structure of a society is conceived of as an institutional framework that either hinders or promotes the development of the individual personality, depending on the society's degree of liberalisation; aggressivity is the psychical consequence of injury to individual self-esteem. Heller at first subscribes to this theoretical model that is critical of both the biologistical and the behaviourist theories of aggression:

> Our impulses assume the form of rage aimed at the humiliation or destruction of other human beings because we are particularist persons, because we do not have self-confidence and self-esteem relying on ourselves,

[11] Emended in light of the German version of the quoted passage; cf. Heller, 1977, pp. 155f. Trans.

because we cannot actualise our potentials, and all this makes us suffer. We react with aggression to individual, isolated frustrations, and we consider them frustrations, because they affect our whole personality, because we conceive of them as an 'offence' against our personality. (Heller, 1979a, p. 88)

Then, however, she contradicts in a critical point the anthropological foundation of this third version of the theory of aggression. The organically rooted potentialities for development of the human species, she asserts, cannot be projected immediately on to an individual subject's capability for action, so that a personality can either authentically unfold itself or else become stunted and atrophied under socio-structural constraints. Rather, the human being's internal nature is formed only in socialisation processes which serve as the mediating connection between the individual's impulsional energies and the institutional system of norms. From this perspective, societal institutions can be understood as objectivations into which the human being's species-specific potentialities for action are gradually objectified; therefore the human being is not naturally endowed from the start with the capabilities that are characteristic of the human species, but only gradually acquires them as integral moments of himself in the process of the appropriation of the institutional system of norms, which process effects his socialisation:

> In my opinion . . . there is no 'species essence', 'human nature', or 'substance' inherent in every individual. There are not 'two' beings concealed in man, an authentic and an inauthentic one, and the function of the objectivations is not to facilitate the development of the inauthentic or impede the development of the authentic.[12] In my opinion particularist or individual personality structures are relationships, the relationship of man to the objectivations of the world and to his self; the forming of the individual relationship is not the development of the 'inner essence', but this development is constituted in the active acquisition of objectivations, the selection between their values, and their constant transformation. (Heller, 1979a, pp. 85–6)[13]

The process of the formation of human beings' 'inner nature' consti-

---

[12] According to the German version of this passage: ' . . . nor do the objectivations have the function of developing the authentic or of hampering its development' (Heller, 1977, p. 152). Trans.

[13] According to the German version of this passage: ' . . . not the development of the "inner essence"; rather, this relationship is constituted through the active appropriation of the objectivations through selection among values and the constant transformation of them' (Heller, 1977, p. 152). Trans.

tutes the socialisation of the human impulsional potentialities that develop organically after, and in conformity with, the systems of objectivations of the historically successive social formations in the praxis of individuals. A social anthropology constructed upon this fundamental premise, which takes the inner plasticity of human motivations as its central point of reference, thus cannot disprove the socio-cultural possibility of human aggression, but can deny its historically universal, anthropologically necessary existence. Aggressive forms of behaviour, asserts Heller, become a possibility of the dynamics of human drives only as a function of the socio-psychical patterns of orientation that are supra-individually implicit in a society's system of institutions:

> Man is not born with inalienable instincts, since he is not born with instinct at all. Nor is he a 'blank page' which may be conditioned by everything according to the spur of the moment. Nor is he, however, an embodiment of the innate essence of the species, of the human substance. Man does have a 'second nature'. This second nature has developed historically and finds incarnation in the objectivations, and in the individuals of the present world, as a matter of reciprocal influence. (Heller, 1979a, p. 96)[14]

In her study of instincts, Heller prepares the transition to her interpretation of Marx's theory presented in her work *The Theory of Need in Marx* with a construction intended to provide a philosophical explanation of history that develops further the social–anthropological premise of the plasticity of the human motivational potential, in opposition to Arnold Gehlen's conservatism in this respect. According to this construction, the process of the human species' history can be conceived of as an objectification of specifically human developmental potentialities – intersubjectivity and consciousness – that becomes universal (*ibid.*, pp. 18ff.). It is quite possible that in this process the supra-individually institutionalised degree of the universality of developmental capacities in the history of the human species has heretofore always surpassed the degree of this universalisation that is at all realisable by the individual subject, namely in all types of class society; on the whole, however,

---

[14] Since the German version of this passage differs from the English version in important respects, I give here my rendering of the German, omitting the sentences for which the published English translation of Heller's book accords in meaning with its German version: 'The human being is not born with immutable instincts, since he comes into being entirely without instincts. Nor is he a "tabula rasa"; i.e., he cannot be conditioned at any given time to do anything whatever . . . This second nature originated historically; it is "embodied" in the interaction upon each other that takes place between the objectivations and the individuals of the present-day world' (Heller, 1977, pp. 164f.). Trans.

human history follows a direction in which human beings' organically rooted capabilities for action gradually expand. In Heller's view, the motivational basis of this emancipatorily oriented, although always uncertain historical process, which follows a continuous spiral of objectivation of human action, subsequent corresponding development of human needs, and expanded objectivation of action, lies precisely in the plasticity of human needs; these needs can develop historically subsequent to, and in conformity with, the objectifications of human actions, from the species-essential objectivations 'in themselves' (labour, language) to species-essential objectivations 'for themselves' (art, science, ethics, politics) (see Heller, 1984, chapter 6).

This construction, which is intended to provide a philosophical explanation of history, also supplies the fundamental framework of the interpretation of Marx proposed by Heller. She interprets Marx's theory uniformly as an anthropologically grounded philosophy of history with a normative intent. In this discussion, certainly, she touches only very briefly on the methodological differences that do after all separate Marx's early writings, whose argumentation is carried out from the standpoint of the theory of subjectivity, from his economic writings, in which the analysis is more from the standpoint of structural theory. According to Heller, Marx grounds the critique of capitalism given in his economic late writings in the anthropological notion, which is central to his analysis, of the potential universality of the human being's needs. As a consequence, he can make a grounded normative critique of the historically established social relations as stages of the distorted fulfilment of human needs. Accordingly, Marx bases his critique of capitalism on a meta-economic concept of need:

> He tends to treat concepts of need as non-economic categories, as historical–philosophical, that is as anthropological value categories, and therefore as not subject to definition within the economic system. (Heller, 1976, p. 27)

Marx's theory recognises three types of need, which are of very different significance in the argument of the theory as a whole. These are: the needs classified according to their objectivations; the anthropological category of the organic need; and the category, appertinent to political economy, of the socially defined need. Of central importance for the purpose of Marx's theory of providing a philosophical explanation of history is the second category, for Marx begins with the anthropological premise of the potential universality of the human being's organic structure of needs. This point of departure assumes a normative role in his theory when it is transformed into the construction of the human being who is 'rich in needs':

> 'Man rich in needs' is thus a consciously philosophical construct and not one which is concocted from empirical facts. (Heller, 1976, p. 44)

In the whole of Agnes Heller's theory, this theory of needs assumes the function of the link joining together the materialist conception of history and the theory of revolution. With the aid of the anthropological concept of a human being who is potentially 'rich in needs' it is supposed to be possible to establish a criterion that is not merely formal, according to which an historically attained social condition can be criticised as a stage in which needs are incompletely satisfied; the same centrally important anthropological notion also serves as the means for identifying the social movements that in a given historical situation truly represent the demand for the satisfaction of these socially unmet, 'radical' needs. It is only through the introduction of this normative construction that the critique of political economy, in her interpretation of which Heller relies principally on the *Grundrisse*, acquires a point of reference beyond the criticised capitalist social relations. For only from the anthropological and normative perspective of Heller's investigation can the capitalist commodity form be grasped as a system of action that forces the qualitative potentialities of human needs into the channels leading to the quantitative, de-sensualised increase of those needs (Heller, 1976, pp. 48ff.).

Human perception as sensuous cognition. The Critical Psychology of Klaus Holzkamp

In recent years, Klaus Holzkamp, together with a few collaborators, has developed the fundamental theoretical framework of a psychology that has claimed for itself the status of a special discipline with a historical–materialist basis. Holzkamp's Critical Psychology seeks to do more than provide a mere ideological critique of traditional psychology, which sees through the interest-linked content of psychological statements, but achieves no advances in understanding the psychical structure of human subjectivity through investigation of those statements. This Critical Psychology translates its claim to systematicity into a theoretical pro-gramme within which the human species' capabilities for action that have grown out of the specifically human form of activity of work are explained by the range of organic possibilities conferred on human beings by natural evolution. Up to now, studies of this kind have been carried out for the phylogenetic production of human consciousness and for the human being's motivational structure and mode of perception (Schurig, 1976; Holzkamp-Osterkamp, 1975 and 1976). The fundamental theoretical framework of these investigations becomes understandable if it is placed in the context of the scientific controversy by means of which Critical Psychology also makes its systematic construction comprehensible to itself.

Holzkamp names two theoretical approaches that, like Critical Psychology, claim to offer a materialist theory of human subjectivity. In his opinion, however, these two approaches both accomplish this goal only in a reductionist manner.

The one approach is based on an economic interpretation of Marx and follows the model of Marx's interpretation of capitalism in its conception of the plexus of social relations of bourgeois societies: it conceives of this complex of relations as constructed wholly out of the logic of capital accumulation, of the valorisation of capital. From the standpoint of this interpretation, the questions regarding socialisation and personality that must be posed and answered by a materialist theory of the human subject become superfluous, inasmuch as the system's economic functional imperatives leave their imprint structurally on the subjects. Thus, the capitalist social structure does not reproduce itself through the individual personality structures, but determines the social subjects even in the very nature of their need-dispositions. All psychological problems can therefore be adequately solved by means of a differentiation of the critique of political economy into a broader range of more specific categories:

> Thus the individual human being appears here completely as the product of objective social influences, and his individuality is reduced to the fact that he is, so to speak, a particular interaction of such influences. Accordingly, if the objective social conditions to which a human being is exposed at his social locus are identified and described with enough specificity, then, so this approach maintains, that is synonymous with the apprehension of his individuality. (Holzkamp, 1977a, p. 32)

For Holzkamp, the second approach claiming to provide a materialist theory of subjectivity is the 'critical theory of the subject'. This approach is complementary to the above-mentioned economic reductionism which conceals the active, action-oriented refraction of the socio-economic structural complex in the individual personality. From the viewpoint of this approach, a thorough interpretation of the Marxist analysis of capital, which is also capable of making the psychical reality of subjects intelligible through its delineation of the functional logic of capitalism, is supposed to suffice to eliminate the sphere of problems pertinent to the theory of personality. In contrast, the critical theory of the subject as a matter of principle seeks the categorial bases of a theory of personality beyond historical materialism, which it identifies with a theory of the logic of the accumulation, or valorisation, of capital. By a 'critical theory of the subject', Holzkamp understands only a critical psychoanalysis. In consequence of the latter's construal of historical materialism, he sees in its attempts to elaborate theoretical constructions only an enterprise complementary to that of economic reductionism. Both approaches do not credit historical materialism with any genuinely psychological theory of the subject, since they wrongly globally equate historical materialism with a socio-economic theory of the capitalist social system:

> According to the conception of the Project Class Analysis and related views, and also according to the conception of the critical theory of the subject, the Marxist theory is only a theory of objective social structures. But in no way is it a theory capable of apprehending human subjectivity as an independent entity, and accordingly, is also incapable of successfully investigating the life activity and the subjectivity of concrete individuals with its own concepts and procedures. (*ibid.*, p. 332)

In this reflection, Holzkamp blurs the theoretical differentiations in which these psychoanalytical theories of the human subject are not based upon the Marxist analysis of capital, but rather attempt to embed their fundamental theoretical model of the personality within the conceptual framework of historical materialism (see Lorenzer, 1971). Nevertheless, he thereby makes clearly visible a significant weakness of these attempts. The current attempts theoretically to integrate psychoanalysis and historical materialism confine personality development to the process of achieving psychosexual identity, even though Marx's early writings should have provided enough suggestive ideas about how the structures of human subjectivity might be reconstructed, taking into consideration the organic conditions under which they emerged, in the full breadth of the affective, cognitive and linguistic dimensions of their development. In point of fact, the mere combination of psychoanalysis and Marxism does not take advantage of the opportunities offered by an anthropological theoretical framework, in which the subject's capabilities for action could be investigated with a view to establishing their organic preconditions.

This laying of a biological foundation for the theory of personality, however, is precisely what Critical Psychology is aiming at. In a certain sense, this is a continuation of one strand of Soviet psychology.

Holzkamp draws on the central anthropological themes of Marxist theory in order to argue for the necessity of a biological grounding of materialist theories of subjectivity. In Critical Psychology's understanding of its theoretical foundation, the possibility of a theory capable of adequately identifying and describing the personality traits specific to capitalism is grounded first of all in the reconstruction of the organic roots of the subjective capacity for action:

> In order to be able adequately to grasp the peculiarity of the individual's development in his own history on the basis of the necessities and the limitations of the prevailing of the individual capacity for action, the fact that human beings are natural beings must be developed in all its implications . . . Here human beings appear in their full corporeality, sensuousness, their capacity for experiencing and suffering. On the one hand, as species beings they dispose over determinate sensuous–practical possibilities of cognitive and world-transforming activity: a brain, sense organs, hands with their 'species-specific' functional possibilities; on the other hand, in their life activity they are constantly running up against the limits of their own nature, are of a fundamental neediness, must eat and sleep, become tired and sick, and cannot escape aging. (Holzkamp, 1977a, p. 332)

Critical Psychology makes its starting point the reconstruction of anthropogenesis. Biology, ethological research on human behaviour and anthropology supply a sufficient quantity of research material to make it possible to describe natural evolution up to the threshold of hominisation as organic evolution effected by the mechanisms of mutation and selection. Only with the development from the primate to the human being are social history's mechanisms of cultural development thrust into natural evolution's mechanisms of organic development. Critical Psychology understands this process of hominisation as a mixed form of evolution that is both organic and social, in which the environmentally necessitated development among the hominids of capacities for active adaptation also produced the organic preconditions for the specifically human form of reproducing life:

For in this period of time, the hominids no longer only adapted themselves to their environment, but began, although at first to a very slight degree, to adapt the environment to themselves by actively working upon it; that is, they began to create their own living conditions themselves. It must be regarded as fairly certain that it was precisely the 'evolutionary advantages' of this transformation of the environment through active operation upon it which reacted on the phylogenetic process in the transitional field between animal and human being in such a way that the development of the 'social' nature of the human being was thereby effectuated; that is, the nature in virtue of which the human being is the sole life form to possess the species-specific biological possibilities of the social preservation of life. (Holzkamp, 1977b, p. 103)

It is only the specifically human mode of reproduction–social labour, that is, a co-operative working upon nature in which the activities of the co-operating individuals are co-ordinated with each other – that causes the mechanism of natural evolution to come to a halt. In the reflexive perfecting of their means of production which rests upon the passing on of knowledge gained from labour, human communities are each historically based upon the preceding one or ones to form the continuity of a social learning process. After the evolutionary stage at which the human being appears, the species-specific evolutionary process follows a sequence of modes of organisation in which the labour process that ensures survival is socially regulated at a higher level of productivity for each successive mode of organisation. Holzkamp's version of Critical Psychology, at least, leaves no doubt about the fact that it is solely human beings' organic capability for co-operative labour, and not additionally the independently originated capability for communicative actions oriented to intersubjectively shared norms (cf. the discussion in Habermas, 1976b, pp. 145ff.), that establishes the conditions for survival and thereby also the developmental mechanism of social history. This a priori choice of an instrumentalist position will also influence the elaboration of the portion of Critical Psychology that pertains to the theory of personality in the narrower sense (see Ottomeyer, 1977, pp. 23ff.).

In the methodological construction of Critical Psychology, the second step is a biologically oriented study of the productive capability that must be developed by a species which ensures its survival through co-operative labour processes. At this point, it makes use of a 'functional–historical' procedure: the psychical phenomena which alone distinguish the human being are analysed to ascertain the function they assume in the circulation of social labour, which ensures reproduction of the human beings carrying out that labour. In this manner, the methodological perspective of the Darwinian theory of evolution is extended to the process of socio-cultural evolution without neglecting the unique level of this type of reproduction. Critical Psychology investigates the specifically human attributes such as the formation of motivation and meaning-oriented perception as psychical capabilities that the human being, vis-à-vis a nature that has to be actively worked upon, must develop under the pressure exerted by the necessity to reproduce himself (Jäger, 1977, pp. 122ff.). From this research perspective there results methodologically the possibility of analysing phylogenesis and ontogenesis as homologous processes. In the course of the human species' evolution, the human being has developed an entire complex of capabilities for action that have been made possible by his organic endowment. In familial processes of socialisation, the child must appropriate to himself these capacities by learning about and participating in the systems of action that have been made socially permanent. In themselves, both processes proceed functionally, since both the species and the individual subject must develop just those capabilities that are required for the preservation of the labour process which is organised in a way specific to each historical period. The second, ontogenetic process of evolution is investigated by Critical Psychology with the aid of the concept of appropriation (Holzkamp, 1973, pp. 188ff.). With respect to the theory of socialisation, this concept is the complement of the central phylogenetic concept of social labour. Critical Psychology took over both categories with their specific meaning from the Soviet tradition of psychology.

Critical Psychology has set itself the task of providing a Marxist theory of personality. At the centre of its research interests, therefore, is the study of personality forms and character structures produced by the social relations of capitalist societies. In the third phase of investigation, attention is turned to the commodity form that was made dominant by bourgeois society; it is investigated as a system of action that restricts and prevents the individual realisation of organic possibilities of development. In this connection, the forms of psychical behaviour are of interest, into which the capitalist labour process socialises the subjects who participate in it:

> Moreover, for each of the analysed functional aspects [of human life] there was established, on the basis of the 'critique of political economy', the relation among living conditions of the concrete individuals in bourgeois society, conditions which are in each particular case specific to the social formation and class to which the individual belongs and to the individual's locus in society, and the given determinacies of form, limitations and dis-

tortions of the realisability of the biological possibilities of development in the individuals' social integration. Thereby the individual limitations were at the same time critically presented as the reverse side of macrosocial possibilities of development, which can become real for each single individual through the qualitative transformation of social relations. (Holzkamp, 1977b, p. 109)

Under capitalist social conditions, individuals can only make their own the segment of capacities for action which makes psychically possible their participation in the capitalist process of reproduction.

Holzkamp bases his psychology of perception on this methodological trisection of investigation into a stage concerned with evolutionary theory that phylogenetically establishes the field of transition from the hominid to the human being; a second, intermediary stage that is anthropological in the narrower sense, and that delineates functionalistically the capabilities essential to specifically human life; and lastly, a kind of restrictional analysis that demonstrates the distortions of these developmental possibilities which are typical of capitalism. In the study entitled 'Sensuous cognition – historical origin and social function of perception', he systematically undertakes to detach the fundamental problems of a psychological theory of perception from their behaviourist or Gestalt-psychological framework, and to solve them within the theoretical horizon of Critical Psychology. The consideration from which this investigation departs is similar to Gehlen's basic theoretical premise with respect to perception. Gehlen assumes that the human being unburdens himself from a life-threatening plethora of stimuli through a representation of his perceptual world by symbols that grows out of his practical experience of things. The human being's confrontation with such a superabundance of stimuli is the presumed result of his organic separation from a system of behaviour ordered by instincts. In Critical Psychology's theoretical framework, the fundamental assumption, which is in principle similar to that of Gehlen, leads to the hypothesis that in the process of socio-cultural evolution, the human being learns to structure his perceptual field with the same significational aspects under which he transforms nature into means for satisfying his needs in the social labour process. Holzkamp's study assumes the burden of proving this thesis, which seeks to make the structure of the human perceptual world comprehensible through recourse to the form of activity that is proper to the human being: work.

Holzkamp begins his investigation with the excitability of organisms at the lowest stage of phylogenetic evolution. At this stage, excitability is synonymous with the ability of environmental stimuli to trigger consummating, life-ensuring activities on the part of the organism. This organically non-specific excitability is a characteristic of the protoplasm even in its most simple forms of organisation. In the subsequent stages of natural evolution, this most primal kind of organismic excitability divides into a non-specific irritability linked to the metabolism and into a specific sensibility that has been uncoupled from the metabolism. These form the phylogenetic pedestal of all higher-level orientational operations of organisms; the organism can now seek out the materials that are signalled to it in its environment through activity that is self-orienting. In this manner, the sensory orientational operations gradually emancipate themselves from the primary, immediate consummative operations, with the result that the organism-relevant environment acquires a greater degree of objectuality as development advances along this path. More and more, the organism comes to grasp the environment that ensures its life as a constant, physically articulated space. Holzkamp demonstrates this using the instinctual movements with which animals react to key stimuli that are of vital importance to them:

> In order for the animals to respond with diverse forms of activity to different, figural–qualitative moments of patterns of stimuli, these stimuli patterns must have been received as 'particular', relatively distinct from their surroundings and relatively constant in their peculiarity. This requires a corresponding physiological endowment, a specific faculty for differentiation and decomposition on the part of the receptor system and of the central neural regions. (Holzkamp, 1973, p. 89)

To be sure, these instinct-bound orientational operations restrict the objectual world that the animal apprehends through sensory activity to the fields of signals that it must perceive and respond to in order to safeguard its life. Only with the hominids has the animal environment completely freed itself from the network of signals ensuring survival and become, as it were, neutral in relation to consummative activity. The hominids' upright carriage, which is supposed to have developed under the environmental pressure for selection of savannahs and veldts, frees the hominid's hand from all locomotive activity, so that in the gradual intertwining of tactile experience, guided by the hand, and visual experience, the physical world is made increasingly perceptually apprehensible in its objectual–spatial solidity. The hominids' capacities for perception thus already possess all the organic properties which are the basis of human perceptual operations:

The most advanced subhuman hominids in the area of transition from animal to human being possessed a degree of adequacy of the perceptual apprehension of objectual world-facts and a degree of capability for exploration of their environment which was free from instinctual fixity and autonomously motivated that went far beyond what was possible for the pongidae. (*ibid.*, pp. 116f.)

Holzkamp explains the peculiarity of *human* perception by the perceptual capabilities that are necessarily presupposed by the co-operative fabrication of tools, which distinguishes the human being from the hominid. By 'social labour' he, like Marx, understands the form of activity in which human subjects, in co-operative relation to one another, give material form to socially generalised intents. In the objectified results of human use-oriented labour, physical reality takes on 'objective' meaning. In this manner, the human being acquires for himself through his work a world that is increasingly composed out of objectifications of his intents, that is, of objectual meanings. The perceptual apprehension of these objectual meanings is a functional component of the human form of the reproduction of life; it therefore distinguishes human perception from all animal modes of perception:

> The adequate perception of objectually meaningful world-facts is, from the very beginning, a necessary moment of the material production and reproduction of social life. The objectual meanings are the orientationally relevant aspect of human work. (*ibid.*, p. 121)

Meaning-oriented perception makes the world apprehensible as a constant, physically compact reality, composed of manipulable and utilisable objects. It comprehends the possibility of the anticipatory perceptual imagination, since human beings must anticipate the result of their labour when they make tools. In this way, Holzkamp can describe human perception as the ability to cognise objectual reality as being meaningfully structured in itself; the human being does not secondarily overlay his world with significations, but gains for himself through his productive labour also his perceptual objects. The world is not per se a chaotic continuum of stimuli, as behaviourism and Gestalt psychology both assume; rather, it is from the start the world that has been worked upon in all respects by human beings, which we also apprehend in our perception.

According to the sensualist fallacy, the (physical) impulses originating from the objective external world and affecting the human being's receptors are in some sense diffuse and unarticulated, and the intuitionally given, objectually articulated perceptual world originates only in the 'physiological' processes triggered in the organism by such impulses. In opposition to this fallacy, we have asserted above that neither the impulses that strike the sense organs, nor the physiological process triggered by the stimulation of the receptors possess an independent reality, but rather that it is, in this regard, a matter of throwing into relief, by abstraction applied to reality, certain moments of sensuous cognition on the level of specificity that is physical–physiological. (*ibid.*, p. 310)

The a priori choice of an instrumentalist position that underlies this theory of perception becomes clear when Holzkamp gives an account of the structure of intersubjective perception; here he employs the unfortunate concept of 'personal objectual meaning' (*ibid.*, pp. 128ff.). According to this concept, in perception the human being also apprehends his co-subject as in himself a meaningful unity; the pre-linguistic horizon of meaning within which moments of reality are perceived here is measured against the co-operative function assumed by the co-subject in the process of the division of labour:

> It can be shown that – just as the material objectual meanings represent the orientationally relevant aspect of objectified results of labour and thus of coherent data – the personal objectual meanings must be regarded as an orientationally relevant aspect of co-operative relations among human beings. (*ibid.*, p. 148)

The framework of action in which the other subject is perceived specifically not from standpoints pertinent to the collective fashioning of objects, but from the standpoint of affectively guided communication, is given no consideration by this theory. From start to finish of his study, Holzkamp disregards the domain of communicative action, which follows other rules than those of the collective fashioning of objects. As a result, human perception is cognitivistically restricted to the cognition of instrumentally relevant structures of meaning, while the dimension of communicatively oriented and affectively guided perception is in this way excluded from consideration. Holzkamp also conceives of the linguistic structuring of reality in a functional circle, in which objects and persons are given an intersubjectively shared linguistic designation in accordance with instrumental functional imperatives.

The most important reason for the 'instrumentalist' shortcoming of Holzkamp's theory and its failure to achieve an adequate apprehension of the dimension of intersubjectivity lies in a dogmatic assumption. Holzkamp considers it to be one of the central propositions of historical materialism that social labour is to be regarded as the solely determinative moment of historical developments, and accordingly he forces phylogenetic and even ontogenetic problems into this framework. This is shown very clearly, for example, by the following 'syllogism', the logic of which is only apparent:

> Just as on the macrosocial scale, objectual social labour must be considered as the fundamental motive moment of historical development, so must the individual's objectual activity be viewed as the motive moment of his 'social integration', when it is a matter of the individual human being. (*ibid.*, p. 53)

However, in this inference neither is the 'antecedent' self-evident (even assuming the premises of historical materialism), nor is the conclusion compelling. It is not self-evident that the dimensions of human, tool-mediated intercourse with nature and of social relations that are condensed in the expression 'objectual social labour' should be made tendentially to contract to the dimension of the domination of nature. Holzkamp finds himself forced (*ibid.*, p. 146) to admit the existence of specifically human social groups with a minimum of objectifying activity; however, he modifies this fact by definitional sleight of hand: as they appear in the area of transition between the animal and man, these social groups are treated as the most immediate precursors of the human being in the full sense of the word. But the problem cannot be disposed of so easily if it can be shown that the revolutionising of social forms is frequently a precondition for the revolutionising of objectual activity, and not the reverse. The assertion that this is impossible, for the simple reason that the regulations of behaviour in the social domain have biologically firmer foundations than those governing commerce with objects, is untenable for many reasons. The findings of Earl Count (1973) regarding the stages of animal sociality, as well as the long delay of a marked improvement in human beings' fabrication of tools and the results of research on dolphins (see Schurig, 1976, pp. 32f.), strongly suggest that a more independent and more effective role should be ascribed to the structure of sociality than is done by Holzkamp. In the research carried out by Volker Schurig, who also belongs to the school of Critical Psychology, the problem is viewed in a much more nuanced manner, but the depth of the theoretical difference that lies at the heart of this problem is not stressed:

> In the light of the present state of knowledge, there seems to be good reason for assuming three components of the origination of consciousness: manipu-

latory and tool-related behaviour, highly differentiated social systems, and a developed intraspecies communication structure. This assumption being made, though, it is necessary that the coupling of linear causal nexuses, for example, by maintaining that the fabrication of tools as a specifically human relation to nature is, as such, already the foundation of human society and of language, be tested by means of alternative hypotheses. The latter can, for example, assume that it is primarily the existence of complex social groups and of a communication system, such as exist among highly developed pongid primates, in conjunction with certain changes in physical structure like upright carriage, the freeing of the hands, etc., that is already the precondition for the fabrication of tools. The genesis of the behaviour designated labour would then be the coinciding of highly developed social and communicational forms with the beginning of the fabrication of tools; however, it is not reducible to any one of these three components. (*ibid.*, p. 36)

Thus a too simply understood 'primacy of labour' in the theory of evolution must be rejected. The same must be done in connection with the problems of an analysis of the present historical period. From Holzkamp's point of view, the spheres of an interaction in the domains outside immediate social production contract to mere epiphenomena. His account of co-operative groups overvalues their objective functions and undervalues the social mechanisms that are in fact operating in them; this is the functionalist fallacy, criticised, for example, by Gehlen and Elias, which leads to postulating a too close relation between the motives of the actors and the objective functions of institutions or social formations. Consequently, the connection with present-day society, which Holzkamp in any case effects only by way of the basic categorial framework of the critique of political economy, is very abstract. These analytical deficiencies have, however, devastating results on both the normative and the ontogenetic levels. Whoever, like Holzkamp, strips the concept of labour of all resonances of duty and toil thereby prevents the historical and transitory character of that concept from becoming apparent, as it does in the writings of Marx. The prospect of a society in which work time has been reduced does not correspond to the categories of Critical Psychology. From the standpoint of ontogenesis, however, the dogmatic assumption of the primacy of production leads to the error of forgetting the scope and the proper dynamics of socialisation processes. The tasks of research on perception conducted from the perspective of Critical Psychology, which Holzkamp names, are all concerned, in an overly pointed manner, with specific problems associated with capitalism (e.g., the subject's relationship to commodities and to money, or to the division of society into classes); but they are not such as to cause us to forget the classical problems of the study of perception. Thus Holzkamp's rejection of an agnosticism on the part of the psychology of perception and his emphasis of the pre-constitutability of the objects of human perception cannot conceal the fact that his theory does not contribute to the elucidation of one of the nodal points of the human subject's cognitive development: the capacity to constitute a 'permanent object' and the linking of this capacity with the development of communicative capabilities (cf. pp. 59ff. of the present work). The concept of 'objectual meaning' enables Holzkamp objectivistically to slip past the problems of the intersubjective constitution of meaning.

Despite his undeniable contributions to the empirical development and the internal systematisation of the Soviet tradition of a psychology of human 'activity', Holzkamp's system of thought remains inadequate at a number of crucially important points, In the problems posed by Holzkamp, there recurs an ambiguity that is to be found already in the Soviet tradition of psychology. In this tradition, Leontiev's work cannot at all be considered the simple continuation of Vygotsky's pioneering efforts. For in the investigations of the former there takes place a progressive neglect of the role of semiotic systems in the analysis of the genesis of action and of the role of culture in the analysis of society. Consequently, what constitutes social process is conceived ever more narrowly by Leontiev.[15] The striking resemblance of Vygotsky's approach to George Herbert Mead's intersubjectivistic pragmatism is thereby made unrecognisable (see Glock, 1986). In this tradition, the category of activity comes increasingly under the dominance of the concept of labour.

Everything that is achieved by Holzkamp's approach must pay the price for the listing of his theory towards instrumentalism. His understanding of perception as 'sensuous cognition', and the fact that he thereby does not separate perception as a merely empirical occurrence from cognition proper as an ideal realm, represent an advance, but at the same time restrict perception to its merely cognitive function. This instrumentalist restriction of perception is made very clearly apparent when Holzkamp's approach is compared with the phenomenological theory of perception of Merleau-Ponty. The latter is, beyond all doubt, the philosophically boldest and most significant contribution to the

---

[15] In recent years, some excellent studies of Vygotsky's work have clearly shown this. They have also given an account of the cultural–historical context of his thought, including his links to literary symbolism. See James V. Wertsch (1985a), Alex Kozulin (1986) and James V. Wertsch (ed.) (1985b).

theory of perception made in this century. As far as the theoretical penetration of the results of empirical research is concerned, Merleau-Ponty's work is without equal. Certainly, it was only in the first stage of his intellectual development that perception was the primary area of his investigations. Later, engaged in a phenomenological exploration of the human being's existential experiences, of his being-in-the-world, he turned his attention more strongly to the phenomenal domains of language and art.

Merleau-Ponty's theory has its beginning in the intention to develop Husserl's phenomenology further, in the form of an existing philosophy. The application of the phenomenological method not just to consciousness, but to the totality of the individual's existential experience, offered a possibility of escaping from the fetters of the classical philosophy of consciousness. Even in his early writings, however, Merleau-Ponty gives to this programme of existential phenomenology, about which a large number of French philosophers were in agreement at that time, a turn that leads it into anthropology. From the outset, he was interested above all by the way in which the human being's organismal body and his consciousness are inseparably intermeshed with each other in every single living-out of human existence. It is his anthropological enquiry that causes Merleau-Ponty to go beyond the scope of existential phenomenology in a second point at the very start of his investigations. In his attempt to show clearly the existential intermeshing of body and mind he had to extend his investigation to include phenomenal domains that are empirically studied by the special sciences. For that reason he was led to integrate the findings of those sciences into the course of his philosophical analysis as having equal importance and validity. This interest for the special sciences, which gives an empirical character to his philosophy, stayed with him; in his last years, it caused him to throw himself upon the findings of psychoanalysis and ethnology with the same enthusiasm with which he had appropriated Gestalt theory in his early work.

His study of Gestalt theory lies in Merleau-Ponty's most productive phase as a writer. It yielded two of his decisively important books: the study entitled *The Structure of Behavior*, which was completed in 1938 (English 1963), and *Phenomenology of Perception*, published seven years later (English 1962). The investigations presented in these two works are situated within a theoretical framework determined by the premise that within the forms of human experience perception has an essential primacy. It is the basis for all human relationships to the world because only in perception does the human being existentially obtain for himself access to the world. Only this premise can explain why, in his first period of intellectual production, Merleau-Ponty occupied himself almost exclusively with perception. For this premise allowed him to regard the analysis of perception as being also the first and the crucially important step of a phenomenology of human being-in-the-world. The study that was to accomplish this task was carried out by Merleau-Ponty in the form of a critique both of the empiricist and of the rationalist theories of perception. In this enterprise, Gestalt theory, which he adopted with enthusiasm, came to his aid. From this theory he developed the thesis that human perception cannot be understood either sensualistically as a merely passive reception of sense impressions, or idealistically as an active constitutional achievement of consciousness; rather, perception is effectuated as a process whereby the world is rendered apprehensible in a manner that confers meaning on it. For their part, the inchoate meanings that thus open up and animate the perceptual process as it were from within have their origin in the action intentions of a corporeally active subject. In and through perception, the human being makes the world apprehensible for himself as an orientational field of possible operations and for the establishment of virtual references of his bodily behaviour.

These theoretical considerations regarding perception have consequences of considerable moment for the determination of the relation between body and mind, which is, after all, of primary importance to Merleau-Ponty in his phenomenological investigation of human beings' existential experience. From these reflections there result the essentials of a critique of the ontological dualism that has come to be taken for granted philosophically in the Cartesian tradition. For if the perceptual process must be conceived of as a process in which the human being, through his bodily behaviour, makes the world apprehensible and confers meaning on it, then body and mind, or consciousness, can no longer be treated as separate entities, as is done in Cartesianism. In the perceptual act, both are fused together to become a single operation, and together they form an indissoluble functional element in the living of human life. The conclusions to be drawn from the foregoing reflections were summarised by Merleau-Ponty in the thesis that from the start the human organismal body is itself a medium of cognitive acts; consciousness, he states, is 'being-towards-the-thing through the intermediary of the body' (Merleau-Ponty, 1962, p. 138).

Whereas Merleau-Ponty regards perception as a centrally important element of the human being's securing of existential certainty for himself, in Holzkamp's writings there is no mention of this overarching significance of perception. Moreover, the notion of 'sensuality' has retained for Holzkamp hardly a trace of the utopian and emancipatory meaning it had for Feuerbach. Holzkamp's insight that perception as sensuous cognition can be developed into a totalising comprehension is spoiled by the exaggerated effort to sublate the individual in the universal. He appoints society, as a collective subject, to be the 'gnoseological subject' and does not enquire about the function of that which is individual for scientific and historical progress. The 'universal' is not presented as arising out of an unboundedness of intersubjective communication, but as an authoritative value in its own right beyond all merely pragmatic and all merely individual interests. Although he argues very strongly that science is the extension of the practical coping with the problems encountered in life, he just as sharply demarcates comprehending cognition, which Marxism is for him, from the everyday 'sensuous experience of the workers' life world'. Here the connection can be seen between the deficiencies of his approach from the standpoint of the theory of intersubjectivity with regard to the objects of study of anthropology and the psychology of perception and, on the other side, the lack in his theory of a notion of individual possibilities of participation in society and in decision-making processes that are free of domination. Thus Holzkamp's 'Critical Psychology' fails to develop an acceptable conception of historical-materialist anthropology.

3

HISTORICAL ANTHROPOLOGY

In an anthropology that focuses attention on the natural preconditions of social action in such a manner and to such a degree that their historical and cultural plasticity becomes evident, a historicisation of anthropology hardly requires lengthy justification. Anthropological theory constitutes a step in the self-reflection of the social and cultural sciences that brings to consciousness the potentialities for human action that have developed in the course of natural evolution in order to understand them as possibilities for socio-cultural progress. 'Historical anthropology' is a legitimate and necessary part of such a project. It reached beyond the traditional history of events as well as social history with its orientation to processes of socio-structural and economic transformation, in order to investigate the historical process of civilisation in which human nature has up to the present day changed and shaped itself within its organically set bounds. Therefore the object of an anthropologically oriented historiography are above all the changes that the human being has historically experienced in his bodily demeanour, in his modes of mental and emotional experiencing, in his patterns of social action, and in his motivations. At present, the building blocks for such an historical anthropology can be obtained chiefly from *historical research on the family*, from the beginnings of a *social history of the body*, and from the French tradition of a *history of 'mentalities'* (see Lepenies, 1977; Hausen, 1977). All these fields of investigation make it vividly clear that anthropology and the science of history are referred each to the other, that they must supplement one another, something that has heretofore been taken for granted very little in Germany. In contrast to France and the countries sharing the Anglo-Saxon tradition, ethnological experience has to a great extent been lacking in Germany as a source on which the development of anthropological theory could draw. In the German tradition, despite its great closeness to historicism, philosophy was the

118

locus of anthropological reflection, and in consequence the historicity of
that reflection's object remained merely an abstract category. Ethnology, however, brings the historical determinacy and mutability of
human nature to consciousness in a wealth of factual data.

Control of affect and the weaving of the social fabric. Norbert Elias's theory
of the civilising process

Norbert Elias's *chef d'oeuvre*, *The Civilizing Process* (vol. 1: 1978; vol. 2:
1982), which was written during the time of the Third Reich, was little
noticed when it was first published in German, but outside of Germany,
by its émigré author. In the decades following the Second World War,
the work led a shadowy existence within sociology. Elias's historical and
interpretative method did not attract the attention of the sociologists,
while his intention to elaborate a great theoretical construction makes
his work remote from the interests and aims of the professional his-
torians. Only in some circles, for example, by Helmuth Plessner and his
students, or by Hans Freyer (1967), was Norbert Elias's study treated as
an unappreciated pioneering effort that produced important results. In
recent years, however, this situation has changed rapidly. Elias's book
has been celebrated as a text that is paradigmatic for an historical
anthropology and has received much belated recognition.[1] The vivid-
ness of the accounts given in it have assured wide interest in the work;
and the claim that it is a rival of sociological theories of evolution and
superior to these because of its historical concreteness also gives Elias's
work a position above the genre of collections of cultural–historical
curiosities.

To understand the rapid growth of interest in Elias's work, which has
led to the formation of a school-like group of followers, it is necessary to
cast a brief glance at the circumstances in which his principal work was
written and at the reasons for the present-day renaissance of interest in
it. The many other writings that we owe to Elias's extraordinary productivity, which has continued unabated into advanced age, will receive
little attention here. In an autobiographical retrospection, Elias tells very
vividly of his classical–humanistic and apolitical education, of his Jewish
origins, and of the slow process whereby he freed himself from neo-

---

[1] The most spectacular instance was certainly the awarding of the Adorno Prize to Elias
by the city of Frankfurt (cf. Elias and Lepenies, 1977).

Kantian, transcendental–philosophical modes of thought.[2] The central motive for his efforts to achieve that liberation was clearly his opposition to the notion of *homo clausus*, that is, to the ostensibly fundamental concept of the human individual who can be conceived of prior to and outside of all social relations and the world. Elias explains Kantian and neo-Kantian epistemology by the illusion of an encapsulated interior life, from which the way to the external world still must be made. For him, this encapsulation is not primordial, but the result of the civilising control of affect:

> Primitively, feelings and their expression belong together. Only gradually is a partition thrust between feelings and gestures or movements of facial muscles, in each case in accordance with the particular pattern of civilisation. Only gradually do the children of internally differentiated societies learn to smile without feeling. And then it seems to human beings that their real self is imprisoned within them and exists without any relation at all to other people. (Elias, 1984, p. 15)

As is true of all significant thinkers whose work is anthropological in character, for Elias the refusal to accept the philosophy of consciousness is of central importance; control of affect and civilisation are the themes, through the investigation of which Elias seeks to escape from the constraints on thought imposed by the philosophy of consciousness. In particular, Karl-Siegbert Rehberg (1979) has opposed Elias's presentation of himself as a solitary thinker, and the reception of his book as an individual stroke of luck, in a detailed interpretation of Elias's work that clearly shows the broader horizon within which it originated. This horizon consists of the various attempts to account for the genesis of the bourgeois world by the emergence of the specific features of bourgeois rationality. Although Elias, who was an assistant to Karl Mannheim, refers to them only little, the investigations of Max Weber, Scheler, Troeltsch and Groethuysen are not far distant from Elias's in their fundamental questions. The originality of Elias's approach lies in the fact that he does not study the bourgeoisie as the bearer of a process of advancing rationalisation, but chiefly the aristocratic upper strata of society, and in another large work the 'court society' in particular (Elias, 1983). This approach raises questions about the relationship of the dynamic established by Elias to the lines of social development that have been stressed by other researchers, but most importantly it makes it

---

[2] Norbert Elias, 'Notizen zum Lebenslauf', in Peter Gleichmann *et al.* (eds.), *Macht und Zivilisation* (Frankfurt, 1984), pp. 9–82.

possible for him to expand his theoretical framework beyond historical reconstruction and to make it into a comprehensive theory. A further original achievement on the part of Elias is that he concerns himself much less than other researchers with the ideological contents of comprehensive interpretative systems, and instead scrutinises principally forms of corporeality and of immediate interaction. Such investigation, however, is a central area of the tasks of historical anthropology and makes study of Elias's work imperative for researchers in this field.

Now, there can be no doubt that in the past decade and a half the question of the limits of the dominant rationality and of the costs of 'our' civilisation has become the focus of discussion and has reanimated the question of the origination of the bourgeois world, and that the subjectivistic shift of the prospects for social change has made any history of the body attractive to social theorists. The combination of these two reasons for interest in Elias's work was further strengthened by the opinion advanced by a number of authors that Elias's approach represents a true alternative to the historical–materialistic theory of history, inasmuch as his analysis of the genesis of the modern state points out fundamental shortcomings in the theory of the state based on Marx's thought (van Benthem van den Bergh, 1977; Matzner, 1979).

An overview of Elias's approach will make it possible to discuss in detail whether his research and its results satisfy the requirements for an historical anthropology and justify the assertion that they are superior to historical materialism.

According to his own account, Elias's study has its origins in 'the experiences in whose shadow we all live, experiences of the crisis and transformation of Western civilisation as it had existed hitherto, and the simple need to understand what this "civilisation" really amounts to' (Elias, 1978, p. xvii). However, Elias does not seek to attain to an understanding of civilisation as a process and to the experience of specific distresses and fears that were engendered by civilisation either by means of an evolutionist faith in a continuous advance of humanity or in an attitude of hostility to civilisation. Instead, he seeks to achieve these goals by ascertaining in an emphatically 'value-free' manner long-term regularities in historical development. Elias's goal is to link a change of personality structures that occurred during long stretches of history with long-term socio-structural processes, but to do so without imputing to historical development conformity with natural laws. His principal thesis comes down to the argument that the establishment of increasing emotional control and self-discipline on the part of the individual actor can only be understood as the product of processes of growing social intertwining, which, on the macrosociological level, manifest themselves in the emergence of the absolutist state as the first form of the modern state. The genesis of a strong, internalised agency of behavioural control appears, then, to be inseparable from the emergence of the modern state's monopoly of violence and taxation.

Elias begins his study with a history of the concepts of 'culture' and 'civilisation'. In particular, he shows how the original antagonism between the German intelligentsia and the upper social stratum around the court was transformed in the opposition of the meanings of these two concepts into a national contrast between the German and the French 'essential character'. This account of the history of the two concepts, which tends to a questionable disparagement of the Rousseauist tradition in France, is only the prelude to Elias's true historiographical accomplishment: his attempt to write a history of manners. He is extraordinarily ingenious in the way he quotes from sources, such as books about proper deportment and rules governing conduct at table, in order to demonstrate and illustrate the historical transformation. The striking passages quoted from these sources leave one in astonishment at all the rules of behaviour that were not a matter of course, and that therefore required mention, rules that today seem to us to be natural and to be taken for granted.

> Nor should one put a piece that one has had in one's mouth back into the communal dish; this, too, is often repeated. Not less frequent is the instruction to wash one's hands before eating, or not to dip food into the saltcellar. Then it is repeated over and over again: do not clean your teeth with your knife. Do not spit on or over the table . . . Do not clean your teeth with the tablecloth. Do not offer others the remainder of your soup or the bread you have already bitten into. Do not blow your nose too noisily. Do not fall asleep at table. (Elias, 1978, pp. 65f.)

With great acuity, Elias traces out the process that brought about progressive psychical distance of the individual from his own body and among the bodies of different individuals, as this process is exhibited in the table manners, the history of eating implements, sleeping customs and bathing habits, sexuality and aggression. However, the thoroughness of documentation and the persuasiveness of interpretation are less marked in the case of sexuality and aggression than in the other parts of Elias's study, a difference which may be due to the source material he prefers. But how does Elias explain the aforementioned process?

It remains to be considered in more detail what change in the social structure actually triggered these psychological mechanisms, what change in external compulsions set in motion this 'civilisation' of affects and behaviour. (Elias, 1978, p. 205)

The second volume of Elias's study is devoted to answering this question. Chiefly through examination of French history from the late Carolingian period onward, Elias reconstructs the mechanisms of the genesis of feudal society and of its transformation into the societal form of the absolutist monarchies. The details of Elias's expositions cannot be reproduced here; but what is striking about them is that the two most important regularities in the processes of this genesis and transformation turn out to be 'competition' and the 'mechanism of monopoly'. Although these two concepts are usually linked to the analysis of capitalism, Elias uses them in an historically comprehensive sense. To be sure, the specificity of their meaning is thereby diminished, and they acquire a strong similarity to the traditional evolutionist concepts 'differentiation' and 'integration' (see Elias, 1977). Historical development is thus conceived in a relatively formal manner in conformity with a linear model:

However complex the leverage of intertwining processes within which the civilization of conduct and experience in European societies takes place may at first sight appear, the basic connections are clear enough. All the individual trends mentioned so far, e.g. the slow rise in the living standards of broad sections of population, the greater functional dependence of the upper class, or the increasing stability of the central monopolies, all these are parts and consequences of a division of functions advancing now more rapidly, now more slowly. With this division of functions the productivity of work increased; this greater productivity is the precondition for the rise of the living standards of ever-larger classes; with this division of functions the functional dependence of the upper classes increases; and only at a very advanced point in the division of functions, finally, is the formation of more stable monopolies of physical force and taxation with highly specialised administrations possible, i.e. the formation of states in the Western sense of the word, through which the life of the individual gradually gains greater 'security'. But this rise in the division of functions also brings more and more people, larger and larger populated areas, into dependence on one another; it requires and instils greater restraint in the individual, more exact control of his affects and conduct; it demands a stricter regulation of drives and – from a particular stage on – more even self-restraint. This is the price, if we may call it so, which we pay for our greater security and related advantages. (Elias, 1982, pp. 310f.)

In addition to giving a summary of Elias's basic idea with respect to the theory of history, this passage shows two things. It shows, first, just how ambivalent Elias's assessment of the civilising process is, how equivocally intensified self-restraint is situated between the two significances of, on the one hand, a liberation making possible self-determination and, on the other hand, a self-restriction that is obviously necessary for safety in social living, but that is nevertheless repressive.[3]

Second, it makes clear just how great is the burden of proof imposed by Elias's historical construction on his notion of the internalisation of external constraints. Only when it is able to identify the anthropological and psychological conditions for the possibility of the assumed tendencies does his construction go beyond the limits of a suggestive combination of long-term lines of development that does not establish causal relations.

Thus, it is all the more surprising to see how little Elias explains the anthropological bases of his socialisation theory. His original procedure – tracing out the historical genesis of the super-ego, loosely following Freud, and then integrating the super-ego into the non-psychological efforts to account for the genesis of the bourgeois world – does not lead him to defining more clearly his theoretical relationship with Freud. To be sure, he mentions differences between his own theory and that of Freud, but he does not set them forth. What does become clear is that he endeavours to lodge the psychoanalytic ideas within the framework of a theoretical model taken from early behaviourism. This is not only true of his continuous talk of 'conditioning'; it also belongs to the substance of his argument. From the closeness of human beings' life in society, Elias concludes that they must inevitably forgo following and fulfilling their drives. This constraint of its drives is exacted from the child by means of fear and disciplinary training in such a manner that the child of itself exhibits the socially desirable behaviour, and is struck with fear at any transgression of social prohibitions. Elias explicitly stresses the necessity of using fear in all upbringing of the young:

> The child and the adolescent would never learn to control his behaviour without the fears instilled by other people. Without the lever of these men-made fears the young human animal would never become an adult deserving the name of a human being. (Elias, 1982, p. 328)

This position, however, deviates also from all versions of psychoanalysis not offering alternative models of upbringing that do not utilise fear, for

[3] This position is very similar to that of Plessner; cf. pp. 85ff. of the present work.

Elias simply assumes the possibility of a shaping of the forces of the drives that partially represses them, but without consequences in the form of inhibitional energies or neurotic disorders. Freud defends the cultural necessity of constraining the drives, while requiring that the demands of society be susceptible to rational justification. Elias, though, aims at demonstrating a linear heightening of the necessity of repressive self-control. He can conceive of the internalisation of such control only as the blind automatic mechanism of behavioural constraints that are invested with fear, not as the internalisation of norms arising from the recognition of their necessity or utility, and that is flexible and accessible to the ego.

> Thus the demands of the drives and the controls of the super-ego collide directly with each other in the individual. The drives wear themselves out in their struggle with the social constraints and find no help in an agency that could enter into dialogue with society about those very constraints. (Wehowsky, 1976, p. 78)

An ego as an independent agency does not exist in Elias's personality model; it is imperceptibly incorporated into the super-ego.

A first criticism of Elias's model of history has already been indicated in the presentation of his theory. This model is much more formalistic and much closer to obsolete evolutionist theories than the wealth of illustrative historical material would lead one to believe. Elias assumes a regularity of the transformation of society's form that remains constant, and that – insofar as it might be at all demonstrable – is not understood as the result of a gaining of autonomy by the institutions that can be undone. Increasing division of functions is not derived from the dimensions of the organisation of production, but instead appears as a linearly growing necessity. 'Competition' is not distinguished from forms of co-operation founded upon solidarity; rather, it appears as a law that cannot be set aside, and that can be eliminated only through the establishment of ever greater units of domination. In a more recent article, Elias (1977) explains his notion of history, associating it explicitly with Darwin's ideas. Like the latter, Elias understands history as purposeless but explainable progress. Now, it is certainly correct that history cannot be explained by the purposeful intentions of the individual actors or of acting collectivities. Instead, the historian must take fundamentally into account the unintended consequences of action, the dynamic that is proper to objectifications and institutionalisations, as well as structural effects of intertwined nexuses of action. However, the tie between the intentions of the individual actors and history must not be severed so drastically as Elias does, precisely because an internal connection with action of the effects and consequences that have become independent can be demonstrated only if the developing situation in which social intertwining occurs is conceived of in terms of categories of action.

The pathos of freedom from valuation with which Elias presents his theory is the logical result of the fact that the problem posed by the values necessarily underlying an historical reconstruction, and that contain features of a desirable future, does not arise solely when the historical development is conceived of evolutionistically in the manner of the nineteenth century. The clearest illustration of the failure to see this shortcoming in Elias's approach is given by the reception of his theory of the formation of the state. It is certainly correct that the formation of the state has a relative autonomy that cannot be resolved into a conformity to certain laws of the mode of production. However, it is completely misleading to seek to combine externally an evolutionistically conceived dynamic of the development of the modes of production with a similar dynamic of forms of the state. What historical materialism lacks is not such a rarefied theory of the state or of the superstructure, but the historically concrete linking together, in each particular instance, of social processes that run their course as though in conformity with natural laws, with action in a pragmatically conceived dimension of 'politics'.[4]

A further indication of the mechanistic dangers implicit in Elias's model becomes apparent when one probes into the statements referring to the extension of the findings gained from study of the upper classes to lower classes or to colonised peoples. The deficiency of Elias's approach does not lie in his concentration on investigating the upper classes; it consists, rather, in his assumption of a diffusion of the phenomena specific to the upper classes. Elias does not understand social strata, classes and peoples on the basis of the patterns of action and the cultural forms established by the social division of labour, but, in the manner of traditional cultural historiography, exclusively in terms of influence and tradition. From Elias's viewpoint, their own forms appear to be only outmoded and barbarous, not as resistant to being supplanted and full of their own possibilities for development.

Owing to his oversimplifying construction of his historical model, though, some findings appear in a false light in Elias's work. Thus it

---

[4] This has been shown in particular by Antonio Gramsci.

cannot be overlooked that he has difficulties in interpreting historical developments that run directly counter to his theoretical construction. This is especially true in the area of sexuality. Elias interprets the relaxation of sexual morality and of the attitude to nudity as liberalisations occurring on the basis of established control of affect and psychical distance from one's own body and the bodies of others. Although this interpretation might be true for certain cultural forms, it precludes consideration of the possibility of a social order that is truly more favourably disposed to the drives and requires less self-restraint. In the area of aggressiveness, Elias's interpretation, namely that there was an increase of its control, does not give an entirely accurate picture of the matter. Elias's reflections lead him to conclude that pre-modern society (cf. Osterloh, 1976) was not at all characterised by unrestrained aggressiveness on the part of its individual members. His account, however, does not mention who was protected by the inviolable commandments enjoining peace, and who was fair prey of unbridled aggressiveness:

> Outbursts of cruelty did not exclude one from social life. They were not outlawed. The pleasure in killing and torturing others was great, and it was a socially permitted pleasure. To a certain extent, the social structure even pushed its members in this direction, making it seem necessary and practically advantageous to behave in this way. (Elias, 1978, p. 194)

The uninhibitedness of aggression does not have to be explained by a general lack of control of affect. Rather, it is due to the sharp demarcation between intrasocietal morality and the morality governing dealings with foreigners. Although peace within social groups was not completely guaranteed by the internalisation of norms ('conscience'), it was brought about to the same extent by ritualised manners and external taboos. However, the permitting of aggression against outsiders and outcasts is part of the fundamental stock of socially integrative mechanisms even today. Elias leads his reader to suppose that there has been a linear decrease in manifest aggression. Yet a gradual replacement of external and ritual means of social integration by possibilities of discursive clarification and settling of intragroup conflicts could also have taken place. For example, George Herbert Mead (1918) has shown, in his analysis of the psychological mechanisms of criminal justice, to what a great degree the existence in society of a friend-and-foe schematisation is the reverse side of the lack of discursive processes of decision-making and of arriving at agreement.

Elias's originality – it has been said – lies in his adducing not only the bourgeoisie but also, in a fundamental manner, the aristocracy to account for the genesis of the rationality of the bourgeois world. The role played by aristocratic absolutism in the imposition of formal rationality is indisputable. Elias does not, however, succeed in making clear the relation between aristocracy and bourgeoisie in this development. In particular, he restricts his examination much too much to the exigencies of social intercourse at the royal court, in the vicinity of the representative of the absolutist system of power, and does not take into consideration the other, new-fashioned social roles that the feudal class had to learn: in addition to that of the 'elegant and refined courtier', the roles of 'disciplined officer', of 'educated official' and of 'land owner who shrewdly manages his estate' (cf. Anderson, 1974). The pressure to adopt rational forms of administration and economic activity would have to be – at least partly – explained by the interest on the part of the aristocracy in exercising control over the peasant masses and in becoming intermeshed with the expanding sectors of bourgeois economic activity. A concrete picture of this dynamic would also show just how little the concepts of monopoly formation and competition do justice to the central phenomenon of absolutism, as it is described by Perry Anderson:

> The increase in the political sway of the royal state was accompanied, not by a decrease in the economic security of noble landownership, but by a corresponding increase in the general rights of private property. The age in which 'Absolutist' public authority was imposed was also simultaneously the age in which 'absolute' private property was progressively consolidated. (Anderson, 1974, p. 429)

Absolutism was not by any means Oriental despotism, for the explanation of which Elias's model offers no possibilities.

The various shortcomings of Elias's construction can be condensed into the following summary: the reduction of the internalisation of norms in the course of socialisation to a quasi-automatic, compulsive guidance of behaviour; the separation of history from the consciously directed action of individuals, groups and classes; the failure to identify and describe the dimension of a politics that is guided by collectively made decisions; the failure to take into consideration discursive forms of decision-making; the passing over of the claims to legitimacy that are necessarily associated with the state's monopoly of violence – all of that blocks the outlook to a future civilisation with less self-restraint and less subjection to a central authority. For Elias, the state is, assessed with a neutrality devoid of valuation, the *supreme co-ordinator and regulator for the functionally differentiated figuration at large* (Elias, 1982, p. 163). Elias's approach hides both the possibility of individual self-determination in one's dealings with oneself, with one's own body, and with others, and the possibility of taking back the state through the social organisation of the 'associated producers'.

The disciplining of the body and decentralised power. Michel Foucault's structuralist analysis of history

At first glance, it is difficult to understand Michel Foucault's investigations as contributions to historical anthropology. Rather, all his studies are shaped by the intent no longer to examine systems of social relations and historical processes for the purpose of ascertaining the historical development of capacities for action implicit in the evolutionary history of the human species, but instead to do the opposite, namely to understand those systems of social relations as subjectless systems of rules which first establish the function and significance of social action. Thus, Foucault's theory is clearly different from every attempt to elaborate an anthropologically grounded social and cultural science. Only indirectly and through critical study of them is it possible to gain from his works suggestions and information useful for the purposes of an historical anthropology.

Foucault's studies apply the basic theoretical model and the concepts of structuralism to the ways in which modern European societies are cognitively and institutionally integrated. The extraordinary importance that these studies have in the present-day situation of social theory is surely due to Foucault's intention to use structuralism's theoretical approach, which was elaborated in linguistics, in order to investigate repeatedly, and in each instance from a different perspective, the forms of knowledge and the systems of institutions which have controlled and integrated modern societies since the epochal transition from the eighteenth to the nineteenth century, a transition that Foucault considers of paramount importance. However, the structuralist approach employed by Foucault in his investigations is distinguished not by its use of the concept of structure. The French structuralism of which Foucault is an adherent differs from other theoretical models in virtue of a thesis that it has taken over from structuralist linguistics, from semiology. The latter holds that the meaning of linguistic utterances is not produced by a creative linguistic subject, but by a structuring agency prior to and underlying consciousness, by a system of linguistic rules. What is conceived by traditional philosophy as that which is 'signified', that is, sensefully meant by a consciousness, whether Hegel's absolute spirit or the transcendental consciousness of the Kantian tradition, is, from the perspective of French structuralism, something passive, something produced by a pre-conscious system of linguistic rules – a *signifié*, something meant 'by language' (cf. Frank, 1977, pp. 13ff.; Lehmann, 1979, pp. 665ff.). The meaning of linguistic utterances as well as of effectuations of actions having practical significance for human life is, therefore, not the cause but the effect of a structural system prior to and underlying consciousness. Jacques Derrida has attempted to give an account of the theoretical tradition which structuralism invokes in its critique of subject-centred ways of thinking:

> Where and how does this decentering, this thinking the structurality of structure, occur? It would be somewhat naïve to refer to an event, a doctrine, or an author in order to designate this occurrence. It is no doubt part of the totality of an era, our own, but still it has always already begun to proclaim itself and begun to *work*. Nevertheless, if we wished to choose several 'names', as indications only, and to recall those authors in whose discourse this occurrence has kept most closely to its most radical formulation, we doubtless would have to cite the Nietzschean critique of metaphysics, the critique of the concepts of Being and truth, for which were substituted the concepts of play, interpretation, and sign (sign without present truth); the Freudian critique of self-presence, that is, the critique of consciousness, of the subject, of self-identity and of self-proximity or self-possession; and more radically, the Heideggerean destruction of metaphysics, of onto-theology, of the determination of Being as presence. (Derrida, 1978, p. 280)

Nietzsche, Freud and Heidegger are included among the antecedents of a kind of thinking that, according to Derrida's and Foucault's interpretation, recognised as invalid the assumption, characteristic of the European philosophical tradition, of a subject of speech and action that freely determines its own intentions. These three thinkers anticipate to a modest degree the structuralist position that the meaning of linguistic utterances and of social actions always makes its appearance only as the effect of a determinate organisation of linguistic signs or of social institutions. Foucault makes this way of thinking, which is critical of philosophy and science, and which combines the critique of the consciousness-centred theoretical tradition with a systematic interest in literatures that burst apart social order, the prerequisite of a social–

historical reconstruction of the cognitive and institutional mechanisms of social integration. Among the structuralists, Foucault is the social historian. He employs the concept of history, to the development of which Louis Althusser also contributed, that describes the historical process in terms of the succession of intrinsically stable systems of rules, the uninterrupted coherence of which, however, is no longer assured by the unifying accomplishments of an historical centre of meaning (see especially Foucault, 1972b, 'Introduction'), in order to write the history of the pre-scientific systems of thought and institutionalised techniques of control guaranteeing the social order of domination in European societies of the modern era. According to Foucault's theoretical hypothesis, it is only these modes of social integration assuring social order that structurally establish the significational content of social actions, the nexus of meaning of all symbolic utterances.

In Foucault's theory, the fundamental structuralist premises and the aspiration to provide social–historical explanation combine with one another in the programme of an 'ethnology of Western culture'. This task is the ganglion that integrates the elements of different traditions used by Foucault and his ever-new research plans into the unity of a theoretical model. In a discussion of his investigations, he himself gave them this name:

> They could be defined as an analysis of the facts of civilisation that characterise our culture, and it would thus be a matter of something like an ethnology of the culture to which we belong. In point of fact, I attempt to place myself outside the culture to which we belong, in order to analyse its formal conditions for the purpose of, so to speak, carrying out its critique; not, however, in order to disparage its accomplishments, but to see how they in fact came into being. By analysing the conditions of our rationality, I also call into question our language, my language, the origination of which I analyse. (Caruso, 1974, p. 13)

Whoever undertakes an ethnological analysis of his own culture must accept the task of making it so alien to himself theoretically that it appears to be just one among all the other cultures. The point of reference of the analysis must be free of all conceptions of rationality and schematisations of reality that are normative in the cultural context under investigation. In the case of Foucault, this epistemological undertaking assumes the form of a theoretical bracketing-out of European assumptions about rationality. His adoption of the model provided by 'ethnology' as the one he will emulate is intended to signal this paradoxical intent: as European ethnology meets with the 'primitive' culture which is alien to it within the horizon of that science's own notions of reality and aspirations to rationality, so will Foucault's ethnology encounter European culture in fictitious ignorance of that culture. With this set of conditions, ethnology poses itself a problem that is, so to speak, one of scientific strategy, and that Claude Lévi-Strauss has formulated with exactitude (Lévi-Strauss, 1974): how can ethnology study an alien culture, its ideas of rationality which are obviously completely unknown to the ethnologists, without destroying them by taking from them by theoretical means their fear-awakening strangeness? This key question of ethnology is a source of much instruction for structuralism, for in this situation the structuralist decision consists in allowing the alien culture to remain the 'Other', to remain hermeneutically incomprehensible, by setting the ethnological researcher the sole task of investigating the anonymous rule-governed processes and events of this culture. Underlying this decision is a critique of all the theoretical attempts to bridge the cultural distance between the ethnologists' own rationality and an at first incomprehensible alien culture by trying to decipher the meaning of the social actions that have been made the object of investigation. The structuralist criticism of the various ethnological efforts to understand alien cultures asserts that every interpretation of an alien culture that seeks to understand the meanings of the actions expressing that culture implicitly contains the destruction of those meanings – for the rationality that is proper to the alien plexus of social relations is allegedly transposed into the ethnologists' own horizon of rationality and in this manner pulverised, so to say.

Foucault implicitly makes use of this insight which was developed by structuralist ethnology in the course of its analysis of non-European cultures, but tailors it to serve the needs of a critical scrutiny of European culture. For him the structuralist concepts and categories are the means for throwing into relief the structures of the socially integrative forms of knowledge and institutional formations, as these are manifested in the historical development of Europe, and they do so all the more plastically the more alien they cause these structures to appear. In Foucault's studies, this programme shifted gradually from an analysis of European systems of thought that was more from the standpoint of sociology of knowledge, to an analysis of modern systems of power from the perspective of the theory of society. Three stages in the development of such an ethnology can be identified in his writings (cf. Fink-Eitel, 1980). The first comprises the investigations, which are in a certain fashion complementary, presented in *Madness and Civilization* (1965) and *The Order of Things* (1970); the second stage is represented by the metatheoretical studies of *The Archaeology of Knowledge* (1972a) and 'The discourse on language' (1972b); in the final stage are joined together his study of the history of French criminal justice, *Discipline and Punish* (1977), and the first three volumes of his originally projected six-volume history of sexuality: *The History of Sexuality: An Introduction* (1978; French title: *La Volonté de savoir*); *The Use of Pleasure* (1985); and *The Care of the Self* (1987).

With *Madness and Civilization*, Foucault began to carry out his programme of a social history of the European systems of social order, a programme that followed the theoretical model of ethnology. This study is, according to its author, a 'history of the Other', of those by means of whose exclusion and legal and social incapacitation the social order of the dominant form of reason is brought about. In the Renaissance, Foucault demonstrates, madness was tolerated and even respected as a kind of existential decision no longer to participate in the rule-governed system of social relations. This social recognition accorded to the insane changes completely in the seventeenth century: reason as argumentation in conformity with established methods obtains the monopoly of knowledge and excludes the insane from the plexus of rational social relations. In the transition from the eighteenth to the nineteenth century, this exclusion of the insane by the dominant form of reason once again undergoes a change: now madness is psychologised, and the insane are incarcerated. Foucault pursues this history with an interest specifically in the phenomenon of non-reason, that is, of madness as the excluded Other; he pursues the 'history of the silence' which exclusive reason does not succeed in hearing but only a 'transgressive thinking', a thinking without hard and fast methodological and conceptual limits. *Madness and Civilization* is the sole work of Foucault guided by the belief that it is possible to reach that which is excluded by reason from society. In this book, his theory is still directly presented as a theoretical development of the possibilities of going beyond the limits of reason – sexuality and the body serve as the models from which we can learn about this 'transgression'. However, such a procedure for enabling, by theoretical means, the experience of insanity to express itself appears to be – as Jacques Derrida (1978, pp. 31–63), especially, has shown – impossible for reasons of essential necessity.

In his next work, *The Order of Things*, Foucault obviously took heed of this epistemologically based criticism. This book can be regarded as an implicit correction of the attempt made in the first study (cf. Fink-Eitel, 1980; Puder, 1972, pp. 315ff.). It, too, takes the jarring experience of an alien rationality, that of a Chinese encyclopedia, as its point of departure, and allows itself to be guided by the irritating laughter elicited by that rationality in order, in this case, to reconstruct the interior, the very core, of European reason itself. The French title of this work, *Les mots et les choses*, formulates the programme of this study: the investigation of the particular fashion in which, in a given culture, the fundamental rules of the linguistic system generally determine the perceptual field, the domain of that which can be scientifically experienced in this culture. The basic thesis formulated by Foucault announces his interest in, and the importance he ascribes to, an epistemology linked to the sociology of culture:

> The fundamental codes of a culture – those governing its language, its schemas of perception, its exchanges, its techniques, its values, the hierarchy of its practices – established for every man, from the very first, the empirical order of things with which he will be dealing and within which he will be at home. (Foucault, 1970, p. xx)

Foucault's investigation is aimed at what he calls the 'historical unconscious' of the sciences. He has in mind the historical regulations of thinking considered from the standpoint of their function of determining the limits and framework of the possibilities of acquiring scientific knowledge. The totality of the fundamental cognitive encodings in a particular epoch are called by Foucault an 'episteme' or epistemological field. Thus *The Order of Things* is an attempt, in the form of a history of science, to trace the discontinuous succession of such epistemes since the Renaissance (on this point, see Sloterdijk, 1972).

In the sequence of Foucault's books, *The Archaeology of Knowledge* is a work of re-orientation and, moreover, an exception. First, it is the only comparatively large study by Foucault that does not investigate the systems of social order of modern Europe by examining social history or the history of science; rather, this book is devoted to the metatheoretical elaboration of the conceptual tools for the analysis of discourse. It is, consequently, the most difficult but conceptually also the least clear of Foucault's writings. In addition, this work is a transitional one: it broadens the theoretical model of the episteme, which assumes a rigid, stable grammar of thinking, to encompass the theoretical model of discourse praxis, which assumes a praxis of speaking governed by unconscious rules. By abandoning the thesis of a rigid, knowledge-generating system of rules, of a code of knowledge that remains constant in an epoch, Foucault gains the possibility of investigating the relation between the discursive praxis of speaking and non-discursive, that is, institutional, political and economic forms of praxis. To be sure, the relationship between socially unconscious linguistic rules and institutional guidance mechanisms remains to a great extent unelucidated in *The Archaeology of Knowledge*; the central concern of this study is the attempt to elaborate a set of theoretical instruments that are quasi-neutral, and that safeguard the fictitious ignorance of the analysis of discourse. These instruments must be so fashioned in every respect that the description of the European modes of rationality as these are embodied in their discourse formations remains free from any tacit adoption or acceptance of the conceptions of reality under investigation.

With *Discipline and Punish* and the first volume of his history of sexuality, Foucault's structuralist analysis of history focuses on a new field of study. Up to his inaugural lecture at the Collège de France, *The Discourse on Language*, which once again programmatically delimits the fields of application of discourse analysis, Foucault's theory has the form of an ethnology of the cognitive and linguistic patterns of social order in modern Europe. From the perspective of this theoretical model, Foucault's own world, that is, European society of the past two hundred years, is to be made alien, strange, and thereby made into a world no different from all the others, and this is to be done for the purpose of enabling the investigator neutrally to contemplate and analyse the integrative systems of knowledge and language of that world. Foucault's new studies adopt this procedure of making their objects alien or strange. They, too, present themselves as historical studies analysing the European world with the regard of someone who is unfamiliar with its horizons of meaning and its interpretative paradigms. The focus of this historically oriented ethnology has shifted, however: the object of structuralist analysis is no longer the forms of knowledge that create social order, but the institutional as well as cognitive systems of the reproduction of power. Foucault himself has often attributed this change of his research's focus to what the Western European Left experienced during the suppression of the revolts in France in May of 1968. The motive for the change of the object of study, according to this explanation, would be the completely unexpected, catastrophic experience of a perfectly functioning system of power that had become proof against social insurrections. The theoretical model of power that grew out of this experience of helplessness compels Foucault to reconstruct the social–philosophical framework he had employed in earlier studies before using it for this new investigation. The integrative systems of knowledge that he had examined in those previous studies were cognitive paradigms for categorising, objectifying and perceiving the world which excluded other, alternative perceptual possibilities and modes of experiencing the world. Thus, in the context of these investigations from the standpoint of the sociology of knowledge, a reference to the forms of experience excluded by the dominant system of rationality, no matter how this reference is conceived theoretically, plays a normative role. In this stage of its evolution, Foucault's historical structuralism still allows the possibility of an external point of reference, which is conceived most often in the terms of *Lebensphilosophie* (cf. Fink-Eitel, 1980; Frank, 1980, p. 19).

Given the new concerns of Foucault's research, this normative image of a plenitude of life free of social ordering, which, although it cannot be grasped theoretically, can be described negatively, must necessarily be lost, owing to his own hypothesis that power relations are socially universal. On the other hand, this re-orientation of his theory has given to the rather functionless, historically contingent paradigms of rationality which he studied in modern Europe a social function that can be defined from the perspective of the theory of society. These paradigms can be analysed as cognitive strategies of rationality which play, in the continuous process of the expansion of institutional systems of power, the role of the media through which power becomes operative – the systems of scientific thought are integral parts of the ongoing process of the establishment and recomposition of power strategies. *Discipline and Punish* and the first volume of *The History of Sexuality* are studies that seek, in a complementary fashion, to provide evidence supporting Foucault's research hypothesis. The first work traces the genesis of institutional and cognitive techniques of control as it is shown in the genesis of the prison system; these techniques of control ultimately lead to the development of the state's modern disciplinary power. The first volume of Foucault's history of sexuality examines the process by which sexuality was made the object of scientific discourse, a process that led not to the liberation of sexuality but to its production and guidance by various forms of power. Admittedly, the two further volumes of *The History of Sexuality* that were published in 1984 shortly before Michel Foucault's death no longer pursue simply an analysis of power. Rather, Foucault has clearly once again made a new theoretical shift in these works which for the first time focuses attention on the dimension of human subjectivity as an independent sphere (cf. Daraki, 1986, *passim*). In his introduction to the second volume of this history, which bears the title *The Use of Pleasure*, Foucault enumerates the corrections and additions that he has made to the original approach of his theory of power since he first elaborated it. The most important of these modifications consists in the fact that the relations of subjects to themselves in every particular instance are to be considered as a crucially important precondition for the success of techniques of power. Henceforth Foucault assumes that it is only by means of 'techniques' of self-formation that subjects historically mould themselves into the individuals who are then administered and manipulated by the corresponding strategies of power. That being so, the first thing that must be ascertained in a history of modern sexuality is the means of self-formation that allowed individuals to become objects of disciplinary power. 'It seemed appropriate', writes Foucault in this introduction, 'to look for the forms and modalities of the relation to self by which the individual constitutes and recognises himself *qua* subject' (1985, p. 6). In the second and third volumes of his history of sexuality, Foucault has pursued this programme by studying such techniques of self-formation, first for the fourth century BC (Foucault, 1985), and then for the first two centuries AD (Foucault, 1987). He cites chiefly philosophical and medical texts in order to ascertain, through examination of the sexual morality of classical antiquity, the forms in which subjects related to themselves as beings defined by their needs. By this means the buried antecedents of the 'desiring subject', which is today both the goal and the object of the disciplinary discourse about sexuality, are to be brought to light.

Viewed in this way, Foucault, would, in fact, in the last two books he completed, no longer understand the human being's subjectivity as merely a domain manipulated by techniques of power, but as an independent, indeed constitutive element in a power structure or system. The assumption that individuals relate to themselves and that their relations to themselves change in the course of history would suffice of itself to take Foucault outside the structuralist framework of argumentation and to link his investigations to questions fruitful for an historical anthropology. Be that as it may, in the most important of his works dealing with the theory of power, Foucault has uncritically adhered to a structuralist theory of history and society. The peculiar character of this theory can best be studied as it is exhibited in the train of argumentation presented in the investigation of the transformation of the European techniques of executing judicial sentences which bears the title *Discipline and Punish*.

The book promises to give an historical description of the development of the European techniques of carrying out judicially imposed penalties. However, the process of change that this set of instruments for social control underwent is not to be followed from the standpoint, at first blush the self-evidently appropriate one, of the humanising and moralising of the techniques of judicial punishment, but instead with the comprehensive intention of analysing ethnologically the structure and the mode of operation of historically successive practices of judicial punishment. The impulse to such a study was given quite some time ago by none other than Claude Lévi-Strauss in his account of his travels, *Tristes Tropiques*:

> But above all, we should realise that certain of our own customs might appear, to an observer belonging to a different society, to be similar in nature to cannibalism, although cannibalism strikes us as being foreign to the idea of civilisation. I am thinking, for instance, of our legal and prison systems. If we studied societies from the outside, it would be tempting to distinguish two contrasting types: those which practice cannibalism – that is, which regard the absorption of certain individuals possessing dangerous powers as the only means of neutralising those powers and even of turning them to advantage – and those which, like our own society, adopt what might be called the practice of *anthropemy* (from the Greek *émein*, to vomit); faced with the same problem, the latter type of society has chosen the opposite solution, which consists in ejecting dangerous individuals from the social body and keeping them temporarily or permanently in isolation, away from all contact with their fellows, in establishments specially intended for this purpose. (Lévi-Strauss, 1974; first published in French in 1955)

The suggestion for research implicitly contained in this passage was clearly adopted by Foucault in *Discipline and Punish*. For the purpose of working out an ethnology of the European penal systems with a social–historical orientation, he studies the great transition in the system of judicial punishment from the corporal punishment of the Middle Ages to the present-day prison system. The beginning and the end of this process of transformation are marked by two historical images which form the introduction to the book and its conclusion. The first is the meticulously detailed depiction of a cruel quartering that took place in 1757 in Paris; the second is the reproduction of a plan drawn in 1836, for a prison-city designed in every detail as a system of control and surveillance. Between these two styles of punishment lies, in Foucault's opinion, the 'birth of the prison', which is the object of his investigation. At first glance, the transformational tendencies that above all had a determinative influence on the decisive phase of radical change in the system of judicial punishment between 1760 and 1840 are the isolation and finally the concealment of the punishment from the public, the moderation of physical suffering in the execution of the punishment, and the growth of abstraction in the methods of punishment, that is, the standardisation of those methods for the same kind of crime.

The chief goal of Foucault's study is to demonstrate that these transformations of the practices of judicial punishment do not follow the guideline of a humanising of the execution of the punishments, of a lessening of the punishments' intensity, but rather on the whole form an integral part of a technology of power having a strategic goal different from the one it previously pursued. Foucault undertakes to show that this process of transformation of the European techniques of judicial punishment had to do with a change of its goal, not with its humanisation. It is certainly true that in the period around 1800 the determination of the punishment to be meted out to convicted criminals and the carrying-out of their sentences are organised around a new entity that has entered into the discourse of criminal justice, namely the human 'soul'. Legal judgments now also take into consideration, when there is sufficient reason to do so, the criminal's psychical state; the techniques of punishment are no longer aimed at injuring the body but at the re-integration of the soul into the civil complex of social relations. The historically new openness to man's inner nature, to his psyche, of the techniques of implementing judicial punishments is, however, only the manifest expression of a new technology of the human body: in the techniques of judicial punishment, human subjectivity becomes accessible only in an effectivising process consisting, on the one hand, in securing possession and a very great degree of control of the criminal's body, and on the other hand in the transformation of these techniques of disciplining the body into a science:

The history of this 'micro-physics' of the punitive power would then be a genealogy or an element in a genealogy of the modern 'soul'. Rather than seeing this soul as the reactivated remnants of an ideology, one would see it as the present correlative of a certain technology of power over the body. It would be wrong to say that the soul is an illusion, or an ideological effect. On the contrary, it exists, it has a reality, it is produced permanently around, on, within the body by the functioning of a power that is exercised on those punished – and, in a more general way, on those one supervises, trains and corrects, over madmen, children at home and at school, the colonized, over those who are stuck at a machine and supervised for the rest of their lives. This is the historical reality of this soul, which, unlike the soul represented by

Christian theology, is not born in sin and subject to punishment, but is born rather out of methods of punishment, supervision and constraint. This real, noncorporal soul is not a substance; it is the element in which are articulated the effects of a certain type of power and the reference of a certain type of knowledge, the machinery by which the power relations give rise to a possible corpus of knowledge, and knowledge extends and reinforces the effects of this power. (Foucault, 1977, p. 29)

The institutional disciplining of the body and the human science which makes it effective are the two sides of the process in which a new stage of the social relations of power came into being at the beginning of the nineteenth century. The fundamental structuralist premise that the explanation of the significational content of social actions is to be found in an anonymous system of rules was given a concrete form by Foucault, and moreover one that connects to the theory of power, in the following thesis: the system of rules which remains unconscious, and which at any given time defines the horizon of meaning of human subjectivity and the scope of its activity, is identical with the paradigm of social power dominant at that time. The social–historical investigation presented in *Discipline and Punish* is intended to demonstrate the validity of this assertion.

The classical system of criminal justice which Foucault examines as it was during the seventeenth and eighteenth centuries interlocks with one another two ritualised treatments of the human body. First, classical criminal justice has two means for eliciting a confession, the truth about the crime being tried. In addition to the oath, which the accused is forced to swear before the interrogation, there is torture, the use of physical violence to exact a truth from the accused. Foucault describes judicial torture as a 'torture of the truth':

Torture was a strict judicial game. And, as such, it was linked to the old tests or trials – ordeals, judicial duels, judgements of God – that were practised in accusatory procedures long before the techniques of the Inquisition. Something of the joust survived, between the judge who ordered the judicial torture and the suspect who was tortured. (Foucault, 1977, p. 40)

Judicial torture is an element of an economy that treats the human body as the place where truth can be obtained. After the evidence has been presented in the trial, and after sentence has been pronounced, this economy of the body is continued in the inflicting of the punishment: in the ceremonial of the public chastisement or execution of the convicted criminal, the latter's body constituted the ceremonial's centre. The judicial torment and execution carried out before the public's eyes contains three principal meanings which are nested one in the other, and which Foucault identifies: (1) execution under torture in the appropriate form continues the work effected by the interrogatory torture by reproducing in public the act of confession; (2) the punitive torment establishes a connection with the crime by establishing a symbolic relationship between the criminal and his crime (the blasphemer's tongue is pierced; the murderer's fist is struck off; etc.); and lastly, (3) the long duration of the public execution that is the conclusion of the judicial ritual constitutes a kind of final examination. This 'festival of torments', as Foucault calls the carrying-out of judicial punishment, is embedded in a host of rituals of domination, in which the sovereign's power manifests itself – the juridico-political heart of the convicted criminal's public torture and execution consists in the fact that it is a 'ceremonial by which a momentarily injured sovereignty is reconstituted' (*ibid.*, p. 48). Thus the brutal public execution of the criminal is no moral anachronism in the age of the enlightened monarchy; rather, physical violence and the rigorous ceremonial subserve the political function of a penal system that is seeking to re-establish not justice but social power:

> We must regard the public execution, as it was still ritualized in the eighteenth century, as a political operation. It was logically inscribed in a system of punishment, in which the sovereign, directly or indirectly, demanded, decided and carried out punishments, in so far as it was he who, through the law, had been injured by the crime. In every offence there was a *crimen majestatis* and in the least criminal a potential regicide. And the regicide, in turn, was neither more nor less, than the total, absolute criminal since, instead of attacking, like any offender, a particular decision or wish of the sovereign power, he attacked the very principle and physical person of the prince. (Foucault, 1977, pp. 53–4)

In its analysis of the further development of the techniques of inflicting judicial punishment, Foucault's social–historical reconstruction encounters a transitional model of penal policy, the grounding of which apparently comes from the critique of the techniques of punitive torture and execution. The reform of criminal justice which has its political and philosophical roots in the bourgeois theories of contract, and which becomes effective in the second half of the eighteenth century, proclaims 'man' as the limit of the legitimacy of punitive authority; the

techniques of judicial punishment were to be moderated and human-
ised. Criminal justice was to punish, not to take vengeance.

Foucault links all of these demands to a political calculation that had
as its goal not at all the mitigation of the techniques of judicial punishment, but the restriction of the monarch's judicial arbitrariness and
the refinement of the agencies for controlling criminality. In Foucault's
view, the reform of criminal justice which was implemented in the latter
part of the eighteenth century, and which was borne upon the spirit of
the Enlightenment, reveals itself to be a phase of far-reaching change in
the European penal economy that, in its critique of royal arbitrariness in
the meting-out of punishment and in its protest against the lack of
principles in such administration of justice, was only laying the ground-
work for a thoroughly rationally organised system of criminal justice that
precisely codified all violations of law and functioned with perfect
consistency:

> In short, penal reform was born at the point of junction between the struggle
> against the super-power of the sovereign and that against the infra-power of
> acquired and tolerated illegalities. And if penal reform was anything more
> than the temporary result of a purely circumstantial encounter, it was
> because, between this super-power and this infra-power, a whole network of
> relations was being formed. By placing on the side of the sovereign the
> additional burden of a spectacular, unlimited, personal, irregular and dis-
> continuous power, the form of monarchical sovereignty left the subjects free
> to practise a constant illegality; this illegality was like the correlative of this
> type of power. So much so that in attacking the various prerogatives of the
> sovereign one was also attacking the functioning of the illegalities. The two
> objectives were in continuity. And, according to particular circumstances or
> tactics, the reformers laid more stress on one or the other. (Foucault, 1977,
> pp. 87–8)

The new techniques of judicial punishment only mitigate the penalties
in order, by means of their refinement, to prevent in a more differentiated manner and more effectively a repetition of the crime. The
inflicting of the judicial punishment is no longer the ritual manifestation
of royal sovereignty, as in the case of public torture and execution, but a
process of presenting a symbol for both preventative and punitive
purposes. The intended result of this structural transformation of the
techniques of judicial punishment is the individualising of the entire
field of delinquency: the possible criminal offences are codified in a
manner that recognises so many distinctions that in many respects the
prescribed punishments are, so to speak, symbolically tailored to the

individual kinds of crimes, so that they acquire the effect of a public instruction and deterrent. Thus the reform of criminal justice which has the outward appearance of a humanisation of the techniques of judicial punishment is in actual fact nothing but the introduction of a technique of carrying out that punishment which increases its effectiveness.

The effect of the reform of criminal justice is, to be sure, both brief and narrow. For, although the prison as the means of penal confinement does not occupy an important place in that reform's system of finely differentiated and symbolic penalties, after only a short time the prison assumes such a great role that it predominates over all other types of punishment. It is true that the prison has its legitimate place even in the arguments that were made for the reform of criminal justice; however, the technique of punishment that with the prison was institutionalised and then also universalised is based on historically new principles. With regard to the prison, it is no longer a matter of the subtly differentiated 'game' of publicly instructive punishments, but of uninterrupted constraint effected by a disciplining of the criminal's body. Whereas the criminal-justice reform interprets judicial punishment as the agency effecting the social re-integration of a juridical subject within the framework of a social contract, in the carceral system the punishment functions as the medium of, in Foucault's words, the 'shaping of an obedient subject' (*ibid.*, p. 129). The extremely great rapidity with which, and the extraordinary extent to which, imprisonment as a technique of punishment gained prevalence pose the historical question that was the impetus of Foucault's study:

> How then could detention, so evidently bound up with an illegality that was denounced even in the power of the prince, become in so short a time one of the most general forms of legal punishment? (Foucault, 1977, p. 120)

In order to be able to answer this centrally important question of his investigation, Foucault takes recourse to a process that is historically earlier and socially much more comprehensive. In the development of a disciplinary power oriented to the organisation of the body and to its training, both as an end in itself and for productive purposes, he sees the process of the formation of an institutional system of power in which the prison assumes a place that is, as it were, taken for granted in the historical moment in which the internal uncertainties and strains of the old system of criminal justice make a new, effective penal technology urgently necessary. The prison originates in the transitional period in which the disciplining technologies of the body that are proper to the monastery, the hospital, the school and the factory, and that originated and evolved in historical independence from one another, enter into an institutional association with each other, and thereby become generalised, so to speak, to constitute a new system of power, that of disciplinary power. These disciplines, which originated in the course of the sixteenth, seventeenth and eighteenth centuries at different loci of socialisation, have in common that they productively train the human body, which is no longer juridically the possession of someone other than the person who is and has a particular body; that is to say that these disciplines enhance the body's effectuality with regard to reality. In these technologies of the body, four kinds of training techniques and knowledge of the body were acquired which subsequently functioned as the base for the universal disciplinary power. First came the technique of the spatial distribution of bodies – in monasteries, schools and workshops, men were assigned to isolating locations or rooms; further, physical activities were thoroughly organised for temporal efficiency–bodily actions were analysed into separate acts that were tailored to the objects (e.g., weapons, tools) to be handled; third, the time of the body's disciplining was itself imposed, analytically and evolutionarily, on an axis, along which developments, instructions and improvements could be planned and organised; and lastly, the body as a functional element became a component of a superordinate functional system (e.g., an army or a factory), so that it could be judged and put into action with a view to enhancing the functioning of a machinery.

The 'individual body', which was first produced both practically and cognitively in these four disciplines of the body, was then productively trained using three training methods. The first consisted in the hierarchised, constant and functional surveillance of activities, which Foucault demonstrates primarily by examining the architectural structuring of hospitals and schools; second, norm-establishing judgment punished the non-justiciable violations of the regulations regarding time and the rules pertaining to the body (Foucault's term for this is 'micro-justice') – in this punitive procedure, the normal is established as a 'principle of coercion'; the third and last method of training is one that unites the functions of the other procedures, namely the strategy of the examination:

> The examination combines the techniques of an observing hierarchy and those of a normalizing judgement. It is a normalizing gaze, a surveillance that

makes it possible to qualify, to classify and to punish. (Foucault, 1977, p. 184)

In this disciplinary agency, the intertwining of power and knowledge, which is typical for disciplinary power in modern Europe as a whole, really acquires for the first time an historically substantive form.

In the examination there is established the monitoring and disciplinary procedure in which, from the viewpoint of Foucault's theory of power, the process of individualisation that began with the modern era of Europe is turned about with respect to social structure. The growth of the 'political axis' of individualisation at first followed the influence exercised by a social stratum in virtue of its power – for example, in feudal systems only the members of the feudal court, who were permitted to gain recognition of themselves as individuals through writing, pictures or rituals, were capable of being individualised. The disciplinary regime reverses this process of individualisation inasmuch as it is precisely the monitored persons whom the examination makes individually capable of being documented:

> In a disciplinary régime, on the other hand, individualization is 'descending': as power becomes more anonymous and more functional, those on whom it is exercised tend to be more strongly individualized; it is exercised by surveillance rather than ceremonies, by observation rather than commemorative accounts, by comparative measures that have the 'norm' as reference rather than genealogies giving ancestors as points of reference; by 'gaps' rather than by deeds. (*ibid.*, p. 193)

In the social-historical development of the controlling examination the European sciences of man gradually become established; for only with the techniques of registration, of making files, and of tabulating data used in the disciplinary procedures, does the individual enter into the purview of the sciences:

> [the birth of the sciences of man] is probably to be found in these 'ignoble' archives, where the modern play of coercion over bodies, gestures and behavior has its beginnings. (*ibid.*, p. 191)

From the outset, institutionalised training of the body and the emerging human sciences are so closely interwoven with one another that knowledge about something cannot be distinguished from power over something. At these points which are crucially important for the elaboration of his power-theory-based ethnology of European culture, Foucault identifies the cognitively directed opening up of new zones of reality so strongly with the social taking possession and supervision of them that he is compelled to regard the human sciences in their entirety as power-giving knowledge. Because he embeds the step-by-step cognition of dimensions of reality directly in the overarching framework of a social domination and supervision of reality, he must completely abandon the essential possibility that scientific knowledge might cognitively open up new areas of unconstrained action.

In the second half of the eighteenth and the first half of the nineteenth century, as Foucault undertakes to demonstrate, the techniques for training the human body and the human sciences, which render each other effective, coalesce into the modern form of disciplinary power that shapes developed European society. This new system of power which productively observes and trains the human body forms the institutional framework in which the prison is only one locus of training among other equally important agencies of supervision. The disciplinary power in which scientific discourses and institutionalised systems of surveillance mutually buttress each other continuously produces and reproduces the social infrastructure over which the declarations of bourgeois law only hang the veil of a humane and just social order. Thus Foucault's study leads to the thesis that the bourgeois legal system has only a formal significance for a society that has long ago been brought into line by unceasing and painstaking processes of surveillance:

> Historically, the process by which the bourgeoisie became in the course of the eighteenth century the politically dominant class was masked by the establishment of an explicit, coded and formally egalitarian juridical framework, made possible by the organization of a parliamentary, representative régime. But the development and generalization of disciplinary mechanisms constituted the other, dark side of these processes. The general juridical form that guaranteed a system of rights that were egalitarian in principle was supported by these tiny, everyday, physical mechanisms, by all those systems of micro-power that are essentially non-egalitarian and asymmetrical that we call the disciplines. And although, in a formal way, the representative régime makes it possible, directly or indirectly, with or without relays, for the will of all to form the fundamental authority of sovereignty, the disciplines provide, at the base, a guarantee of the submission of forces and bodies. The real, corporal disciplines constituted the foundation of the formal, juridical liberties. The contract may have been regarded as the ideal foundation of law and political power; panopticism constituted the technique, universally widespread, of coercion. It continued to work in depth on the juridical structures of society, in order to make the effective mechanisms of power function in

opposition to the formal framework that it had acquired. The 'enlighten-ment', which discovered the liberties, also invented the disciplines. (Fou-cault, 1977, p. 222)

Foucault sees the explanation of the effectiveness of modern systems of power in his historical process of a scientifically guided disciplining of the human body that penetrates even into the innermost domains of its voluntary motions. In these modern systems of power, the prison, whose institutional process of origination Foucault's study seeks to trace out, is a functional subsystem among other systems of socialisation that train the human body. Foucault traces the development of these other dis-ciplines of the body, namely those of the military, the school and manufacture, back into the seventeenth century; however, he locates the emergence of the prison system in the early nineteenth century. In his view, it is only on the basis of historically developed disciplinary power that the prison succeeds in gaining general recognition and acceptance. The historical inaccuracy of this thesis, however, indicates a weakness, from the standpoint of the theory of society, of the analysis of power underlying Foucault's structuralist conception of history.

As Foucault himself shows in some parts of his study, the emergence of disciplinary surveillance is first of all linked to the centralisation of the material resources required for warfare, administration and production in the hands of an authority having discretionary power; in France, this centralisation of all administrative discretionary power was ac-complished by the absolutist state, which in its mercantilist form also accelerated the development of the capitalist economic system. This centralised administrative system of the absolute monarchy of the sev-enteenth century is, certainly, also the historical soil in which corporally disciplinary confinement (e.g., in workhouses or shelters) has its roots. In 'the pertinent period of the first half of the nineteenth century', writes Heinz Steinert (1978, p. 40) in a critique of Foucault that draws its arguments from social history, 'it was not a matter of the "birth of the prison", but of its further development and perfecting, of its recognition by the judicial system, on the periphery of which it had for a long time been playing a crucially important role'. Like the other disciplines of the body, the prison as an instrument of social control originates in the social sphere of the centralised state apparatus of French absolutism. In the aftermath of the bourgeois revolution in France, it is, as the pre-eminent penal instrument, only accorded a greater value juridically and put into general use.

If this social–historical criticism is valid, then the validity of a key thesis of Foucault's structuralist analysis of power also becomes questionable. A central argument of his theory of power attacks the localisation, in theories of society, of power in state apparatuses; in contrast, Foucault seeks to achieve a decentralising of the concept of power (see Foucault, 1980a). This part of Foucault's theory of power is obviously directed against the privileging of the political system of power in the theory of domination, as this is done above all by Althusser's structural Marxism (cf. Althusser, 1971). For a concept of power that is restricted in its applicability to the institutions of the state, Foucault substitutes a 'microphysics of power' that traces power relations back to their genesis in social microprocesses, in local 'confrontations' in factories, families and schools. In comparison with Althusser's theory of power, which is limited to the manipulative strategies and procedures of the state, this theoretical model clearly represents a great advance, as it makes us aware of the reproduction of power relations in a society's everyday conflicts; for only in this fashion can it be shown that a social system of power maintains itself solely through the quotidian and inconspicuous fighting-out of conflicts between opposed interests and the resolution of social tensions. This theory of power, however, does not take into consideration the fact that institutionalised strategies of power, which structurally decide such ongoing social conflicts in advance, are tied to the concentration of actual discretionary authority over administrative and military establishments or over means of production. In *Discipline and Punish*, Foucault is able to ascribe the development of different disciplinary techniques, which ultimately coalesced into the modern disciplinary power, to such diverse loci and to such different points in time only because he downplays the establishment and the rendering effective of the disciplinary institutions by the centralised administration of the absolutist state. Only thus is he able to decompose the concept of power that guides his structuralist analysis of history into a particular form of momentary and constantly repeated collisions among a certain number of individuals (see Foucault, 1979), without systematically taking into consideration the force issuing from a centralised authority having discretionary power. In consequence, the dimension of class struggles, that is, the conflicts among social classes having different degrees of structural power, becomes completely insignificant in Foucault's social–historical investigations in comparison with the anonymous mechanisms of power encompassing forms of knowledge and strategies of power.

The explanation for these shortcomings of Foucault's theory of power is given only by the fundamental structuralist model which forms the framework for his new social–historical studies. The structuralist criticism which Foucault makes of the equation of the conscious intentions guiding human actions with actual social reality, an equation which is a tenet of the philosophy of history, permits him to account for systems of norms and value-orientations through underlying strategies of power, in accordance with which the former are systematically generated. Foucault often carries out this step of his analysis in an ironically presented reversal of Hegel's position: the moral forms of consciousness embodied in the institutions of civil society, and in which Hegel, from the viewpoint of this philosophy of history, sees the definitive realisation of moral freedom, are for Foucault merely the cultural veil concealing the effective prevalence in society of a power that keeps watch over society's members with extreme thoroughness.[5] At the same time, though, Foucault is compelled by his own basic structuralist premises to rule out, on principle, a reaction of the legal forms that have been established on the conditions of social intercourse. From his standpoint, a society's network of everyday actions and its system of norms, which is institutionalised in its legal system, are always torn asunder from the outset into the two dimensions of the social base that has been productively organised by the disciplinary power in the society and, on the other hand, the moral superstructure that denies the reality of this power. In order to hold that the plexus of social interrelations can be split in this way, Foucault must have interpreted that plexus of interrelations in its entirety as a complex of microconfrontations, that is, of strategic actions. Only then can he assume that complicated power strategies prevail without exception in a society's everyday conflicts. Thus, Foucault's structuralist analysis of history requires that society shrink down to a sphere of ongoing strategic confrontations which constitutes the social medium for the anonymous transformation process of the power systems.

The price for the assumption of an omnipresence of productive power strategies which Foucault's social–historical theory of power must therefore pay is the systematic exclusion of a domain of non-strategic action, namely that of communicative action. This type of social action, which is the co-ordination of goal-directed actions by means of agreement, achieved through the use of symbols, upon a shared definition of a given situation, could have made it clear to

[5] Cf., for example, the image of Napoleon presented in *Discipline and Punish* (p. 217), which is obviously ironically opposed to Hegel's view of Napoleon.

Foucault that the social relations of a society must have as an integral part moral orientations and normative regulations which assist from day to day this continuously necessary process of reaching agreement: social systems of actions are normally founded upon the consensual recognition of normative behavioural expectations. Thus a stock of moral orientations and social norms forms, in every particular instance, the historical background before which occur the persisting conflict situations in which a system of power reproduces itself. However, then the moral and practical regulations embodied by a legal system during a certain historical period cannot be separated at all from forms of social intercourse, as Foucalt undertakes to do even in his fundamental premises; only because he denies the consensual component of a social order, hence the measure of agreement upon a particular moral order which is structurally necessitated in whatever manner, is he able to regard a society's institutionalised system of norms as a mere cultural superstructure in relation to the actually operative strategies of power and to neglect them. Just as, in Foucault's eyes, every theoretical opening up of new domains of human subjectivity coincides from the very beginning with the strategical taking possession of and gaining control over these domains of subjectivity, so every legal system also assumes, from the standpoint of his analysis of history, the same function, to wit that of merely concealing the reality of the disciplinary power in a society. Because Foucault, from the start, reduces the entire domain of social action to a sphere of persisting confrontations between different instances of power, he can no longer take into consideration in a nuanced manner the intrasocietal significance and the possibly progressive character of scientific knowledge and of moral forms of consciousness.

Now, it is this task that has guided the efforts of Jürgen Habermas and his collaborators to elaborate a theory of socio-cultural evolution. At the centre of his reconstruction of historical materialism there stands the process of historical progress which, on the basis of the development of the forces of production, thus of broadening social domination of nature, gradually liberates the socio-cultural core of consensual action from determination by relations of force or power. In this theory, therefore, those forms of action effecting the social integration of human beings, which are categorically excluded from the outset in Michel Foucault's structuralist analysis of history, advance into the foreground.

Moral evolution and domination of nature. Jürgen Habermas's theory of socio-cultural evolution

The interpretation of historical materialism as a theory of socio-cultural evolution which Jürgen Habermas has been working on does not itself constitute a contribution to historical anthropology. Rather, anthropological facts and themes have entered in such a substantial manner into this theoretical project, of which the analytical framework has so far been elaborated, and which has been illustrated by the evolutionary genesis of class societies (Habermas, 1976b; Eder, 1976), that those facts and concerns have not themselves been made the object of historical analysis, but instead determine the categorial presuppositions of the theory as a whole. The theory of socio-cultural evolution is conceived of programmatically as a new interpretation of historical materialism that has learned from the advances made by the social and cultural sciences since Marx, and that is safeguarded from dogmatic shortcomings. In its fundamental theoretical premises, the theory of socio-cultural evolution is the result of the continuous critical examination of his own thought in which Habermas, beginning with his first writings, has developed ever further his own interpretation of Marxism. Through examination of the stages of Habermas's achievement of clarity and certainty about his theory, therefore, the central aims and the guiding substantive themes of his reconstruction of historical materialism can be identified and formulated.

Habermas's first attempts to interpret Marx's theory (see Habermas, 1973b, pp. 195ff. and 1977b, pp. 387ff.) are informed by the difficulties which were encountered by a politically motivated updating of Marxism in the fifties. The experience of a restoration of capitalism in the Federal Republic of Germany that was forced by the state seemed to make the mere further application, without modification, of Marx's analysis of capitalism impossible; Stalinism, which as a political formation had entered the awareness of many Marxists only through the de-Stalinisation of the fifties, awakened doubts about the basic ethicalness of Marxist theory. In the relevant interpretations of Marx in these years, Marxism itself assumed either a de-historicised or a de-economised form. In Soviet Marxism, Marx's theory was so radically ontologised into a dialectical universal science, and in post-war Western Marxism so strongly neutralised into a philosophical theory of alienation, that interest in a practically oriented critique of capitalism is scarcely to be found in either of them. In this situation of Marxist theory, Habermas returns to Marx's early writings in order to make evident again the importance, from the standpoint of the theory of science, of Marxism as a critical theory of society.

Habermas begins by differentiating his interpretation of Marxism from the two dominant ways of interpreting it. In opposition to the Soviet-Marxist version of historical materialism, Habermas adduces, in this early phase, the empirical and historical references of the argumentation of Marx's theory: historical materialism cannot be understood as a theory of the developmental laws of universal history, as it is informed both normatively and with regard to political praxis by the experience of contemporary history. In this connection, Habermas owes to Merleau-Ponty's interpretation of Marxism (Merleau-Ponty, 1973) his conviction that Marxist theory cannot extract an immanent meaning of history from the evolution of society, but rather utilises in philosophical analysis of the present historical period the openness of historical processes for the formulation of a meaning of history that must still be realised politically (see esp. Habermas, 1971b, pp. 424ff.; E. H. Walter, 1967, pp. 425ff.). The historical preconditions of the attainment of this goal of historical praxis, however, cannot be fixed pre-empirically in a theory of proletarian revolution, but must be established through sociological analysis of historical reality. Consequently, Marxist theory must rely strictly on empirical knowledge and philosophical interpretation of the present historical period. In opposition to the anthropological or existentialist de-politicisation of Marxist theory in post-war Western philosophy, Habermas adduces the connection to praxis of the argumentation of Marx's theory: historical materialism does not aim solely at the empirically grounded analysis of the present era, but is theoretically completed only with the attainment through political praxis of its declared goal of emancipation. Moreover, historical materialism, like all theories, is itself grounded in the historical and political complex of interests that is also its object of study. Thus the fundamental propositions of Marxist theory cannot be interpreted philosophically as contemplative analyses of a particular historical period, but only as determinations of the capitalist social plexus which provide guidance for action. Habermas attempts to combine historical materialism's empirical, sociological grounding and its practical and political orientation in the programme of an *empirically falsifiable philosophy of history having a practical intent*. In empirically grounded social research, Marxist theory investigates the complex of interrelations out of which capitalist crises arise in order to make it possible, through philosophical critique giving guidance to action, to eliminate politically the causes of those crises (see Habermas, 1973b, pp. 212ff. and pp. 276ff.).

However, the theoretical framework which this materialist philosophy of history establishes quite soon shows obvious weaknesses. Historical materialism's claim to lead to emancipation cannot be convincingly justified by the philosophical interpretation of the present era alone, nor can the social possibilities of socialist praxis and the structure of capitalist social systems be established solely by means of empirical social research. The empirically falsifiable philosophy of history with practical intent does not of itself suffice to provide the analytical possibilities of a materialist explanation of history. For that reason, in his subsequent writings Habermas pursues the problems of the achievement by Marxist theory of a clear understanding of its methods and their basis, as well as the politico-economic problems posed by an analysis of capitalism founded upon empirical evidence. Even in his first essays, Habermas had limited the validity of the labour theory of value to the period of liberal capitalism, in order to take into account in an adequate manner the changed constellation of conditions obtaining in late capitalist societies (*ibid.*, pp. 222ff.). However, it is the first component or strand of reflection of Habermas's theory that is chiefly relevant for his elaboration of historical materialism. For the reflections from the standpoint of the theory of science, by means of which he undertakes to determine the methodological structure of a critique of society that is directed to political praxis, quickly lead to an emendation of Habermas's original philosophy of history.

In his essays on the positivism controversy (1970a, pp. 9ff. and pp. 39ff.), Habermas advances pragmatist arguments that burst asunder critical theory's traditional line of argument against positivism. Unlike Adorno, who draws upon the work of Alfred Sohn-Rethel, Habermas does not link the positivist notion of science to the necessity for abstraction inherent in the exchange of commodities, but instead accounts for that notion by mental operations that are an integral part of human beings' manipulative fashioning of nature. In the pragmatism of Habermas's epistemology, the rules governing the performance of instrumental activities, which form the culturally invariant action-basis of social production, assume a role that is played in Sohn-Rethel's sociogenetic epistemology by the rules of abstraction proper to the exchange activities which become universal with the spread of capitalism (Sohn-Rethel, 1970). From the standpoint of Habermas's line of argument, therefore, the scientistic model of science only gives explicit formulation to the mental operations which are pre-scientifically already implicit in the technical praxis whereby human beings dispose over nature. This scientific model becomes positivism of the kind that is the object of critique only with its extension to social reality as a field of enquiry. It is only the claim to universal applicability and validity which positivism associates with its explanatory model that can be called into question epistemologically, not the rules of cognition themselves which positivism formulates from the standpoint of the theory of science.

Of course, this reflection, which was originally intended to subserve the critique of positivism, compels Habermas also to situate the human sciences in terms of the theory of action. For if the formation of theories by the natural sciences is to be rooted in the process of achieving and extending domination of nature that has taken place in the course of the human species' history, then the formation of theories by the human sciences must be related back to a similar process of pre-scientific experience, through which process the human species reproduces itself practically. Habermas asserts that Marx's distinction between forces of production and relations of production has its origin in the distinction between the two forms of action, 'instrumental' and 'communicative' praxis (see Habermas, 1973b, pp. 142ff.; Arnason, 1980; Honneth, 1982), in order to be able to ground pragmatically the difference between the formation of natural–scientific and social–scientific theories in the fact that the process of social reproduction proceeds along two tracks. Just as the natural sciences follow the cognition-directing interest in instrumental disposition over nature, the social sciences allow themselves to be guided by interest in the preservation and expansion of intersubjective communication and agreement, an interest which became a matter of necessity for the survival of the species with its dependence on language (see Habermas, 1973b, pp. 142ff.).[6] For Habermas, historical materialism can now no longer, as was still the case in his early interpretation of Marxism, be grounded in a social complex of interests which is determined solely by the historical constellations of conditions obtaining at the time in question; rather, historical materialism must understand itself as the result of the historical process of the human species' reproduction of itself. It becomes a theory, which in its design follows the methodological model of psychoanalysis, of the educational process that has taken place in the course of the human

---

[6] No consideration has been given here to Habermas's vacillation between a two-dimensional (labour/interaction) and a three-dimensional (labour/language/domination) structure of his theoretical model of interests.

species' history. According to this theory, processes of collective self-reflection are triggered by the theoretical reconstruction of the repression of social relations of interaction through the dominant power in society. As psychoanalysis aims at individual liberation from a pathologically distorted individual biography by means of the theoretically guided interpretation of that life history, historical materialism, in the interpretation of the history of the species, aims at collective emancipation from a history of domination that heretofore has come into being and proceeded spontaneously, that is, a history that has hitherto resembled a natural process in that it has not been guided by human reflection. Habermas no longer understands the Marxist theory of history as a philosophy of history that is grounded in the experience of the present historical period, but instead as a critical theory of the species' history (see esp. Habermas, 1971a, particularly chapter 3).

The framework within which Habermas anchors this interpretation of historical materialism is derived from the theory of action and is informed by the fundamental epistemological problem to the solution of which this framework is intended to make a substantive contribution: Habermas is interested primarily by the cognitive achievements that are systematically woven into the effectuation of instrumental and communicative actions. He develops the concepts of action which he requires for answering this question at first on a categorial level that is characterised on the one side by Gehlen's anthropological theory of action and on the other side by the sociology based on the theory of action that stands in the tradition originating with Mead. In this tradition, the field of investigation of the social sciences is understood as a reality consisting of the plexus of interrelations which the socially integrated subjects produce directly or indirectly through their social actions; it is only through their actions which are reciprocally referred to one another that the members of society generate, with their interpretations of their action situations, the social reality which sociology then encounters. The special theoretical position of sociology is the result of the peculiarity of its domain of investigation, which is pre-structured by the interpretation of the subjects of social action. This fundamental premise is adopted by Habermas in the version formulated by George Herbert Mead's approach, based on the latter's theory of intersubjectivity. Here social action is conceived of as a communicative process in which at least two subjects co-ordinate their purposive actions with each other through agreement upon a shared definition of their situation, effected by means of symbols. The process of a symbolically mediated interaction requires of the actors continuous interpretative operations in which they must reciprocally decipher each other's intentions with respect to their actions for the purpose of reaching agreement about the action-situation. This theoretical model of action, which Habermas develops further through a reconstruction of communicative speech acts, a path that has been followed by analytic philosophy (see Habermas, 1976a, pp. 174ff.), determines the categorial structure of his theory of society; he conceives of the whole range of modes of social praxis on the basis of this type of action, so that all actions that are socially directed, but not oriented to communication and the establishment of agreement, become practical variants of communicative action. The concept of communicative action is thereby promoted to a key concept in Habermas's interpretation of historical materialism that is both normative and empirical. On the one hand, it serves for the analysis of the empirical process in which plexuses of social relations culturally reproduce themselves and accomplish their social integration in processes of communication and agreement, no matter how distorted these processes might be. At the same time, the model of communicative action is supposed to provide the normative yardstick by which the degree of freedom of plexuses of social relations is to be assessed according to the freedom from coercion of their forms of communication.

The emancipatory importance that the concept of communicative action thereby acquires in Habermas's theory leads to the shrinking of the function of the concept of labour. Within the categorial framework of this theory of the human species' history, the latter concept has only the task of identifying the substrate of action on which the social forces of production develop, a development from which the processes of communicative action can be distinguished. Habermas adopts the concept of labour on the categorial level at which Gehlen's anthropological theory of action formulated it. As has been shown, in that theory instrumental action constitutes the practical medium in which the system of drives, perception and voluntary movement, which is organically in disorder in the human being, continuously reorganises itself. Habermas makes use of this anthropological consideration in order to complete his theory of the human species' history with determinations appertinent to the theory of action that characterise action directed to physical objects. The concept of communicative action is intended to account for the forms of social interaction by means of an anthropologically rooted structure of rules; the concept of instrumental action is supposed to account in the same way for the modes of action directed to objects, and that are the means by which human beings exercise domination over nature. In instrumental actions, a subject assesses his activity according to the success with which it is able to manipulate physical objects for a preconceived end; thus the kind of action called labour is dependent on the knowledge of technical rules which have been ascertained empirically through manipulative commerce with things.

On this foundation provided by the theory of action, Habermas distinguishes between the potential for practical and moral rationalisation that is inherent in communicative actions because they are in themselves aimed at ways of communication that are free from domination and the potential for technical rationalisation that is an integral moment of the manipulative fashioning of nature. This distinction, which analytically separates the process of the human species' historical development into two dimensions of rationalisation, is intended to make easily graspable the effacing of the difference between technical progress and political emancipation which is characteristic of late-capitalistic societies:

> While *instrumental action* corresponds to the constraint of external nature and the level of the forces of production determines the extent of technical control over natural forces, *communicative action* stands in correspondence to the suppression of man's own nature. The institutional framework determines the extent of repression by the unreflected, 'natural' force of social dependence and political power, which is rooted in prior history and tradition. A society owes emancipation from the external forces of nature to labor processes, that is to the production of technically exploitable knowledge (including the 'transformation of the natural sciences into machinery'). Emancipation from the compulsion of internal nature succeeds to the degree that institutions based on force are replaced by an organisation of social relations that is bound only to communication free from domination. This does not occur directly through productive activity, but rather through the revolutionary activity of struggling classes (including the critical activity of reflective sciences). Taken together, both categories of social practice make possible what Marx, interpreting Hegel, calls the self-generative act of the species. (Habermas, 1971a, p. 53)

With this distinction Habermas grounds his theory of the history of the human species, which follows at first the methodological model of psychoanalysis. The distinction is supposed to shed light on the relationship between the process of the development of the forces of production, on the one hand, and the process of political and moral progress, on the other. Whereas in instrumental rationalisation the technical equipment, the organisational engagement and the training of the workers are gradually improved, so that the human species increasingly frees itself from the constraint of external nature, it is only advances in the internal structure of communicative action that secure liberation from relations of social constraint. In the process of communicative rationalisation social movements make men conscious of the power relations that structurally deform the practically effective background consensus which is, so to say, the foundation of a plexus of social relations, of a society. The process of political and moral progress is therefore tied to collective advances in understanding gained in the sphere of social interaction. Even at the threshold of this bifurcation of the history of the human species, the shape of the evolutionary theory is beginning to emerge into which Habermas will later seek to convert historical materialism. Before Habermas could arrive at this theory itself, though, a further self-correction of his interpretation of Marxism was required.

Up to this point Habermas has understood history as a universal process in which the human species constitutes itself as the subject of world history in instrumental and interactive education processes. However, objections to this notion of history have been made by H. M. Baumgartner, who criticised the idealist historical fiction of a unitary subject of history:

> How is the educational process, which itself presupposes the unity of the species subject, supposed to be conceived without equivocations in the notion of education in general, if the totality and unity of the subject as themselves historical events appear only within this process. (Baumgartner, 1972, p. 299)

A historical materialism that is conceived of as the 'self-reflection of the historical process of the human species' education presupposes by that very fact the unitary bearer of historical development that is, however, supposed to come into being only through the self-reflective elucidation of history. By taking over arguments from systems theory, Habermas sought to correct this idealist fallacy of his theory (see Habermas, 1971c, p. 179 and 1973a, pp. 389ff.); he is convinced that the functionalist systems theory provides the most plausible theoretical model for conceiving the historical process as an objectively meaningful process of development, independent of the presupposition of a single general subject of history:

> Since the collective subject of a meaning-constituted life world, which is borrowed from transcendental philosophy, proves to be misleading at least in sociology, the concept of system recommends itself to us. Social systems are units that can solve objectively posed problems by means of suprasubjective learning processes. (Habermas, 1971c, p. 271)

But this insight of systems theory can be made fruitful for historical materialism only when that theory's social–scientific reductionism can be overcome. In his critique of functionalism's claim to universal validity, Habermas attempts to show that systems theory's restriction of socio-cultural development to the level of systemic adaptation alone fails to take into account just that dimension of development in which societies must also reproduce themselves by means of moral and practical processes of communication and agreement (Habermas, 1971c; Döbert, 1973). Historical materialism can make the functionalist concept of system into a component of its theory of social development only if it understands instrumental and interactive learning processes as problem-solving dimensions of social systems in which the latter reproduce themselves. The implications of this consideration are worked out in Habermas's theory of socio-cultural evolution.

When he took over into his version of historical materialism the category of 'evolution', Habermas adopted a concept that had behind it a highly problematical semantic history in the tradition of Marxist theory. In Kautskian Marxism, as in Bernstein's revisionism (cf. von Weiss, 1965), Marx's reflections on the materialist conception of history had been reformulated into a sociological theory of social evolution and expanded into a general theory of the human species' progress with the aid of the concept of adaptation formulated by the Darwinian theory of evolution. In this interpretation of Marxism, the concept of evolution assumed the theoretical function of giving to the Marxist theory of social development the methodological objectivity and rigour of the natural sciences: through the evolutionarily necessary growth of the forces of production, the development of society compels the progress of the social relations of production. Politically, this concept of evolution served as the legitimating basis of what has been described as the social–democratic tenet that socialism would come to pass merely through the passage of time, and that the proponents of socialism needed only to wait. With respect to the political and practical status of Marxism in Kautsky's theoretical programme, Karl Korsch (1971) described that programme as a 'Darwinisation' of Marxism; Walter Benjamin (1974, p. 691) criticised as a 'positivistic' conception of progress the unilinearity of this Marxist evolutionary theory which is tailored exclusively to the growth of the productive forces at the disposal of humanity. From the perspective of a critical Marxism, therefore, a historical materialism interpreted in terms of evolutionary theory can apparently be interpreted as an objectivist theory of progress that has become blind to historical retrogressions. Lastly, from the standpoint of the structuralist theory of history, the theory of evolution is a prime example of that philosophy of history which theoretically guarantees historical progress with the fiction of a subject of history that unfolds or realises itself gradually (cf. Foucault, 1972b).

Habermas's theory of socio-cultural evolution undertakes to refute such criticisms by means of an older fundamental premise. Historical materialism, even in its evolutionary interpretation, is to remain self-reflectively referred to its context of political realisation – thus it must not be objectivistically separated from the contexts in which praxis occurs (see Habermas, 1976b, pp. 129ff.; on the point just discussed, p. 130). Furthermore, the newer social–scientific concept of evolution, which Habermas also takes over into his theory, has abandoned the strong implications of classical evolutionary theory. In it, the older assumption of a continuity, irreversibility and unilinearity of social development has been replaced by attenuated assumptions about the rationally reconstructable direction of socio-cultural evolution (cf. Parsons, 1966; Nisbet, 1969, especially chapter 3). Habermas subscribes to this weak concept of evolution, with the result that his theory of socio-cultural evolution no longer has to assume the burden of proof for an actually existing, gradual process of social progress that necessarily determines all social cultures in the course of history, but only has to demonstrate the logical necessity of successive stages of development of socio-cultural formations. This logic of socio-cultural progress is not converted directly into the empirical course of history; rather, this logic's realisation is determined by contingent events of history.

Now, Habermas adopts this concept of evolution, which is character-istic for neo-evolutionism, in the form of an hypothesis about the developmental logic of human beings' instrumental and interactive forms of rationality. It is supposed to be possible, using developmental logic, to extract the evolutionary trend of socio-cultural systems from the 'anthropologically deep-seated systems of rules' embodying the culturally invariant structures of instrumental and communicative action. According to this thesis, the evolution of human societies does not follow only the pattern of the development of the productive forces (technical and cognitive learning ability), as postulated by Kautskian Marxism, but moreover the pattern of the development of the relations of production (moral and practical learning ability). The presuppositions contained in this idea are of decisive importance for the construction of Habermas's evolutionary theory. Habermas gives detailed formulation to these presuppositions by setting forth a sequence of moral learning successes underlying the development of the relations of production that parallels the sequence, which was assumed by Marx, of instrumental learning successes underlying the development of the forces of production:

> Whereas Marx localized the learning processes important for evolution in the dimension of objectivating thought – of technical and organizational knowledge, of instrumental and strategic action, in short, of *productive forces* – there are good reasons meanwhile for assuming that learning processes also take place in the dimension of moral insight, practical knowledge, communicative action, and the consensual regulation of action conflicts – learning processes that are deposited in more mature forms of social integration, in new *productive relations*, and that in turn first make possible the introduction of new productive forces. The rationality structures that find expression in world views, moral representations, and identity formations, that become practically effective in social movements and are finally embodied in institutional systems, thereby gain a strategically important position from a theoretical point of view. (Habermas, 1979a, pp. 97f.)

Processes of evolutionary transformation can be understood only as socio-cultural learning processes. Thus, this process of social learning which is tied to the transmission of knowledge by means of language replaces, on the socio-cultural plane, the process of genetic mutation that is the motor force of natural evolution. The supra-individual learning processes which are stabilised in social organisations and institutions remain systematically dependent on the learning capabilities and levels of consciousness of socially integrated subjects: the learning successes of a given social system, which are given permanence for historically determinate periods of time in the forces and the relations of production, rest upon the processes of consciousness of social groups. For this reason, Habermas, in a second step, undertakes to structure, in accordance with developmental logic, the two socio-culturally intermeshed learning processes in homology with the learning processes of individual subjects. Following the theory of the individual's psychological development proposed by Piaget's Geneva School, which understands ontogenesis as a constructive learning process on the part of the subject that develops itself from stage to stage through confrontation with, and solution of, cognitive and moral problems, Habermas maintains that the universal learning stages of socio-cultural development can also be reconstructed in the analytically distinguishable dimensions of cognitive–instrumental knowledge and interactive knowledge (labour/interaction) as logically necessary sequences. The stages that on this premise can then be constructed for the development of the forces of production and the relations of production establish the formal level of consciousness on which, on the one hand, the natural environment is made the object of human labour, and on the other hand the social world is morally integrated. As the rationalisation of instrumental action is expressed in technically ever more effective forces of production, so does the logic of the rationalisation of communicative action follow the direction of an increasing universalisation of moral norms that are embodied in the legal organisation of a society:

> Cognitive developmental psychology has shown that in ontogenesis there are different stages of moral consciousness, stages that can be described in particular as preconventional, conventional and postconventional patterns of problemsolving. The same patterns turn up again in the social evolution of moral and legal representations. (*ibid.*, p. 99)

Thus from the perspective of developmental logic, the history of the human species can be conceived of as a process that replicates the ontogenesis of the individual consciousness on the level of socio-cultural learning processes in the two dimensions of cognitive–purposive consciousness and of cognitive–moral consciousness. This view, however, fails to take into consideration the reciprocal dependence and internal dynamisation of the two developmental logics. From this perspective, the instrumentalist versions of a dialectic of the forces of production and the relations of production have as their basis the thesis that the state of the production techniques, that is, the cognitive knowledge embodied in the forces of production, historically determines the relations of production. Habermas assumes another developmental dynamic between the forces of production and the relations of production. While he also understands the development of the forces of production as a fundamental, problem-generating mechanism driving social development, he allows the actual realisation of a higher capability of the forces of production to remain dependent on moral and practical restructuring of the relations of production. In this manner, the moral learning process of the human species acquires an historically productive function because, in reaction to the pressure of social problems but following a developmental logic of its own, it brings to consciousness organisational rules of communicative action in stages, each of which is normatively more mature than the preceding one. The practical institutionalisation of these rules for the purpose of social integration is what first structurally permits an application of technically and strategically more highly developed knowledge. The explanation of social evolution in terms of developmental logic thus adduces system-threatening problems, which in the case of a particular society are located in the historically contingent conditions in which the society is set, in order to identify the moral learning process, which must pass through distinct stages, and which, along with the reorganisation of social integration, also permits the overcoming of the threat to the system and thereby the evolutionary further development of the technical–strategic system of action:

> In explaining the transition from one social formation to the other we must explain the institutional core of the new organizational principle – e.g., a differentiated state system in the transition to archaic high cultures, and a differentiated economic system (with a complementary state) in the transition to the (at first capitalist) modern era. With such explanations (a) we go back to system-problems which constitute evolutionary challenges because they put excessive demands on the steering capacity of the old forms of society, and (b) we return to the evolutionary learning process that produces a new principle of organization. Social evolution occurs in two stages insofar as it takes place both in the learning and adaptation processes on the *respectively given* learning level (until its structural possibilities are exhausted), *and* in those improbable evolutionary leaps that lead to *new* learning levels. A society can learn in a constructivistic sense by accepting the evolutionary challenges before which the available steering capacity fails and by meeting them through the full use and *institutionalisation* of the overflowing individual potentials (already collectively accessible in world views). Here the first step is the establishment of a new form of social integration (via family, forms of state organization, universalistic exchange and legal traffic with corresponding collective identities, such as tribe, empire, nation, etc.). Only this new form of social integration in which the new learning level that is to be explained according to a logic of development is expressed, makes possible a further increase of system complexity, for example, the social use of productive forces, the formation of new forms of society, new media, etc. (Habermas, 1979b, pp. 31f.)

A theory of social evolution that makes use of this pattern of explanation has, however, completely detached itself from the real historical process which it is supposed to help structure from the point of view of social progress. The explanation of socio-cultural evolution by developmental logic must abstract from the determinate complex of events and from the unique experiences within whose historical framework social groups act historically with momentous consequences; it must do so in order to be at all able to analyse the evolutionary process in which general learning successes, that is, learning successes which are by their essential character specific to the human species, become generally accepted and effective. Historical materialism in the form of Habermas's evolutionary theory must penetrate historical happenings in order always to identify only the formal levels of consciousness, which, as realised stages of anthropologically fixed structures of action, form the cognitive infrastructure of social systems; it must therefore ignore the processes of interaction that are guided by what has been learned from experience and the collective processes of interpretation by means of which and through which all conditions pre-given by the system first become at all relevant for human action and thereby formative of historical situations. On the methodological level, Habermas has transformed this criticism into a peculiarity of all evolutionary theories founded upon developmental logic, without, however, entirely taking into account the consequences of this step for the theoretical status of historical materialism:

> Let us assume that instead of rational history of individual technical or scientific innovations, the discovery of bronze metallurgy, the discovery of blood circulation, or the origin of the theory of relativity, the rational history, of technology or of modern science, is to be told. Such a 'history' could no longer be 'told', in the strict sense, for the rational model that would have to be discovered for technology and modern science could no longer be arranged as a rational reconstruction of *special* tasks and *particular* learning processes.
>
> Rational models of this kind would not reconstruct *just any* competence, but one of universal scope – generic competencies as claims to validity of technology or science are not epoch-dependent and culture-specific, but universally binding. (Habermas, 1979b, pp. 17f.)

In order to maintain the claim that the theory of socio-cultural evolution comprehends and accounts for the development of the structures, which are referred to each other, of communicative and instrumental action, Habermas rigorously separates from each other narrative historiography and reconstructive developmental logic. This separation, however, has consequences that considerably weaken the explanatory power of historical materialism. For example, in the historical research that comes to the assistance of Habermas's evolutionary theory in order to elucidate the historically contingent conditions in which an exemplary historical case of social evolution is situated, the historical material itself is seen from the perspective of the determinations of reconstructive developmental logic. Thus, the historical process, in its experiential breadth and its evenimential density, is examined with a view solely to finding the historical evidence that scientifically substantiates the hypothesis of developmental logic regarding the sequence of stages of communicative and instrumental rationalisation. A possible consequence of this approach is that the researcher loses sight of historically innovative action that expresses itself in social movements without responding directly or intentionally to a problem threatening the social system. This criticism can be illustrated by means of an ambiguity of the concept of learning, which is a key concept of Habermas's evolutionary theory. On the one hand, evolutionary learning processes in which advances in technical and moral understanding are obtained socially and passed on culturally constitute, on the socio-cultural level, the mechanism that succeeded the process of genetic mutation of natural, subhuman evolution (see Habermas, 1976b, pp. 186ff.). According to Habermas, such instrumental and moral learning processes occur on the level of the whole society following the same pattern in which the individual subject in the individual learning process learns from the problems for action which are of central importance for socialisation. Habermas therefore attempts to project the structure of the ontogenetic learning process on to the process of evolutionary learning:

> I shall assume two series of initial conditions for evolutionary learning processes of society: on the one hand, unresolved system problems that represent challenges; on the other, new levels of learning that have already been achieved in world views and are latently available but not yet incorporated into action systems and thus remain institutionally inoperative. (Habermas, 1979, pp. 121f.)

However, with regard to moral and practical progress, the actual historical bearers of such evolutionary learning processes are often social movements, in which consciousness is attained of orientations of action that are socially superior and constitute a normative advance. Therefore, at all the points which he wants to use to document historically the process of moral learning, Habermas must have recourse to a social phenomenon that is hardly compatible with evolutionary classifications.

For social movements, the empirical bearers of advances in moral and practical understanding, do not 'learn' in reaction to system-threatening dangers, but in the collective experiencing of, and the co-operative opposition to, injustice arising out of the nature of the social system (cf. Moore, 1978). Consciousness of social repression and social injustice is not the same as the perception of unsolved problems in the social system. Consequently, in Habermas's theory of socio-cultural evolution the key concept of 'social learning' must necessarily contain an unresolved ambiguity that makes it possible to encompass the process of systemic learning and socially revolutionary learning processes within a single concept, although the two phenomena in question are very different from each other.

In this problem a danger manifests itself that is characteristic of the evolutionary version of historical materialism as a whole. Inasmuch as they must be aimed exclusively at identifying and describing the universal rules informing social action, the categories of this theory can no longer be translated systematically into a framework of historiographical categories that would be open enough to explain the genesis and collective development of socially critical, system-bursting orientations of action which are tied to everyday plexuses of experience. Thus the actual history of social movements becomes completely insignificant in comparison with the logical sequence in which systems of norms, each of which is based on the preceding one, have evolutionarily achieved general recognition and acceptance. Thereby the categories and concepts employed by the theory of socio-cultural evolution have become so remote from the experiential plexus of the real historical happening that they can hardly be translated back into the action perspectives of collective actors. If it were conceived as an evolutionary theory in this fashion, historical materialism would have relinquished every possibility of providing explanatory interpretations of history that intervene instructively in a present-day situation of social confrontations. Because the explanatory evolutionary models are constructed without any possibility of linking them back hermeneutically to the unique experiential situation of subjects acting in the present, they cannot be introduced into historical praxis for the purpose of supplying practical orientation for the acting subjects. If that is the case, however, then the evolutionary theory that had conceived of itself as a logic of development would have pretended to the status of a foundational science, instead of understanding itself as a step of anthropological reflection in the course of substantive research by the social and cultural sciences.

It is true that the position occupied by the evolutionary model in the totality of Habermas's theory of society has changed again in his subsequent writings. Through further elaboration of a universal pragmatics, which serves to elucidate systematically the linguistic infrastructure of communicative action (Habermas, 1976a), and through intensified study of systems theory, for the purpose of investigating the tendencies of domains of action organised according to purposive rationality to become autonomous, Habermas has striven to strengthen and deepen the basis of his theory of society with its structural duality. Although his theoretical efforts reach into the most diverse areas of knowledge, they are nevertheless all aimed at the same goal of providing, by means of the theory of communication, the foundation of a critical theory of society. With their aid, Habermas intends to demonstrate that the rationality of communicative action is such a fundamental condition of social development that the tendencies towards instrumental reification can be criticised as one-sided forms of social rationalisation, that is, as forms the orientation of which is solely purposively rational. In *The Theory of Communicative Action*, the two volumes of which were published in German in 1981, this programme assumes for the first time a systematic shape. The results of Habermas's diverse researches are combined here into a single theory, in which the rationality of communicative action is reconstructed within the framework of a speech-act theory, elaborated into the foundation of a theory of society in the course of an examination of the history of sociological theories from Weber to Parsons, and finally made into the point of reference of a critical analysis of the present historical period.

Within this theory of society, the theory of socio-cultural evolution has been left only with the function of serving as a kind of secondary theoretical affirmation of the processes of the evolution of consciousness that have made possible a real separation of communicatively integrated and systemically organised domains of action, of the life world and the social system. However, that evolutionary theory has, as such, retained all the difficulties contained in it from the very start.

SUGGESTED READING

Introduction

The reader who wants to reflect on the status of anthropology in relation to the social sciences can begin by comparing the positions presented in the following works: Wolf Lepenies and Helmut Nolte, *Kritik der Anthropologie* (Munich, 1971); Dietmar Kamper, *Geschichte und menschliche Natur: Die Tragweite gegenwärtiger Anthropologie kritik* (Munich, 1973). A recent contribution to this discussion is Gernot Böhme, *Anthropologie in pragmatischer Hinsicht* (Frankfurt, 1985).

A lexicon article published in 1958 continues to serve as an overview of the problems and the questions that anthropology deals with: Jürgen Habermas, 'Philosophische Anthropologie', reprinted in Jürgen Habermas, *Kultur und Kritik* (Frankfurt, 1973), pp. 89–111. A detailed overview, which is somewhat confusing owing to the lack of cross-references, is provided by Hans-Georg Gadamer and Paul Vogler (eds.), *Neue Anthropologie* (7 vols., Stuttgart, 1972–4).

The reader who is looking for an excellent and graphic overview of the more ethnologically than philosophically influenced anthropology of the Anglo-Saxon variety will find it in Marvin Harris, *Culture, Man, and Nature: An Introduction to General Anthropology* (New York, 1971). Of the pertinent French literature, the following works should be mentioned: Edgar Morin, *Le Paradigme perdu: La nature humaine* (Paris, 1973); André Leroi-Gourhan, *Le Geste et la parole* (2 vols., Paris, 1964 and 1965).

Feuerbach and Marx

The writings of Feuerbach that are of chief interest in the present context come from the period 1842–3, in particular 'Principles of the philosophy of the future', written in 1843. The writings in question are collected in Ludwig Feuerbach, *The Fiery Brook: Selected Writings*, trans. with an introduction by Zawar Hanfi (New York, 1972). In addition to 'Principles' (pp. 175–245), this volume contains 'Preliminary theses on the reform of philosophy' (pp. 153–73) and 'The necessity of a reform of philosophy' (pp. 145–52). Knowledge of the area in which Feuerbach's substantive accomplishments chiefly lie can be gained from Ludwig Feuerbach, *The Essence of Christianity*, trans. by M. Evans (G. Eliot) (New York, 1957).

Of the works on Feuerbach, the following can be especially recommended: on the rehabilitation of sensualism, Alfred Schmidt, *Emanzipatorische Sinnlichkeit: Ludwig Feuerbachs anthropologischer Materialismus* (Munich, 1973); on the rehabilitation of 'altruism', i.e., of Feuerbach's theoretical framework of intersubjectivity: Karl Löwith, *Das Individuum in der Rolle des Mitmenschen* (Munich, 1928) (reprinted: Darmstadt, 1962); Karl Löwith, 'Ludwig Feuerbach und der Ausgang der klassischen deutschen Philosophie', *Logos*, 17(1928), 323–47.

A thoroughgoing study of the early Feuerbach (prior to 1842) is given in Carlo Ascheri, *Feuerbachs Bruch mit der Spekulation* (Frankfurt, 1969). An examination of the relationship between Feuerbach and Marx that is outstanding from the philological viewpoint is Werner Schuffenhauer, *Feuerbach und der junge Marx: Zur Entstehungsgeschichte der marxistischen Weltanschauung* (Berlin [GDR], 1972). An excellent comprehensive interpretation of Feuerbach, including the little-known late work, is offered by Marx Wartofsky, *Feuerbach* (Cambridge, Mass., 1977).

Marx used Feuerbach's anthropological materialism as the foil of his critique of the Hegelian dialectic in *The Economic and Philosophical Manuscripts*, written in 1844 (Marx and Engels, *Collected Works*, vol. 3, pp. 229–346, esp. pp. 326ff.); he presents in a concentrated manner his critique of Feuerbach in his 'Theses on Feuerbach' (Marx and Engels, *Collected Works*, vol. 5, pp. 3ff.). This critique is given a broad development in *The German Ideology: Critique of Modern German Philosophy*, written jointly by Marx and Engels in 1845–6 (*Collected Works*, vol. 5, pp. 19ff.; see esp. chapter 1; also important for the present discussion are the manuscripts of Marx and Engels printed in the appendix to the aforementioned work). In 1886 Friedrich Engels once again wrote a summary of the meaning and importance of Feuerbach's philosophy: 'Ludwig Feuerbach and the end of classical German philosophy', in Karl Marx and Friedrich Engels, *Selected Works in One Volume* (New York, 1968), pp. 596ff.

An important and still very noteworthy interpretation of Marx's relation to Feuerbach and the Left Hegelians is given in Karl Löwith's book *From Hegel to Nietzsche* (New York, 1984). Also important for our enquiry is Alfred Schmidt, *The Concept of Nature in Marx* (London, 1971). The special methodological status of Marx's critique of political economy in relation to his early writings is demonstrated above all in the following interpretations: Helmut Reichelt, *Zur logischen Struktur des Kapitalbegriffs bei Karl Marx* (Frankfurt, 1970); Hans-Jürgen Krahl, 'Zur Wesenslogik der Marxschen Warenanalyse', in Hans-Jürgen Krahl, *Konstitution und Klassenkampf* (Frankfurt, 1971), pp. 31ff. Another of the very early works in which the theoretical peculiarity of *Capital* was investigated is that of the Czech philosopher Jindřich Zelený, *Die Wissenschaftslogik bei Marx und 'Das Kapital'* (Frankfurt, 1968)'

The interpretations of Marx have become practically innumerable. Of these, the works that consider at some length and in some detail the anthropological dimension of Marx's theory are: Helmut Dahmer and Helmut Fleischer, 'Karl Marx', in Dirk Käsler (ed.), *Klassiker des soziologischen Denkens*, vol. 1 (Munich, 1976), pp. 62ff. (see also the bibliography of secondary literature, pp. 368ff.); Lawrence Krader, *Ethnologie und Anthropologie bei Marx* (Munich, 1973); also useful are the short studies by Erhard Lucas: 'Die Rezeption Lewis H. Morgans durch Marx und Engels', *Saeculum*, 15(1964), 153ff.; Erhard Lucas, 'Marx' Studien zur Frühgeschichte und Ethnologie 1880–1882: Nach unveröffentlichten Exzerpten', *ibid.*, pp. 326ff.

The Marxist discussion of anthropology

With respect to the interpretation of Feuerbach and the critique of anthropology, Althusser's most important work is certainly Louis Althusser, *For Marx* (New York, 1969). The article entitled 'Feuerbach's "philosophical manifestoes"' gives an examination and critique of Feuerbach's anthropological materialism. Also of interest in connection with Althusser's interpretation of Marx's early writings is the volume of essays *Marxismus und Ideologie* (Berlin, 1973). Althusser's interpretation of Marx's theory is systematically elaborated in Louis Althusser and Etienne Balibar, *Reading 'Capital'* (London, 1970). A text that is very important for the critique of the 'humanistic' problematic of the young Marx, but that was omitted from the English edition of *Reading 'Capital'*, has been published separately: Jacques Rancière, *Der Begriff der Kritik und die Kritik der politischen Ökonomie* (Berlin, 1972). (Cf. the French edition of Althusser and Balibar.)

A first overview of the international discussion of Althusser is given by the special issue of the journal *dialectiques* 15/16 (Paris, 1976) entitled 'Lutte de classe et théorie en Europe de l'Ouest', which is about his work and thought. In France, the proponents of structural Marxism have themselves criticised their original theory; cf. Louis Althusser, *Essays in Self-Criticism* (Atlantic Highlands, NJ, 1976). A comprehensive interpretation has been offered by Saül Karsz, *Theorie und Politik: Louis Althusser* (Frankfurt and Vienna, 1976). After entering extensively into the British discussion of Marxism (cf., e.g., the journals *New Left Review* and *Economy and Society*), the structuralist interpretation of Marxism has been globally criticised by Edward P. Thompson, *The Poverty of Theory and Other Essays* (London, 1978), pp. 193ff. A good overview of the developments in French Marxism is provided by Mark Poster, *Existential Marxism in Postwar France: From Sartre to Althusser* (Princeton, 1985). Martin Jay, *Marxism and Totality: The Adventures of a Concept from Lukàcs to Habermas* (Cambridge, 1984) is also a succinct and precise study. Of the contributions to the German discussion should be mentioned: Axel Honneth, 'Geschichte und Interaktionsverhältnisse: Zur strukturalistischen Deutung des Historischen Materialismus', in Urs Jaeggi and Axel Honneth (eds.), *Theorien des Historischen*

Materialismus (Frankfurt, 1977), pp. 405ff. A detailed critique of structuralist Marxism, which also takes into consideration positions of critical theory, is Jóhann P. Arnason, *Zwischen Natur und Gesellschaft: Studien zu einer kritischen Theorie des Subjekts* (Frankfurt and Cologne, 1976).

The international discussion of Sève's ideas was marked by a broad range of diversity. We give here only a small selection from the contributions to the French discussion of Sève that are especially worth reading. It must be noted that Sève deals with some of the opinions and criticisms of his theory in the afterword to the third French edition of his book.

Tony Andreani, 'Marxisme et anthropologie', *L'homme et la société*, 15(1970), 25–75; Jean-François Le Ny, 'Une autre science psychologique?', *La Pensée*, 147(1969), 47–60; Dimitri Voutsinas, a review of Sève's book in *Bulletin de Psychologie*, 24(1970–1), 836–56; and lastly the article by Adam Schaff, 'Au sujet de la traduction française de la VIᵉ thèse de Marx sur Feuerbach', *L'homme et la société*, 19(1971), 157–67, which Sève rebutted in detail.

Preliminary remarks on the German tradition of 'philosophical anthropology'

Max Scheler's essay 'Zur Idee des Menschen', first published in 1914, is generally considered to be the first clear sign of the emerging intellectual movement 'Philosophical Anthropology'. It was reprinted in Max Scheler, *Vom Umsturz der Werte: Gesammelte Werke 3* (Bern, 1955), pp. 171–96. The true manifesto of this school, however, is Max Scheler, *Man's Place in Nature*, trans. and with an introduction by Hans Meyerhoff (New York, 1981; first published 1928). The work by Martin Heidegger to which the remarks in our discussion refer is *Being and Time* (New York, 1962), which first appeared as a special issue of *Jahrbuch für Philosophie und phänomenologische Forschung*, 8(1927). Contemporary interpretations of this current of thought and of its relationship to Heidegger are: (the most important) Joachim Ritter, *Über den Sinn und die Grenze der Lehre vom Menschen* (1933), reprinted in: Joachim Ritter, *Subjektivität* (Frankfurt, 1974), pp. 36–61; Friedrich Seifert, 'Zum Verständnis der anthropologischen Wende in der Philosophie', *Blätter für Deutsche Philosophie*, 8(1934–5), 393–410; Theodor Haering, 'Die philosophische Bedeutung der Anthropologie', *Blätter für Deutsche Philosophie*, 3(1929–30), 1–32.

A lucid interpretation of the relationship between Heidegger and Philosophical Anthropology is given by Helmut Fahrenbach, 'Heidegger und das Problem einer "philosophischen" Anthropologie', in Vittorio Klostermann (ed.), *Durchblicke: Martin Heidegger zum 80. Geburtstag* (Frankfurt, 1970), pp. 97–131. Based in large part upon the foregoing interpretation is Helmuth Plessner, 'Der Aussagewert einer philosophischen Anthropologie', in Helmuth Plessner, *Die Frage nach der Conditio Humana: Aufsätze zur philosophischen Anthropologie* (Frankfurt, 1976), pp. 180–97.

Since the theories of Gehlen and Plessner are treated at length in the present study, only a few of the other representatives of philosophical anthropology will be mentioned here: Erich Rothacker, *Probleme der Kulturanthropologie* (Bonn, 1948); Erich Rothacker, *Philosophische Anthropologie* (Bonn, 1966); Victor von Weizsäcker, *Der Gestaltkreis: Theorie der Einheit von Wahrnehmen und Bewegen* (Stuttgart, 1973; first published Leipzig, 1940. Our discussion does not do justice to the importance of this work); and Ludwig Klages, *Der Geist als Widersacher der Seele* (Leipzig, 1929).

Ernst Cassirer, *An Essay on Man: An Introduction to a Philosophy of Human Culture* (New Haven, Conn. and London, 1944) was written during the author's emigration and under the strong influence of American thought and empirical studies, and was first published in English.

Of high quality but purely philosophical is Paul Ludwig Landsberg, *Einführung in die philosophische Anthropologie*, 2nd edn (Frankfurt, 1960; first published 1934).

Very weak is Werner Sombart, *Vom Menschen: Versuch einer geistwissenschaftlichen Anthropologie* (Berlin, 1938).

Arnold Gehlen

The classical work by Gehlen, the reading of which in its entirety cannot be replaced by any summaries of it, is Arnold Gehlen, *Der Mensch: Seine Natur und seine Stellung in der Welt* (Frankfurt, 1971; first published 1940). Also important is this author's principal work on cultural anthropology: *Urmensch und Spätkultur* (Frankfurt, 1964; first published 1956). A collection of introductory texts, written in an easily understandable manner, is offered by Arnold Gehlen, *Anthropologische Forschung* (Reinbek, 1968; first published 1961). Gehlen gives an autobiographical self-presentation in 'Ein anthropologisches Modell', *The Human Context*, 1 (1968), 1–10. His early writings are partly collected in *Die Theorie der Willensfreiheit und frühe philosophische Schriften* (Neuwied, 1965). Very well suited as an introduction to Gehlen's thought is also the collection of essays *Studien zur Anthropologie und Soziologie* (Neuwied, 1963) (esp. 'Zur Systematik der Anthropologie', pp. 11–63). For the present discussion, the writings in which Gehlen gives a critique of contemporary culture and an evaluative analysis of the present historical period are of less interest than the others. A complete edition of his works is currently being published by Klostermann-Verlag.

A very important interpretation of the early Gehlen and thus a crucial contribution to the understanding of anthropology has been presented by Dietrich Böhler, 'Arnold Gehlen: Die Handlung', in Josef Speck (ed.), *Grundprobleme der großen Philosophen: Philosophie der Gegenwart II* (Göttingen, 1973), pp. 230–80; with respect to the enquiry from the standpoint of the theory of intersubjectivity from which it sets out, this study was preceded by Karl-Otto Apel, *Arnold Gehlens 'Philosophie der Institutionen' und die Meta-Institution der Sprache*, reprinted in Karl-Otto Apel, *Transformation der Philosophie*, vol. 1 (Frankfurt, 1973), pp. 197–221. A sharp but accurate critique of Gehlen's last work of some length, 'Moral und Hypermoral', which has a similar point of departure, was written by Jürgen Habermas, 'Arnold Gehlen: Imitation of substantiality', in his *Philosophical–Political Profiles* (Cambridge, Mass., 1983), pp. 111–28.

In addition to the largely affirmative study of Gehlen to be found in Friedrich Jonas, *Die Institutionenlehre Arnold Gehlens* (Tübingen, 1966), there are other critical accounts of the whole of Gehlen's work that consider it from a number of different perspectives. Substantial and clear is Johannes Weiß, *Weltverlust und Subjektivität: Zur Kritik der Institutionenlehre Arnold Gehlens* (Freiburg, 1971). M. de Mey, 'Anthropologie philosophique et psychologie génétique: Une confrontation de l'anthropologie philosophique d'Arnold Gehlen avec la psychologie génétique de Jean Piaget', *Studia philosophica Gandensia*, 2(1964), 41–67, draws a parallel with Piaget's psychology that is instructive with regard to the substantive content of Gehlen's anthropology.

George Herbert Mead

Of Mead's writings, the one that is best known by far is *Mind, Self, and Society* (Chicago, 1934). However, this book represents only a small part of Mead's work, and moreover does so in a form bearing all the defects arising from its origin in posthumously published students' transcripts of Mead's lectures. The best way, therefore, to reach an understanding of Mead's thought is by means of the articles that he himself prepared for publication in many different journals and newspapers. See the volume of Mead's articles, George Herbert Mead, *Selected Writings*, edited by Andrew Reck (Indianapolis, 1964).

The most reliable American monograph on Mead's work is David L. Miller, *G. H. Mead: Self, Language, and the World* (Austin, Texas, 1973). The study of Mead's thought is advanced further in the articles by Gary Allan Cook, 'The development of G. H. Mead's social psychology', *Transactions of the Ch. S. Peirce Society*, 8(1972), 167–86; Gary Allan Cook, 'G. H. Mead's alleged behaviorism', *Journal of the History of the Behavioral Sciences*, 13(1977), 307–16. Misleading but frequently cited is Maurice Natanson, *The Social Dynamics of G. H. Mead* (Washington, 1956).

From the German literature on Mead, Konrad Raiser, *Identität und Sozialität: G. H. Meads Theorie der Interaktion und ihre Bedeutung für die theologische Anthropologie* (Munich, 1971) is usable, despite its mainly theological frame of reference. One of the authors of the present work has written a comprehensive reinterpretation of Mead's work: Hans Joas, *G. H. Mead: A Contemporary Re-Examination of his Thought* (Cambridge, England, 1985). Joas's book contains the most comprehensive bibliography of Mead's writings to date, as well as an extensive bibliography of secondary literature on Mead.

A collection of important new contributions to the discussion of Mead's work has been made available in Hans Joas (ed.), *Das Problem der Intersubjektivität* (Frankfurt, 1985).

Helmuth Plessner

Plessner's oeuvre is now easily accessible in a complete edition of his writings published by the Suhrkamp-Verlag. Helmuth Plessner himself composed an overview of his intellectual development, which can be found in Ludwig J. Pongratz (ed.), *Philosophie in Selbstdarstellungen*, vol. 1 (Hamburg, 1975), pp. 264ff. The first work by Plessner in which the intention of elaborating a biologically grounded hermeneutics of the human senses is clearly discernible is certainly *Die Einheit der Sinne: Grundlinien einer Aesthesiologie des Geistes* (Bonn, 1923; 2nd edn, 1965); the ideas informing this study are developed further in the article written jointly by Plessner and Frederik J. J. Buytendijk: 'Die Deutung des mimischen Ausdrucks', *Philosophischer Anzeiger*, 1(1925), 72ff. The book that appeared five years later, *Die Stufen des Organischen und der Mensch* (Berlin, 1928; 3rd edn, 1975), develops the hierarchical biological schema that thenceforth formed the horizon, in the sense of a philosophy of nature, of Plessner's writings. The investigation *Laughing and Weeping: A Study of the Limits of Human Behavior* (Evanston, Ill., 1970), first published in Switzerland in 1941, and which is the prime example of Plessner's anthropological hermeneutics, appeared, in the original German version, together with the studies *Das Lächeln* and *Anthropologie der Sinne*, in the volume entitled *Philosophische Anthropologie* (Frankfurt, 1970). Additional short anthropological studies have been collected in the volume of essays *Die Frage nach der Conditio Humana* (Frankfurt, 1976). The project of a political anthropology occupied Plessner's thoughts as early as 1924, as shown by *Grenzen der Gemeinschaft* (Bonn, 1972), which is intended to be an anthropologically grounded critical evaluation of the contemporary era; in a certain sense, this political interest is given further expression in the lecture published in 1935, in which Plessner, admittedly, argues more in terms of intellectual history: *Die verspätete Nation* (republished: Frankfurt, 1974) (original title: *Das Schicksal deutschen Geistes im Ausgang seiner bürgerlichen Epoche*, Zürich, 1935). Also useful in this regard are the two volumes in which Plessner's political–sociological essays are collected: *Diesseits der Utopie* (Frankfurt, 1974) and *Zwischen Philosophie und Gesellschaft* (Frankfurt, 1979).

Two studies of Plessner's work are Günther Dux, 'Helmuth Plessners philosophische Anthropologie im Prospekt: Ein Nachwort', in Helmuth Plessner, *Philosophische Anthropologie* (Frankfurt, 1970), pp. 253ff and Hermann Asemissen, *Die exzentrische Position des Menschen*, in Joseph Speck (ed.), *Grundprobleme der großen Philosophen: Philosophie der Gregenwart II* (Göttingen, 1973), pp. 146ff. Problem-oriented, critical secondary literature on Plessner's anthropology is otherwise extremely rare.

Because of its excellence, Jürgen Habermas's review of Plessner's lecture, *Die verspätete Nation*, must be singled out for special mention; it is contained in the German edition of his *Philosophisch-politische Profile* (Frankfurt, 1971), pp. 222ff.

Agnes Heller

To date, Agnes Heller has published three studies intended to delineate the framework of a projected five-volume social anthropology: *The Theory of Need in Marx* (London, 1976; German edn, 1976); *Instinkt, Aggression, Charakter* (Berlin, 1977; the larger part of this work has been published in English as *On Instincts*, Assen, the Netherlands, 1979); and *A Theory of Feelings* (Assen, the Netherlands, 1979; German edn, 1980). The purpose of Heller's social anthropology can be adequately understood only when her intermediate position between a more sociological theory of everyday life and a Marxist ethics is taken into account; on her theory of everyday life, see Agnes Heller, *Everyday Life* (London, 1984; German edn, 1978). On the grounding of a Marxist ethics, see Agnes Heller, 'Jenseits der Pflicht: Das Paradigmatische der Ethik der deutschen Klassik im Oeuvre von Georg Lukács', *Revue internationale de philosophie*, 27(1973), 439ff.; *Hypothese über eine marxistische Theorie der Werte* (Frankfurt, 1972) (abridged version of the study published under the title 'Towards a Marxist theory of value', *Kinesis*, 5(1972); and, most recently, *Beyond Justice* (Oxford, 1987).

   The most important discussion of the 'Budapest School' has taken place in Italy. There the journal *aut aut* devoted a double issue (nos. 157–8, 1977) exclusively to the late works of Lukács and the Budapest School; especially noteworthy among the articles in this double issue is Amadeo Vigorelli, 'Critica del socialismo burocratico e teoria della vita quotidiana nella scuola di Budapest', *ibid.*, pp 74ff. In the subsequent double issue, Heller dealt at length with the Italians' comments on, and criticisms of, her writings; her response is entitled 'Un prologo piu che un epilogo: Replica sulla teoria dei bisogni e della vita quotidiana', *ibid.*, pp. 2ff. Regarding the reception in Italy of Heller's work, see also Pier Aldo Rovatti's foreword to the Italian edition (Milan, 1974) in Agnes Heller, *Theorie der Bedürfnisse bei Marx* (Berlin, 1976), pp. 7ff. Other contributions to the discussion of Heller's theory of need are to be found in the American journal *Telos*; see, for example, Jean Cohen's review of 'The theory of need in Marx', *Telos*, 33(1977), 170ff.; Laura Boella, 'Radicalism and needs in Heller', *Telos*, 37(1978), 112ff. An assessment of the significance and implications of Heller's theory of everyday life is undertaken in Hans Joas's foreword to the German edition of Agnes Heller, *Everyday Life* (Frankfurt, 1978), pp. 7ff.

Critical Psychology

The principal works of 'Critical Psychology' are: Klaus Holzkamp, *Sinnliche Erkenntnis: Historischer Ursprung und gesellschaftliche Funktion der Wahrnehmung* (Frankfurt, 1973); Ute Holzkamp-Osterkamp, *Grundlagen der psychologischen Motivationsforschung* (2 vols., Frankfurt, 1975–6); Klaus Holzkamp, *Grundle-*

gung der Psychologie (Frankfurt, 1983); Volker Schurig, *Die Entstehung des Bewußtseins* (Frankfurt, 1976).

Alternative approaches to the establishment of an anthropological basis of the psychology of perception are offered by the work of Jean Piaget, but especially by the writings of Maurice Merleau-Ponty; see the latter's *Phenomenology of Perception* (New York, 1962) and *The Structure of Behavior* (Boston, 1963). A volume of essays by Merleau-Ponty has been published by John O'Neill: *Phenomenology, Language and Society* (London, 1974). An excellent account of this philosopher's work is given in Bernhard Waldenfels, *Phänomenologie in Frankreich* (Frankfurt, 1983). To be recommended is the book by Samuel B. Mallin, *Merleau-Ponty's Philosophy* (New Haven, Conn. and London, 1979).

The question is important whether 'Critical Psychology' and the Soviet psychology of the Leontiev school represent a continuation of the legacy of Lev Vygotsky. See the latter's *Thought and Language* (Cambridge, Mass., 1962) and *Mind in Society* (Cambridge, Mass., 1978). An excellent study of Vygotsky is the book by James V. Wertsch, *Vygotsky and the Social Formation of Mind* (Cambridge, Mass., 1985).

Historical anthropology

In addition to Norbert Elias's studies, and certainly also Michel Foucault's investigations of the history of knowledge, the following studies of the history of socialisation and the family are important: Philippe Ariès, *Centuries of Childhood* (London, 1962); Edward Shorter, *The Making of the Modern Family* (New York, 1975); Lloyd DeMause, *The History of Childhood* (New York, 1974); and Jean-Louis Flandrin, *Families of Former Times* (Cambridge, Mass., 1979).

Norbert Elias

Elias's principal work, on which his fame is based, is *The Civilizing Process* (2 vols., New York, 1978 and 1982) (first published: Basel, 1939). Also of interest are his *The Court Society* (New York, 1983) and *Über die Zeit* (Frankfurt, 1981).

The secondary literature on Elias is often insistently venerative. Regarding the formation of an Elias school, see Peter Gleichmann *et al.*, *Materialien zu Norbert Elias' Zivilisationstheorie* (Frankfurt, 1979). (This volume contains the highly informative and interesting contribution by Karl-Siegbert Rehberg, pp. 101–69.) A second volume on Elias, prepared by the same editors, was published in 1984: *Macht und Zivilisation* (Frankfurt, 1984). See also the Festschrift *Human Figurations: Essays for Norbert Elias* (Amsterdam, 1977).

The most interesting critiques of Elias's work have been made by Wehowsky and Buck-Morss: Andreas Wehowsky, *Studie zu Norbert Elias: Über den Prozeß der Zivilisation*, master's dissertation in sociology, Free University of Berlin, 1976; Andreas Wehowsky, 'Uns beweglicher machen als wir sind: Überlegungen zu Norbert Elias', *Ästhetik und Kommunikation*, 30(1977), 8–18; Susan

Buck-Morss, a review of Elias's work in *Telos*, 37(1978), 181–98.

Michel Foucault

Michel Foucault's writings are easily accessible in English. All of his larger works have been translated; in addition, collections of his articles and essays are available. In listing the titles of his books here, we follow the division of the development of Foucault's theories that we proposed in our discussion, and that we owe to the excellent article by Hinrich Fink-Eitel, 'Foucaults Analytik der Macht', in Friedrich Kittler (ed.), *Die Austreibung des Geistes aus den Geisteswissenschaften* (Paderborn, 1980), pp. 38ff.

Michel Foucault, I. *Madness and Civilization: A History of Insanity in the Age of Reason* (New York, 1965); *The Order of Things: An Archaeology of the Human Sciences* (New York, 1970); *Birth of the Clinic: An Archaeology of Medical Perception* (New York, 1973); II. *The Archaeology of Knowledge* (New York, 1972); 'The discourse on language', in *The Archaeology of Knowledge*; III. *Discipline and Punish: The Birth of the Prison* (New York, 1977); *The History of Sexuality*, vol. 1, *An Introduction* (New York, 1978); vol. 2, *The Use of Pleasure* (New York, 1985); vol. 3, *The Care of the Self* (New York, 1987). In addition, collections of essays by Foucault and interviews with him have been published. Some of these are: Michel Foucault, *Power, Truth, Strategy*, edited by Meaghan Morris and Paul Patton (Sydney, Australia, 1979); *Power/Knowledge: Selected Interviews and Other Writings 1972–1977*, edited, with an afterword, by Colin Gordon (New York, 1980); *Language, Counter-Memory, Practice: Selected Essays and Interviews*, edited by Donald F. Bouchard and translated by Sherry Simon (New York, 1980). These edited volumes contain important supplementary material on the theory of power that Foucault was endeavouring to found in his last historical studies.

Understanding of the socio-philosophical framework in which Foucault situated his studies presupposes familiarity with French structuralism. An introduction to this subject that is still very instructive and worth reading is given by François Wahl (ed.), *Einführung in den Strukturalismus* (Frankfurt, 1973). See especially Wahl's article, which, like the others, was published separately in its French version, *Philosophie: La philosophie entre l'avant et l'après du structuralisme* (Paris, 1973). See also Gilles Deleuze, 'Woran erkennt man den Strukturalismus?', in François Châtelet (ed.), *Geschichte der Philosophie*, vol. 8 (Frankfurt, Berlin and Vienna, 1975), pp. 169ff.; John Sturrock (ed.), *Structuralism and Since: From Lévi-Strauss to Derrida* (Oxford, 1979). Useful studies showing the philosophical and linguistic presuppositions of French structuralism have been written by Manfred Frank; see, for example, his *Das Sagbare und das Unsagbare* (Frankfurt, 1980).

Foucault's writings have been and continue to be the subject of intense international discussion. A bibliography that undertakes to record the discussion of the first two phases of the development of Foucault's theory has been prepared by F. H. Lapointe und W. Seitter: 'Bibliographie der Schriften über Michel Foucault', *Philosophisches Jahrbuch*, 81(1974), 202ff. An excellent comprehensive overview of Foucault's theory is given in Hubert L. Dreyfus and Paul Rabinow, *Michel Foucault, Beyond Structuralism and Hermeneutics*, 2nd edn (Chicago, 1983). A collection of important articles on Foucault's work can be found in David Couzens Hoy (ed.), *Foucault: A Critical Reader* (Oxford, 1986). Of the growing number of publications on Foucault, the following books are also of interest: Charles C. Lemert and Garth Gillan, *Michel Foucault, Social Theory and Transgression* (New York, 1982); Mark Poster, *Foucault, Marxism and History* (Oxford, 1984); Barry Smart, *Foucault, Marxism and Critique* (London, 1983). An interesting account of Foucault's theory, which remains, however, very much within the framework of that theory, is offered in the book written by Foucault's friend: Gilles Deleuze, *Foucault* (Paris, 1986). Foucault's oeuvre is critically discussed in Axel Honneth, *Kritik der Macht* (Frankfurt, 1985), and in Jürgen Habermas, *The Philosophical Discourse of Modernity* (Cambridge, Mass., 1987).

Jürgen Habermas

The development and the purpose of Habermas's theory of socio-cultural evolution can be best understood by tracing back the path that Habermas followed in his advance from his early attempt to elaborate a Marxist 'philosophy of history with practical intent' to the theoretical project that he is currently engaged in. Therefore, only those works by Habermas will be named here, in the order of their succession, that document this course of theoretical development. The original theoretical model is presented principally in the essays contained in the volume *Theorie und Praxis* (Frankfurt, 1971; the fourth, expanded edition); most of the essays contained in the foregoing volume are available in English in *Theory and Practice* (Boston, 1973). The articles on epistemology contributed by Habermas to the 'positivism controversy' develop the arguments that have compelled him to undertake an expansion of the fundamental concepts of historical materialism; they have been published in a volume containing the study 'Zur Logik der Sozialwissenschaften', intended as a review of the literature on the logic of the social sciences; Jürgen Habermas, *Zur Logik der Sozialwissenschaften* (Frankfurt, 1970). Relevant to the documentation of Habermas's theoretical development are the two articles 'Analytische Wissenschaftstheorie und Dialektik', pp. 9ff. and 'Gegen einen positivistisch halbierten Rationalismus', pp. 39ff. In connection with the theory of society, Habermas has developed the distinction between 'labour' and 'interaction', chiefly in the last three essays of *Toward a Rational Society* (Boston, 1970); of these, the essays entitled 'Technology and science as "ideology"' and 'Labor and interaction: Remarks on Hegel's Jena *Philosophy of mind*' are especially important. The latter essay has also been published in English as chapter 4 of *Theory and Practice*. Epistemologically, the distinction between labour and interaction is the central theme of Habermas's extensive investigation *Knowledge and Human Interests* (Boston, 1971). The critical study of social–scientific systems theory that is important for Habermas's construction of his theory of socio-cultural evolution, and that he began already in the Parsons critique contained in *Zur Logik der Sozialwissenschaften*, is given systematic expression in his debate with Niklas Luhmann: Jürgen Habermas and Niklas Luhmann, *Theorie der Gesellschaft oder Sozialtechnologie?* (Frankfurt, 1971); in this regard it is also useful to consult the study by Rainer Döbert, *Systemtheorie und die Entwicklung religiöser Deutungssysteme* (Frankfurt, 1973). Habermas's *Legitimation Crisis* (Boston, 1975) already presents, in rough outline, the basic premises of his theory of socio-cultural evolution, although the focus here is, of course, on the book's main topic. To date, this theory has been presented chiefly in the sketches of investigations and the outlines of the theory gathered together in the volume *Zur Rekonstruktion des Historischen Materialismus* (Frankfurt, 1976). A historical–material example of the mode of argumentation of historical materialism that has been further developed in accordance with Habermas's theory of evolution is provided by the study of Klaus Eder, *Die Entstehung staatlich organisierter Gesellschaften* (Frankfurt, 1976). Habermas has summed up his theoretical endeavours in *Theorie des kommunikativen Handelns* (2 vols., Frankfurt, 1981). Both volumes have been translated into English: *The Theory of Communicative Action* (Boston, 1985 and 1987).

Very good interpretations of the presuppositions and the basic premises of Habermas's theory are given in two studies by Albrecht Wellmer: *Kritische Gesellschaftstheorie und Positivismus* (Frankfurt, 1969), and 'Kommunikation und Emanzipation', in Urs Jaeggi and Axel Honneth (eds.), *Theorien des Historischen Materialismus*, pp. 465ff. A first extensive and comprehensive overview of the development of Habermas's theory is available in the book by Thomas McCarthy, *The Critical Theory of Jürgen Habermas* (Cambridge, Mass., 1979). Important contributions to the discussion of Habermas's thought, accompanied in each case by lengthy responses by Habermas, have been collected in David Held and John Thompson (eds.), *Habermas: Critical Debates* (London, 1982), and Axel Honneth and Hans Joas (eds.), *Kommunikatives Handeln* (Frankfurt, 1986).

BIBLIOGRAPHY

(This bibliography contains only works quoted or cited in the text of this book; further references are to be found in the Suggested reading section.)

Althusser, Louis, 1969 *For Marx* (New York, Pantheon).

1971 *Lenin and Philosophy and Other Essays* (London, New Left Books).

1976 *Essays in Self-Criticism* (Atlantic Highlands, NJ, Humanities Press).

Althusser, Louis, and Etienne Balibar, 1970 *Reading 'Capital'* (London, New Left Books).

Anderson, Perry 1974 *Lineages of the Absolutist State* (London, New Left Books).

Ariès, Philippe, 1962 *Centuries of Childhood* (London, Cape).

Arnason, Jóhann P., 1980 'Marx und Habermas', in Axel Honneth and Urs Jaeggi (eds.), Arbeit, *Handlung, Normativität: Theorien des Historischen Materialismus II* (Frankfurt, Suhrkamp), pp. 137–84.

Baumgartner, Hans Michael, 1972 *Kontinuität und Geschichte* (Frankfurt, Suhrkamp).

Benjamin, Walter, 1974 'Über den Begriff der Geschichte', in *Gesammelte Werke*, vol. 1 (Frankfurt, Suhrkamp), pp. 691–704.

Benthem van den Bergh, G. van, 1977 'Is a Marxist theory of the state possible?', in Peter Gleichmann *et al.* (eds.), *Human Figurations: Essays for Norbert Elias* (Amsterdam, Sociologisch Tijdschrift).

Berki, R. N., 1979 'On the Nature and Origins of Marx's Concept of Labor', *Political Theory*, 7, 35–56.

Berlin, Isaiah, 1980 *Against the Current* (London, Hogarth Press).

Böhler, Dietrich, 1973 'Arnold Gehlen: Die Handlung', in Josef Speck (ed.), *Grundprobleme der großen Philosophen: Philosophie der Gegenwart II* (Göttingen, Vandenhoeck und Rupprecht), pp. 230–80.

Breccia-Boella, Laura, 1974 'Philosophie und Politik in der "Budapester Schule"', in Andras Hegedüs *et al.* (eds.), *Die Neue Linke in Ungarn*, vol. 2 (Berlin, Merve), pp. 5–23ff.

Brede, Karola, 1976 'Interaktion und Trieb', in Klaus Menne *et al.* (eds.), *Sprache, Handlung und Unbewußtes* (Kronberg, Scriptor), pp. 135–78.

Bubner, Rüdiger, 1973 *Dialektik und Wissenschaft* (Frankfurt, Suhrkamp).

Caruso, Paolo, 1974 'Gespräch mit Michel Foucault', in Michel Foucault (ed.), *Von der Subversion des Wissens* (Munich, Hanser), pp. 7–31.

Cassirer, Ernst, 1944 *An Essay on Man: An Introduction to a Philosophy of Human Culture* (London, Oxford University Press).

Cerutti, Furio, 1970 'Hegel, Lukács, Korsch: Zum dialektischen Selbstverständnis des Kritischen Marxismus', in Oskar Negt (ed.), *Aktualität und Folgen der Philosophie Hegels* (Frankfurt, Suhrkamp), pp. 195–210.

Conze, Werner, 1972 'Arbeit', in *Lexikon der politisch-sozialen Begriffe der Neuzeit*, vol. 1 (Stuttgart, Kleff-Cotta), pp. 154–215.

Count, Earl, 1973 *Being and Becoming Human: Essays on the Biogram* (New York, Van Nostrand).

Daraki, Maria, 1986 'Foucault's journey to Greece', *Telos*, 67, 87–110.

DeMause, Lloyd, 1974 *The History of Childhood* (New York, Psychohistory Press).

Derrida, Jacques, 1978 *Writing and Difference* (Chicago, University of Chicago Press).

Döbert, Rainer, 1973 *Systemtheorie und die Entwicklung religiöser Deutungssysteme* (Frankfurt, Suhrkamp).

Eder, Klaus, 1976 *Die Entstehung staatlich organisierter Gesellschaften: Ein Beitrag zu einer Theorie sozialer Evolution* (Frankfurt, Suhrkamp).

Elias, Norbert, 1978 and 1982 *The Civilizing Process*, 2 vols. (New York, vol. 1: Urizen Books; vol. 2: Pantheon).

1983 *The Court Society* (Oxford, Blackwell).

1977 'Zur Grundlegung einer Theorie sozialer Prozesse', *Zeitschrift für Soziologie*, 6, 127–49.

Elias, Norbert and Wolf Lepenies, 1977 *Zwei Reden* (Frankfurt, Suhrkamp).

Engels, Friedrich, 1968 'Ludwig Feuerbach and the end of classical German philosophy', in Karl Marx and Friedrich Engels, *Selected Works in One Volume* (New York, International Publishers), pp. 596ff.

Feuerbach, Ludwig, 1957 *The Essence of Christianity* (New York, Harper & Row 1972).

1972 *The Fiery Brook: Selected Writings* (New York, Verlag).

Fichte, Johann Gottlieb, 1970 *The Science of Rights* (London, Routledge).

Fink–Eitel, Hinrich, 1980 'Foucaults Analytik der Macht', in Friedrich Kittler (ed.), *Die Austreibung des Geistes aus den Geisteswissenschaften* (Paderborn, Schöningh), pp. 38ff.

Flandrin, Jean-Louis, 1979 *Families in Former Times* (Cambridge, Mass., Cambridge University Press).

Foucault, Michel, 1965 *Madness and Civilization: A History of Insanity in the Age of Reason* (New York, Pantheon).

1970 *The Order of Things: An Archaeology of the Human Sciences* (New York, Pantheon).

1972a *The Archaeology of Knowledge* (New York, Pantheon).

1972b 'The discourse on language', in Michel Foucault, *The Archaeology of Knowledge* (New York, Pantheon) (first published under the title 'Orders of discourse', *Social Science Information*, 10, April 1971).

1973 *Birth of the Clinic: An Archaeology of Medical Perception* (New York, Pantheon).

1976 *Über Strafjustiz, Psychiatrie und Medizin* (Berlin, Merve).

1977 *Discipline and Punish: The Birth of the Prison* (New York, Pantheon) (first published in French, 1975).

1978 *The History of Sexuality*, vol. 1, *An Introduction* (New York, Pantheon) (French title: *La Volonté de savoir*).

1979 'Power and norm: Notes', in Michel Foucault, *Power, Truth, Strategy* (Sydney, Australia, Verlag), pp. 59ff.

1980a 'Body/Power', in Michel Foucault, *Power/Knowledge: Selected Interviews and Other Writings 1972–1977* (New York, Pantheon), pp. 55ff.

1980b *Language, Counter-Memory, Practice: Selected Essays and Interviews* (New York, Pantheon).

1985 *The History of Sexuality*, vol. 2, *The Use of Pleasure* (New York, Pantheon).

1987 *The History of Sexuality*, vol. 3, *The Care of the Self* (New York, Pantheon).

Frank, Manfred, 1977 *Das individuelle Allgemeine: Textstrukturierung und -interpretation nach Schleiermacher* (Frankfurt, Suhrkamp).

1980 'Schmerzbetäubung oder Die Welt als Wunsch und Repräsentation', *Frankfurter Rundschau* (12 January).

Freyer, Hans, 1967 *Theorie der gegenwärtigen Zeitalters* (Stuttgart, Deutsche Verlagsanstalt).

Gadamer, Hans-Georg and Paul Vogler (eds.), 1972–4 *Neue Anthropologie* (7 vols., Stuttgart, Enke).

Gehlen, Arnold, 1927 *Zur Theorie der Setzung und des setzungshaften Wissens bei Driesch* (Leipzig) (Dissertation).

1963 *Studien zur Anthropologie und Soziologie* (Neuwied).

1964 *Urmensch und Spätkultur*, 2nd edn. (Frankfurt and Bonn, Athenäum).

1968a *Anthropologische Forschung* (Reinbek, Rowohlt).

1968b 'Ein anthropologisches Modell', *The Human Context*, 1, 1–10.

1969 *Moral und Hypermoral* (Frankfurt, Athenäum).

1971 *Der Mensch: Seine Natur und seine Stellung in der Welt*, 9th edn. (Frankfurt, Athenäum).

1980 *Man in the Age of Technology* (New York, Columbia University Press).

Gerratana, Valentino, 1976 'Sur les difficultés de l'analyse du stalinisme', *dialectiques*, 15/16, 43–53.

Glock, Hans-Joachim, 1986 'Vygotsky and Mead on the self, meaning, and internalisation', *Studies in Soviet Thought*, 31, 131–48.

Habermas, Jürgen, 1968 *Technik und Wissenschaft als 'Ideologie'* (Frankfurt, Suhrkamp).

1970a *Zur Logik der Sozialwissenschaften* (Frankfurt, Suhrkamp).

1970b *Toward a Rational Society: Student Protest, Science, and Politics* (Boston, Beacon Press).

1971a *Knowledge and Human Interests* (Boston, Beacon Press).

1971b *Theorie und Praxis* (Frankfurt, Suhrkamp).

1971c 'Theorie der Gesellschaft oder Sozialtechnologie?: Eine Auseinandersetzung mit Niklas Luhmann', in Jürgen Habermas and Niklas Luhmann, *Theorie der Gesellschaft oder Sozialtechnologie* (Frankfurt, Suhrkamp), pp. 142–290.

1971d *Philosophisch–politische Profile* (Frankfurt, Suhrkamp).

1973a *Kultur und Kritik* (Frankfurt, Suhrkamp).

1973b *Theory and Practice* (Boston, Beacon Press).

1975 *Legitimation Crisis* (Boston, Beacon Press).

1976a 'Was heißt Universalpragmatik?' in Karl-Otto Apel (ed.), *Sprachpragmatik und Philosophie* (Frankfurt, Suhrkamp), pp. 174–272.

1976b *Zur Rekonstruktion des Historischen Materialismus* (Frankfurt, Suhrkamp).

1978 *Knowledge and Human Interests* (London, Heinemann) (with a new afterword by the author).

1979a *Communication and the Evolution of Society* (Boston, Beacon Press).

1979b 'History and Evolution', *Telos* No. 39, 5–44.

1983 *Philosophical–Political Profiles* (Cambridge, Mass., MIT Press).

1985 and 1987 *The Theory of Communicative Action*, 2 vols. (Boston, Beacon Press).

1987 *The Philosophical Discourse of Modernity: Twelve Lectures* (Cambridge, Mass., MIT Press).

Haering, Theodor, 1929–30 'Die philosophische Bedeutung der Anthropologie', *Blätter für Deutsche Philosophie*, 3, 1–32.

Hammer, Felix, 1967 *Die exzentrische Position des Menschen: Methode und Grundlinien der philosophischen Anthropologie Helmuth Plessners* (Bonn, Bouvier).

Harris, Marvin, 1971 *Culture, Man, and Nature: An Introduction to General Anthropology* (New York, Thomas Crowell).

Hausen, Karin, 1977 'Historische Familienforschung', in Reinhard Rürup (ed.), *Historische Sozialwissenschaft* (Göttingen, Vandenhoeck und Rupprecht), pp. 59–95.

Heidegger, Martin, 1962 *Being and Time* (New York, Harper Brothers).

Heller, Agnes, 1976 *The Theory of Need in Marx* (London, Allison & Busby).

1977 *Instinkt, Aggression, Charakter* (Berlin, VSA).

1979a *On Instincts* (Assen, the Netherlands, Van Gorcum).

1979b *A Theory of Feelings* (Assen, the Netherlands, Van Gorcum).

1984 *Everyday Life* (London, Methuen).

1987 *Beyond Justice* (Oxford, Basil Blackwell).

Henrich, Dieter, 1971 *Hegel im Kontext* (Frankfurt, Suhrkamp).

Hillach, Ansgar, 1978 'Ästhetisierung des politischen Lebens: Benjamins faschismustheoretischer Ansatz – eine Rekonstruktion', in Burkhardt Lindner (ed.), *Links hätte sich alles noch zu enträtseln . . . Walter Benjamin im Kontext* (Frankfurt, Syndikat), pp. 127–67.

Holzkamp, Klaus, 1973 *Sinnliche Erkenntnis: Historischer Ursprung und gesellschaftliche Funktion der Wahrnehmung* (Frankfurt, Athenäum).

1977a 'Kann es im Rahmen der marxistischen Theorie eine Kritische Psychologie geben?' *Das Argument*, 103, 316–36.

1977b 'Die kategoriale und theoretische Erfassung der Vermittlung zwischen konkreten Individuen und ihren gesellschaftlichen Lebensbedingungen durch die Kritische Psychologie', in Karl-Heinz Braun and Klaus Holzkamp, *Kritische Psychologie*, Kongreßbericht, vol. 1 (Cologne, Pahl-Rugenstein), pp. 101–10.

Holzkamp-Osterkamp, Ute, 1975–6 *Grundlagen der psychologischen Motivationsforschung* (2 vols., Frankfurt, Campus).

Honneth, Axel, 1977 'Geschichte und Interaktionsverhältnisse: Zur strukturalistischen Deutung des Historischen Materialismus', in Urs Jaeggi and Axel Honneth (eds.), *Theorien des Historischen Materialismus* (Frankfurt, Suhrkamp), pp. 405–49.

1982 'Work and Instrumental Action, *New German Critique*, 26, 31–54.

Hooff, J. A. R. A. M. van, 1972 'A comparative approach to the phylogeny of laughter and smiling', in Robert A. Hinde (ed.), *Non-verbal Communication* (Cambridge, Cambridge University Press), pp. 209ff.

Husserl, Edmund, 1941 'Phänomenologie und Anthropologie', *Philosophy and Phenomenological Research* 2, 1–14.

Jäger, Michael, 1977 'Wissenschaftstheoretische Kennzeichnung der funktional-historischen Vorgehensweise als Überwindung der Beschränktheit der traditionellen psychologischen Wissenschaftspraxis', in Karl-Heinz Braun and Klaus Holzkamp, *Kritische Psychologie*, Kongreßbericht, vol. 1 (Cologne, Pahl-Rugenstein), pp. 122–39.

Joas, Hans, 1978a 'George H. Mead', in Dirk Käsler (ed.), *Klassiker des soziologischen Denkens*, vol. 2 (Munich, C. H. Beck), pp. 7–39.

1978b 'Einleitung', in Agnes Heller, *Das Alltagsleben* (Frankfurt, Suhrkamp), pp. 9–24.

1979 'Intersubjektivität bei Mead und Gehlen', *Archiv für Rechts- und Sozialphilosophie*, 65, 105–21.

1985 *G. H. Mead: A Contemporary Re-Examination of his Thought* (Cambridge, Mass., Polity Press).

Kamper, Dietmar, 1973 *Geschichte und menschliche Natur: Die Tragweite gegenwärtiger Anthropologiekritik* (Munich, Hanser).

Kofler, Leo, 1967 *Der asketische Eros* (Vienna, Europa-Verlag).

Korsch, Karl, 1971 *Die materialistische Geschichtsauffassung und andere Schriften* (Frankfurt, Europäische Verlagsanstalt).

Kozulin, Alex, 1986 'The concept of activity in Soviet psychology: Vygotsky, his disciples and critics', *American Psychologist*, 41, 264–74.

Krader, Lawrence, 1973 *Ethnologie und Anthropologie bei Marx* (Munich, Hanser).

Krahl, Hans-Jürgen, 1971 *Konstitution und Klassenkampf* (Frankfurt, Neue Kritik).

Lacan, Jacques, 1977 *Ecrits* (London, Tavistock).

Lang, Hermann, 1973 *Die Sprache und das Unbewußte: Jacques Lacans Grundlegung der Psychoanalyse* (Frankfurt, Suhrkamp).

Lehmann, Hans Thies, 1979 'Das Subjekt als Schrift: Hinweise zur französischen Texttheorie', *Merkur*, 33, 665–77.

Leontiev, Alexei N., 1973 *Probleme der Entwicklung des Psychischen* (Frankfurt, Athenäum).

Leontjew, Alexei N. and Alexander R. Luria, 1958 'Die psychologischen Anschauungen L. S. Wygotskis', *Zeitschrift für Psychologie*, 162, 165–205.

Lepenies, Wolf, 1967 'Handlung und Reflexion: Aspekte der Anthropologie Arnold Gehlens', *Soziale Welt*, 18, 41–66.

1977 'Probleme einer Historischen Anthropologie', in Reinhard Rürup (ed.), *Historische Sozialwissenschaft* (Göttingen, Vandenhoeck und Rupprecht), pp. 126–59.

Lepenies, Wolf and Helmut Nolte, 1971 *Kritik der Anthropologie* (Munich, Hanser).

Lévi-Strauss, Claude, 1974 *Tristes Tropiques* (New York, Atheneum).

Lippe, Rudolf zur, 1976 'Anthropologie für wen?', in Dietmar Kamper and Volker Rittner (eds.), *Zur Geschichte des Körpers: Perspektiven der Anthropologie* (Munich, Hanser), pp. 91–129.

Lorenz, Konrad, 1970–1 *Studies in Animal and Human Behavior* (2 vols., Cambridge, Mass., Harvard University Press).

Lorenzer, Alfred, 1970 *Sprachzerstörung und Rekonstruktion* (Frankfurt, Suhrkamp).

Lorenzer, Alfred *et al.*, 1971 *Psychoanalyse als Sozialwissenschaft* (Frankfurt, Suhrkamp).

Löwith, Karl, 1984 *From Hegel to Nietzsche* (New York, Garland Publishers).

Lucas, Erhard, 1964a 'Die Rezeption Lewis H. Morgans durch Marx und Engels', *Saeculum*, 15, 153–76.

1964b 'Marx' Studien zur Frühgeschichte und Ethnologie 1880–1882: Nach unveröffentlichten Exzerpten', *Saeculum*, 15, 327–43.

Márkus, György, 1978 *Marxism and 'Anthropology': The Concept of Human Essence in the Philosophy of Marx* (Assen, the Netherlands, Van Gorcum).

Marx, Karl, and Friedrich Engels, 1970a *Die deutsche Ideologie*, *MEW*, vol. 3 (Berlin [GDR]).

1970b *Thesen über Feuerbach*, *MEW*, vol. 3 (Berlin [GDR]).

1970c *Das Kapital*, *MEW*, vol. 23 (Berlin [GDR]).

1970d   *Ökonomisch-philosophische Manuskripte*, *MEW*, Ergänzungsband, part I (Berlin [GDR]).

1975   *Collected Works*, vols. 3 and 5 (London, Lawrence and Wishart).

Matzner, Egon, 1979 'Die Soziogenese des Staates nach Elias und Schumpeter: Ihr Beitrag zu einer Theorie staatlicher Interventionen', Wissenschaftszentrum Berlin, discussion paper 57.

Mead, George Herbert, 1918   *The Psychology of Punitive Justice*, *American Journal of Sociology*, 23 (1917/18), 577–602.

1932   *The Philosophy of the Present* (La Salle, Ill., Open Court).

1934   *Mind, Self, and Society* (Chicago, University of Chicago Press).

1936   *Movements of Thought in the Nineteenth Century* (Chicago, University of Chicago Press).

1938   *The Philosophy of the Act* (Chicago, University of Chicago Press).

1964   *Selected Writings*, edited by Andrew Reck (Indianapolis, Bobbs–Merrill).

Merleau-Ponty, Maurice, 1962   *Phenomenology of Perception* (New York, Humanities Press).

1963   *The Structure of Behavior* (Boston, Beacon Press).

1973   *Adventures of the Dialectic* (Evanston, Ill., Northwestern University Press).

Misch, Georg, 1947   *Vom Lebens- und Gedankenkreis Wilhelm Diltheys* (Frankfurt, Schulte-Bulmke).

Moore, Barrington, 1978   *Injustice: The Social Basis of Obedience and Revolt* (White Plains, NY, M. E. Sharpe).

Nisbet, Robert A., 1969   *Social Change and History* (New York, Oxford University Press).

Nolte, Helmut, 1971   *Über gesellschaftstheoretische Implikationen des Aggressionsbegriffs*, in Wolf Lepenies and Helmut Nolte, *Kritik der Anthropologie* (Munich, Hanser), pp. 103–40.

Osterloh, Karl-Heinz, 1976   'Die Entstehung der westlichen Industriegesellschaft und die Revolution der Interaktionsweisen: Europäischer Kulturwandel als psychosoziales Problem', *Archiv für Kulturgeschichte*, 58, 340–70.

Ottmann, H., 1981   'Der Mensch als Phantasiewesen: Arnold Gehlens Theorie der Phantasie', in Alfred Schöpf (ed.), *Phantasie als anthropologisches Problem* (Würzburg, Königshausen & Neumann), pp. 159–76.

Ottomeyer, Klaus, 1977   'Interaktion und Selbstbewußtsein im Konzept der gegenständlichen Tätigkeit', in Karl-Heinz Braun and Klaus Holzkamp (eds.), *Kritische Psychologie*, Kongreßbericht, vol. 2 (Cologne, Pahl-Rugenstein), pp. 23–38.

Parsons, Talcott, 1966   *Societies: Evolutionary and Comparative Perspectives* (Englewood Cliffs, NJ, Prentice-Hall).

Plessner, Helmuth, 1959   *Die verspätete Nation: Über die politische Verführbarkeit bürgerlichen Geistes* (Stuttgart/Berlin/Cologne/Mainz, Kohlhammer).

1970a *Philosophische Anthropologie* (Frankfurt, S. Fischer).
1970b *Laughing and Crying: A Study of the Limits of Human Behavior* (Evanston, Ill., Northwestern University Press).
1972 *Grenzen der Gemeinschaft: Eine Kritik der sozialen Radikalismus* (Bonn, Bouvier).
1974 *Diesseits der Utopie* (Frankfurt, Suhrkamp).
1975 *Die Stufen des Organischen und der Mensch*, 3rd edn. (Berlin and New York, de Gruyter).
1976 *Die Frage nach der Conditio Humana* (Frankfurt, Suhrkamp).
1979 *Zwischen Philosophie und Gesellschaft* (Frankfurt, Suhrkamp).
Puder, Martin, 1972, 'Der böse Blick des Michel Foucault', *Neue Rundschau*, pp. 315–24.
Rancière, Jacques, 1972 *Der Begriff der Kritik und die Kritik der politischen Ökonomie* (Berlin, Merve).
Rehberg, Karl-Siegbert, 1979 'Zu den katalysatorischen Wirkungschancen einer Soziologie aus dem Exil: Norbert Elias', in Peter Gleichmann *et al.* (eds.), *Materialien zu Norbert Elias' Zivilisationstheorie* (Frankfurt, Suhrkamp), pp. 101–69.
1985 'Form und Prozeß: Die Theorie der Intersubjektivität als eine Lehre von Menschen: G. H. Mead und die deutsche Tradition der Philosophischen Anthropologie', in Hans Joas (ed.), *Das Problem der Intersubjektivität*. (Frankfurt, Suhrkamp), pp. 60–92.
Reichelt, Helmut, 1970 *Zur logischen Struktur des Kapitalbegriffs bei Karl Marx* (Frankfurt, Europäische Verlagsanstalt).
Riedel, Manfred, 1973 'Hegel und Marx: Die Neubestimmung des Verhältnisses von Theorie und Praxis', in Manfred Riedel, *System und Geschichte: Studien zum historischen Standort von Hegels Philosophie* (Frankfurt, Suhrkamp), pp. 9–44.
Ritter, Joachim, 1974 *Subjektivität. Sechs Aufsätze* (Frankfurt, Suhrkamp).
Rovatti, Pier Aldo, 1976 'Vorwort', in Agnes Heller (ed.), *Theorie der Bedürfnisse bei Marx* (Berlin, VSA), pp. 7–21.
1977 'Bruch und Grundlegung: Zu einer phänomenologischen Kritik an Althusser', in Bernhard Waldenfels *et al.* (eds.), *Phänomenologie und Marxismus*, vol. 1 (Frankfurt, Suhrkamp), pp. 178–96.
Schaff, Adam, 1970 *Marxism and the Human Individual* (New York, McGraw-Hill).
Scheler, Max, 1981 *Man's Place in Nature* (New York, FS & G).
Schmidt, Alfred, 1973 *Emanzipatorische Sinnlichkeit* (Munich, Hanser).
Schnädelbach, Herbert, 1983 *German Philosophy 1831–1933* (Cambridge, Mass., Cambridge University Press).
Schuffenhauer, Werner, 1972 *Feuerbach und der junge Marx*, 2nd edn. (Berlin [GDR], Deutsche Verlag der Wissenschaften).
Schulz, Walter, n.d. *Philosophie in der veränderten Welt* (Pfullingen, Neske).
Schurig, Volker, 1976 *Die Entstehung des Bewußtseins* (Frankfurt, Campus).
Seidel, Alfred, 1927 *Bewußtsein als Verhängnis* (Bonn, F. Cohen).

Seifert, Friedrich, 1934–5 'Zum Verständnis der anthropologischen Wende in der Philosophie', *Blätter für Deutsche Philosophie*, 8, 393–410.

Sève, Lucien, 1978 *Man in Marxist Theory and the Psychology of Personality* (Hassocks, Harvester Press).

Siep, Ludwig, 1979 *Anerkennung als Prinzip der praktischen Philosophie. Untersuchungen zu Hegels Jenaer Philosophie des Geistes* (Freiburg, Alber).

Sloterdijk, Peter, 1972 'Michel Foucaults strukturale Theorie der Geschichte', *Philosophisches Jahrbuch*, 79, 161–84.

Sohn-Rethel, Alfred, 1970 *Geistige und körperliche Arbeit* (Frankfurt, Suhrkamp).

Steinert, Heinz, 1978 'Ist es denn aber auch wahr, Herr F.? "Überwachen und Strafen" unter der Fiktion gelesen, es handle sich dabei um eine sozialgeschichtliche Darstellung', *Kriminalsoziologische Bibliographie*, 19/20, 30–45.

Taylor, Charles, 1975 *Hegel* (Cambridge, Mass., Cambridge University Press).

Theunissen, Michael, 1975 'Krise der Macht: Thesen zur Theorie des dialektischen Widerspruchs', in Wilhelm Raimund Beyer (ed.), *Hegel Jahrbuch 1974* (Cologne, Verlag), pp. 318–29.

Wahl, François, 1973 *Philosophie: la philosophie entre l'avant et l'après du structuralisme* (Paris, Seuil).

Walter, Emil H., 1967 'Die prekäre Vermittlung von Theorie und Praxis in unserer nachrevolutionären Epoche: Anmerkungen zur Geschichtsphilosophie Maurice Merleau-Pontys und Jürgen Habermas', *Archiv für Rechts- und Sozialphilosophie*, 53:3, 415–31.

Wehowsky, Andreas, 1976 'Studie zu Norbert Elias: Über den Prozeß der Zivilisation', master's dissertation in sociology, Free University of Berlin.

Weiss, Andreas von, 1965 *Die Diskussion über den Historischen Materialismus in der deutschen Sozialdemokratie 1891–1918* (Wiesbaden, Harrasowitz).

Wertsch, James V., 1985a *Vygotsky and the Social Formation of Mind* (Cambridge, Mass., Harvard University Press).

1985b (ed.), *Culture, Communication, and Cognition: Vygotskian Perspectives* (Cambridge, Mass., Harvard University Press).

INDEX